STUDENT STUDY GUIDE
for use with
PSYCHOLOGY
FIRST CANADIAN EDITION

JOHN W. SANTROCK

University of Texas at Dallas

JOHN O. MITTERER

Brock University

Prepared by

GREGORY H. CUTLER

Bay de Noc Community College

JOHN O. MITTERER

Brock University

**McGraw-Hill
Ryerson**

Toronto Montréal Burr Ridge, IL Dubuque, IA Madison, WI New York San Francisco
St. Louis Bangkok Beijing Bogotá Caracas Kuala Lumpur Lisbon London Madrid
Mexico City Milan New Delhi Santiago Seoul Singapore Sydney Taipei

McGraw-Hill
Ryerson Limited
A Subsidiary of The McGraw·Hill Companies

STUDENT STUDY GUIDE
for use with
Psychology
First Canadian Edition

ISBN: 0-07-087201-5

1 2 3 4 5 6 7 8 9 10 CP 0 9 8 7 6 5 4 3 2 1

Printed and bound in Canada

Senior Sponsoring Editor: Veronica Visentin
Associate Sponsoring Editor: Marianne Minaker
Marketing Manager: Ralph Courtney
Supervising Editor: Julie van Veen
Production Coordinator: Nicla Dattolico
Printer: Canadian Printco

Contents

Introduction to the Study Guide

This Student Study Guide will assist you as you read Santrock and Mitterer's *Psychology*, First Canadian edition. Each chapter has the following features:

The Big Picture: Chapter Overview. Read this brief chapter summary first to prepare yourself for the topics being presented. Read it again at the end to help identify any gaps in your understanding of the material.

Learning Objectives. First examine them to get a sense of what you should focus on in the chapter. Then return to them following your reading to assure you can do what each objective outlines. If not, go back and reread those relevant portions of the chapter.

The Guided Review. A challenging and comprehensive fill-in-the-blank activity, this exercise will help you point out the terms or sections of the chapter you need to review. Challenge yourself by covering the answers and resist the temptation to peek until you have provided them yourself. Each answer is page referenced to the text to help you pinpoint the material with which you are struggling.

Explorations in Psychology. This exercise asks you to summarize the material found in each "Explorations in Psychology" text feature and to relate it to the chapter material.

In Your Own Words. In this exercise you develop your own examples and applications of chapter material. Try to make connections between your own ideas and experiences and what is presented in each chapter. The more you make these associations, the more meaningful will be the material, and the better will be your understanding.

Correct the Incorrect. Your task in this activity is to determine if the statements provided are correct or incorrect. If incorrect, make the necessary changes to correct it. The correct statement and text page reference are found immediately below each statement.

Practice Test. Containing multiple-choice questions, these items are similar to those given during a class exam. The correct answer appears directly under each question along with information explaining why the other options are incorrect.

On Being A Successful Student

In our years of teaching psychology, we have noticed that the successful students . . .

1.   . . . are well organized To organize, make use of a calendar. Clearly indicate deadlines for papers, exam dates, and other important dates. Keep your course outlines in a safe place so that you can refer to them during the term. Know the office hours and office phone numbers of your instructors. Make and adhere to a weekly schedule for yourself that builds in all the important activities, including class time, work time, study time, and relaxation time.

2.   . . . come to class. Both casual observation and the results of research studies show that students who attend class do better than those who do not. Come to class - it's that simple.

3.   . . . read the material before going to class. This will give you a better idea what the lecture will be about. This also helps you organize your note-taking while in class.

4.   . . . take good notes and review them. Outline your lectures using roman numerals and letters for the major and minor points. This technique can be particularly effective if the instructor lectures from an outline. Review your notes as soon as possible after class. Remember: using someone else's notes is not the same as using your own.

5.   . . . focus on key terms and concepts. A large and important part of most introductory courses consists of learning the language of the field you are studying.. Monitor whether or not you are "getting it." Keep asking yourself, "Does this make sense?"

6.   . . . prepare for exams. Find out as much as you can about the exam beforehand. Try to study always in the same place that is quiet and well-lit on a regular basis. Generally you study most efficiently when you study alone. Take breaks— it is certainly time to take a break when you reach the end of a

page and then realize you haven't retained a word. The type of test you are going to take should dictate how you prepare for it, e.g., for essay exams ask yourself essay questions and write out good answers. Solid preparation, a good night's sleep the night before, and relaxing instead of cramming should help minimize test anxiety. If necessary, seek the advice of a counselor. Many universities now offer courses designed to help deal with test anxiety.

7. . . . do not psych themselves out. In general, students who set learning goals tend to do better and enjoy their classes much more than students who set performance goals.

Good luck with your studies. You are about to go on a great adventure learning and applying psychology!

Gregory H. Cutler
Bay de Noc Community College, June 1999

John O. Mitterer
Brock University, April, 2000

Chapter 1 - What is Psychology?

The Big Picture: Chapter Overview

Psychologists define their field as the scientific study of behavior and mental processes and rely upon systematic methods to observe, describe, predict, and explain behavior. The history of psychology is rooted in philosophy, biology, and physiology. The first scientific psychology laboratory was developed by Wundt in 1879. Working in his laboratory in Germany, Wundt studied consciousness with Titchener expanding Wundt's work. Their approach, which emphasized the importance of conscious thought and classification of the mind's structures, was called structuralism. William James, the first psychologist in the United States, emphasized the functions of the mind in adapting to a changing world; his approach was called functionalism.

There are seven main contemporary approaches in psychology. The behavioral approach focuses on using science to study how the environment influences behavior. In the social cognitive theory, behavior is seen as determined by environmental conditions and how thoughts affect the impact of those conditions on behavior. The unconscious mind, conflict between biological instincts and society's demands, and early family experiences characterize the psychoanalytic approach. In the humanistic approach, people are seen as having the capacity for personal growth, freedom to choose their own destiny, and as possessing positive qualities. The cognitive approach focuses on mental processes such as attention, perception, memory, thinking, and problem-solving. The brain and nervous system and their relationship to behavior, thought, and emotion are the areas of interest in the behavioral neuroscience approach. The evolutionary psychology approach argues for the importance of adaptation, reproduction, and survival of the fittest in explaining behavior. The newest perspective, the sociocultural approach, emphasizes that culture, ethnicity, and gender are necessary to understanding behavior, thought, and emotion. Most psychologists take an eclectic approach, selecting and using the best in each approach.

There are several principles and themes that exert great influence on our lives and on psychology. Biological processes, like those of the brain, have powerful influences on behavior. Repeated experiences acting as environment processes can wire or rewire the brain. Mental processes matter since they allow us to remember, make decisions, plan, set goals, and be creative. Other people and our relationships to them matter in the social world. The culture in which we grew up and live in now has a significant impact on our behavior and mental processes. Individual variations that make us unique from one another matter in psychology and in life. Science matters because it can give us more objective knowledge and understanding than can personal interpretations. Macro and micro approaches in psychology give it conceptual diversity, which stimulates us to think. Paradoxes and controversies matter in psychology because psychology's diversity leads to different approaches, such as scientific and applied research. Another theme is that of critical thinking. Critical thinking matters since it involves reflecting and productive thinking, as well as evaluating evidence.

Majoring in psychology gives an individual knowledge and understanding of mind and behavior and important skills like research skills, critical thinking skills, and writing skills. An undergraduate degree in psychology can be useful in a variety of jobs. A graduate degree in psychology expands the opportunities, allowing one to use skills and knowledge in many settings. The areas of specialization in psychology are many. Clinical and counseling psychologists specialize in the diagnosis and treatment of psychological problems. A community psychologist focuses on providing accessible care for people with problems. A psychologist who conducts basic research using an experimental strategy specializes in experimental psychology. Physiological psychology and neuroscience examines biological processes and their role in behavior. Developmental psychologists are concerned with human development; a social psychologist studies social interactions, relationships, social perceptions, and attitudes. If a psychologist focuses on the relatively enduring traits and characteristics of individuals, the specialization is personality psychology. In school and educational psychology, the psychologist examines children's learning and adjustment in school. The setting of industrial/organization psychology is the workplace, where the psychologist focuses on the workers and the organizations that employ them. In cross-cultural psychology, there is attention given to the role of culture in understanding behavior, thought, and emotion. The importance of promoting the research and study of women characterizes the specialization known as the psychology of women. In health psychology, there is a multidimensional approach to health that emphasizes psychological factors, lifestyle, and the nature of the health care delivery system. The field of psychology that applies psychological concepts to the legal system is forensic psychology. A relatively new specialization is health psychology; it attempts to apply the principles of psychology to improving sport performance and enjoying sports participation.

Learning Objectives

When you have studied the material in this chapter, you should be able to:

1. define psychology. (p. 5)
2. identify the two disciplines from which psychology emerged. (p. 6)
3. distinguish among the following early psychologists and their approaches to psychology: Wundt and Titchener (structuralism) and William James (functionalism). (pp. 6-7)
4. distinguish among the seven contemporary approaches to psychology and identify contributions to each approach:
    -   behavioral (p. 8)
    -   psychoanalytic (p. 9)
    -   humanistic (p. 10)
    -   cognitive (p. 11)
    -   behavioral neuroscience (p. 11)
    -   evolutionary (p. 12)
    -   sociocultural (p. 13)
5. explain what is meant by an eclectic approach. (p. 14)
6. discuss why biology, environment, mental processes, social world, culture, and individual variations all matter in the study in psychology. (pp. 17-20)
7. discuss the importance of systematic methods in the study of psychology. (pp. 20-21)
8. explain why conceptual diversity, paradox, and controversy help to advance the study of psychology. (p. 21)
9. list five thinking strategies essential to good critical thinking. (p. 22)
10. summarize and relate the material from *Explorations in Psychology: From Horoscope to the Sex Lives of Tigers* to the material on critical thinking. (p. 23)
11. discuss the skills to be gained from a career in psychology. (p. 24)
12. identify the various areas of specialization in psychology. (pp. 24-28)

Guided Review

Exploring Psychology

Psychology is the scientific of behavior and mental processes. The term behaviour refers to everything that we do that can be directly observed. Mental processes refer to the thoughts, feelings, and motives that are not directly observable. Because psychology is a science, it uses systematic methods to observe, describe, predict, and explain behavior. Influenced by the field of philosophy, psychology emerged as a science in the nineteenth century. Darwin developed the concept of natural selection.

In 1879, Wundt developed the first scientific laboratory in psychology. His work was popularized in the United States by Titchener. Their approach emphasized the importance of conscious thoughts and a classification of the mind's structure and become known as structuralism. William James, meanwhile, examined the mind's ability to adapt to the environment, in an approach called functionalism. Pavlov and Watson emphasized measuring overt behavior as they rejected inferences about the conscious mind in the approach called behavioural approach. In this approach, behavior is influenced by the environmental determinants. Social cognitive theory stresses that thought modifies the impact of the environment on behavior. According to this perspective, imitation is an important process by which we learn about the world.

Freud believed that the key to understanding mind and behavior rested in the unconscious part of the mind. Freud's approach is known as the psychoanalytic approach. In explaining behavior, Freud argued that people were heavily influenced by biological and _____ instincts. These instincts conflicted with the demands of society. Contemporary psychoanalytic theories place more emphasis on _____ experiences. Another approach in contemporary psychology stresses a person's capacity for personal growth, freedom of choice and the positive qualities of people, which is called humanistic approach. These psychologists believe individuals control direct their own lives. Two psychologists who influenced this approach are _____ and _____.

In the cognitive approach, there is an emphasis on mental processes involved in knowing. This type of psychologist views the mind as a(n) active and aware problem-solving system. Within this approach, there is a perspective that studies how individuals perceive information. It compares the human mind with a computer. An approach that gives the brain the central nervous system primary roles in understanding behavior, thoughts, and emotions is called behavioral neuroscience.

The evolutionary approach examines the conditions that allow individuals to survive or to fail. According to this approach, the mind has _____ in such a way to increase the chance of survival. The _____ approach to psychology stresses the importance of culture, ethnicity, and gender. The term _____ refers to the behavior patterns, beliefs, and other products of a particular group of people that are passed from one generation to the next. _____ is based on cultural heritage, nationality characteristics, race, religion, and language. By the year 1996, only _____ of all Canadians had their origins in the British Isles and France. The sociocultural dimension of being female or male is _____, while _____ refers to the biological dimension of being female or male. Many psychologists taken a(n) _____ approach, which allows one to select and use whatever is considered best in each approach.

20% - p. 13

gender/sex - p. 13

eclectic - p. 14

Psychology and Life: What Matters

The behavioral neuroscience and evolutionary approaches argue that _____ processes have powerful influences on behavior. The fact that different environments alter brain development suggests that _____ processes matter. At the center of the cognitive approach is the assumption that we are _____ beings in addition to being biological and environment beings. Parents, teachers, peers, friends and partners play important roles in our lives; this illustrates that the _____ matters. The sociocultural approach focuses on how _____ influences us. Since two people are different and our biological and experiential legacies interact to produce unique composites of mind and behavior; this summarizes how _____ variations matters. Often personal experiences and individual observations are flawed. Psychology is a _____ and can provide more objective knowledge and observations. A complete portrait of mind and behavior occurs in psychology because it is conceptually _____. Psychology is a field characterized by paradoxes and _____. To understand the complex nature of mind and behavior requires thinking reflectively and productively, and evaluating the evidence; this is called _____.

biological - p. 17

environmental - p. 17
mental - p. 18

social world - p. 19
culture - p. 19

individual - p. 20

science - p. 20

diverse - p. 21
controversies - p. 21

critical thinking - p. 22

Psychology's Careers and Areas of Specialization

A career in psychology will be greatly expanded by a _____ degree in psychology. Most psychologists work in _____ and private practice settings. More psychologists specialize in _____ and _____ psychology than in any other area. A branch of medicine practiced by physicians who specialize in abnormal behavior and psychotherapy is _____. Providing accessible care for people with psychological problems is the primary goal for _____ psychology. A psychologist who conducts basic research in such areas as sensation and perception, memory, and emotion specializes in _____ psychology. The areas that focus on the biological processes in behavior are called _____ psychology and _____ _____. Biological and environmental factors are considered in a specialization called _____ psychology which examines our development from conception to death.

graduate - p. 24
educational - p. 24
clinical/counseling - p. 24

psychiatry - p. 25

community - p. 25

experimental - p. 25
comparative - p. 25
behavioral neuroscience - p. 25
developmental - p. 27

People's social interactions, social perceptions, and relationships are studied by _____ psychologists. The area that studies the relatively enduring traits and characteristics of individuals is called _____ psychology. The specialization that is concerned with children's learning and adjustment in school is called _____ psychology. The specialization concerned with workers and the organization that employs them is called _____ psychology. The role of culture in understanding behavior, thought, and emotion is

social - p. 27

personality - p. 27
educational - p. 27

industrial/organizational -p. 27

examined by _____ psychology. The psychology of women emphasizes the importance of promoting the _____ and _____ of women. Working in physical and mental health areas, a _____ psychologist studies the relationships among psychological factors, _____, and the nature of health care delivery factors. _____ psychology applies psychological concepts to the legal system. Improvement of _____ _____ is part of sport psychology as well as improving sports _____.

cross-cultural - p. 27
research - p. 27
study - p. 27
health - p. 27
lifestyle - p. 27
Forensic - p. 27
sports performance - p. 28
participation - p. 28

Explorations in Psychology

To respond to the questions and exercises presented in this section, please write your thoughts, perspectives, and reactions on a separate piece of paper.

Explorations in Psychology: From Horoscopes to the Sex Lives of Tigers

- What does the word "skepticism" mean to you? Does it have a bad connotation to you?
- Have you ever had an experience with one of the phenomena listed in this section?
- If so, how might a person who practices skepticism explain your experience?
- What does a belief in horoscopes give people?
- What would you say to a person who has totally bought into one of the phenomena listed in this section?

In Your Own Words

To respond to the questions and exercises presented in this section, please write your thoughts, perspectives, and reactions on a separate piece of paper.
- ✓ Put the definition of psychology into your own words.
- ✓ What are some examples of mental processes that you have experienced in the last 10 minutes?
- ✓ List some things about you that have been influenced by the culture in which you live. (Hint: Don't overlook the obvious.)
- ✓ Thinking about how individual variations matter; list some things about you that are unique.
- ✓ Based on your experiences and what you've learned so far in this course, what about people fascinates you the most?
- ✓ Imagine that you work for an advertising agency. Your team is creating television commercials for each of the perspectives. Your part of the project is to write a catchy jingle or slogan for each perspective.
- ✓ Make up titles of fictitious books that could have been written by Wundt, James, Freud, Skinner, Berry, Simon, and Sperry. Try writing book titles for books on clinical psychology, developmental psychology, forensic psychology, and the psychology of women. The titles should reflect the perspective or specialization. Be creative!
- ✓ Chapter One discusses several specializations of psychology. Which one sounds most appealing to you? If you could create a new specialization in psychology, what would it be?

Correcting the Incorrect

Carefully read each statement. Determine if the statement is correct or incorrect. If the statement is incorrect, make the necessary changes to correct it. Then look directly under the statement for the correct statement and page reference in the textbook.

1. Psychology is the scientific study of people's psychological problems and how to help those people.
   - ❑ *Psychology is the scientific study of behavior and mental processes. (p. 5)*
2. Mental processes include thoughts, feelings, and motives that cannot be observed directly.
   - ❑ *Mental processes include thoughts, feelings, and motives that cannot be observed directly. (p. 5)*

3.   Since mental processes are not directly observable, they are actually not real.
      ❑   *Mental processes are not directly observable, but they are nonetheless real. (p. 5)*
4.   As a philosophy, psychology uses systematic methods to observe, describe, predict, and explain behavior.
      ❑   *As a science, psychology uses systematic methods to observe, describe, predict, and explain behavior. (p. 5)*
5.   Charles Darwin established the first psychological laboratory.
      ❑   *Wilhelm Wundt established the first psychological laboratory. (p. 6)*
6.   Wundt and Titchener developed an approach called functionalism.
      ❑   *Wundt and Titchener developed an approach called structualism. (p. 7)*
7.   The first psychologist in the Germany was William James.
      ❑   *The first psychologist in the United States was William James. (p. 7)*
8.   Behaviorists, like Freud and Rogers, would say that the environment determines behavior.
      ❑   *Behaviorists, like Watson and Skinner, would say that the environment determines behavior. (p. 8)*
9.   Social cognitive theory focuses on unconscious motives.
      ❑   *Social cognitive theory focuses on how thoughts modify the impact of environment on behavior. (p. 8).*
10.   B. F. Skinner suggested psychology should study the mind.
      ❑   *B. F. Skinner suggested psychology should not study the mind. (p. 8)*
11.   Behaviorism emphasizes the scientific study of behavior and its environmental determinants.
      ❑   *Behaviorism emphasizes the scientific study of behavior and its environmental determinants. (p. 8)*
12.   In structuralism, there is an emphasis on the role that the unconscious mind plays in behavior, thought, and emotion.
      ❑   *In the psychoanalytic approach, there is an emphasis on the role that the unconscious mind plays in behavior, thought, and emotion. (p. 9)*
13.   Freud developed the psychoanalytic approach.
      ❑   *Freud developed the psychoanalytic approach. (p. 9)*
14.   The psychoanalytic approach stresses how people can choose their own destiny.
      ❑   *The humanistic approach stresses how people can choose their own destiny. (p. 10)*
15.   In the information processing approach, the human mind is compared to a computer.
      ❑   *In the information processing approach, the human mind is compared to a computer. (p. 11)*
16.   The cognitive perspective focuses on behaviors that increase organisms' reproductive success.
      ❑   *The evolutionary perspective focuses on behaviors that increase organisms' reproductive success. (p. 12)*
17.   Ethnicity is based on nationality characteristics, race, religion, and language.
      ❑   *Ethnicity is based on nationality characteristics, race, religion, and language. (p. 13)*
18.   The sociocultural dimension of being female or male is called sex.
      ❑   *The sociocultural dimension of being female or male is called gender. (p. 13)*
19.   Natural selection states that organisms best adapted to their environment are likely to survive, reproduce, and pass on their characteristics to their offspring.
      ❑   *Natural selection states that organisms best adapted to their environment are likely to survive, reproduce, and pass on their characteristics to their offspring. (p. 12)*
20.   Behavioral neuroscientists study the brains of sea slugs.
      ❑   *Behavioral neuroscientists study the brains of sea slugs. (p. 11)*
21.   If a psychologist selects and uses whatever is considered best in each approach, she is taking an eclectic approach.
      ❑   *If a psychologist selects and uses whatever is considered best in each approach, she is taking an eclectic approach. (p. 14)*
22.   Biological factors play a minor role in behavior, thought, and emotion.
      ❑   *Biological factors play a major role in behavior, thought, and emotion. (p. 17)*
23.   The brains of animals that experienced enriched environments weigh more and have more neural connections.
      ❑   *The brains of animals that experienced enriched environments weigh more and have more neural connections. (p. 18)*

24.   Religion is a cultural area of study in psychology that has not been neglected.
    ❑   *Religion is a cultural area of study in psychology that has been neglected.* (p. 19)
25.   Personal experience is never based on individual observation and interpretations.
    ❑   *Personal experience is based on individual observation and interpretations.* (p. 20)
26.   Since psychology is a science, it readily accepts simple explanations of behavior.
    ❑   *Since psychology is a science, it does not readily accept simple explanations of behavior.* (p. 21)
27.   There is no difference between clinical psychology and psychiatry.
    ❑   *There are differences between clinical psychology and psychiatry.* (p. 24)
28.   Experimental psychology focuses on basic research in sensation and perception, learning, and emotion.
    ❑   *Experimental psychology focuses on basic research in sensation and perception, learning, and emotion.* (p. 25)
29.   Comparative psychology and behavioral neuroscience focus on providing accessible care for people with psychological problems.
    ❑   *Community psychology focuses on providing accessible care for people with psychological problems.* (p. 25)
30.   Forensic psychology is the field of psychology that studies changes through the lifespan.
    ❑   *Developmental psychology is the field of psychology that studies changes through the lifespan.* (p. 27)
31.   If you are a psychologist who studies attitudes, then you are probably a social psychologist.
    ❑   *If you are a psychologist who studies attitudes, then you are probably a social psychologist.* (p. 27)

Practice Test

1.   Psychology is best defined as the
    a.   study of perception and memory.
    b.   investigation of the human psyche.
    c.   scientific study of conscious and unconscious processes.
    d.   scientific study of behavior and mental processes.

    a.   no; psychology is more than the study of just perception and memory
    b.   sorry; this is not the best definition
    c.   even though psychology does study conscious and unconscious processes, this is not the best answer
    d.   THAT'S CORRECT; psychology is best defined as the scientific study of behavior and mental processes

2.   As you read the definition of psychology you begin to think about examples. Of the following, which one is the best example of behavior?
    a.   planning your weekend activities
    b.   adding two numbers in your head
    c.   a two-year-old boy coloring a picture
    d.   thinking about this question

    a.   planning is an example of a mental process since it cannot be directly observed
    b.   adding is an example of a mental process since it cannot be directly observed
    c.   CORRECT; coloring a picture is behavior since it can be directly observed
    d.   thinking is an example of a mental process since it cannot be directly observed

3.   A team of researchers wants to study aggressive behavior in adolescents. The researchers plan to use observations to describe, make predictions about, and explain adolescents' aggressive behavior. Which of the following best describes what these researchers are doing?
    a.   They are trying to define mental processes.
    b.   They are identifying environmental determinants of behavior.
    c.   They are studying peer pressure.
    d.   They are following the scientific method.

a.	aggression is behavior, not a mental process	
b.	no; observations in description, predictions, and explanation are part of the scientific method	
c.	the researchers might be studying peer pressure, but this is not the best answer	
d.	CORRECT; this option best describes what the researchers are doing	

4. The definition of psychology is made up of several parts. Which part refers to "thoughts, feelings, and motives"?
   a. scientific study
   b. behavior
   c. contexts
   d. mental processes

a.	scientific study refers to using systematic methods
b.	behavior is anything you do that is directly observable
c.	contexts is not a component of the definition
d.	YES; thoughts, feelings, and motives are examples of mental processes

5. What is the main difference between philosophers and psychologists?
   a. the types of questions they ask about human behavior
   b. the causes they presume for human behavior
   c. the debate of the question how people acquire knowledge
   d. the methods they use for obtaining evidence

a.	philosophers and psychologists often ask the same questions
b.	no, both may acknowledge the same causes of behavior
c.	no, both debate
d.	YES; philosophers think to obtain evidence; psychologists use the scientific method

6. The British naturalist Charles Darwin is best known for his suggestion that
   a. organisms that are best adapted to their environment survive and pass on their characteristics to their offspring
   b. consciousness experience is made up of structure
   c. psychology should focus only on observable behavior not the mind
   d. people have freedom to choose their own destiny

a.	YES; this is the idea of natural selection
b.	this describes structuralism, not Darwin
c.	focusing on observable behavior was Skinner's suggestion
d.	freedom to choose is a basic tenet of the humanistic approach

7. A structuralist would have been most interested in studying
   a. the unconscious.
   b. dreams.
   c. conscious thought.
   d. behavior.

a.	no; structuralism focused on conscious thought
b.	no
c.	YES; structuralism attempted to examine the structure of conscious thought
d.	no; the emphasis of structuralism was on conscious thought, not behavior

8. The mind's content is to Titchener as the mind's function is to
    a. Wundt.
    b. James.
    c. Watson.
    d. Darwin.

a.	Wundt is associated with structuralism, as is Titchener
b.	THAT'S RIGHT; William James studied how the mind adapted to the environment
c.	Watson is related to behaviorism, which discounted the role of the mind
d.	Darwin is best known for the theory of evolution

9. Structuralism is to _____ as functionalism is to _____.
    a. Wundt; Titchener
    b. Skinner; Wundt
    c. James; Bandura
    d. Wundt; James

a.	both Wundt and Titchener are associated with structuralism
b.	Skinner is associated with the behavioral approach; Wundt is associated with structuralism
c.	James is associated with functionalism; Bandura is associated with social cognitive theory
d.	THAT'S RIGHT; Wundt is associated with structuralism and James is associated with functionalism

10. You believe that the environment determines behavior. What approach would you be most likely to side with?
    a. psychoanalytic
    b. humanistic
    c. behavioral neuroscience
    d. behavioral

a.	the psychoanalytic focuses on unconscious influences
b.	the humanistic approach says that people control their own lives, not the environment
c.	the behavioral neuroscience argues that the brain and nervous system determine behavior
d.	YES; environmental conditions determine behavior

11. Which of the following was most similar to Ivan Pavlov in his approach to psychology?
    a. William James
    b. Erik Erikson
    c. John B. Watson
    d. Wilhelm Wundt

a.	James is associated with functionalism
b.	Erikson's views are more similar to Freud's and the psychoanalytic approach
c.	YEAH; Watson and Pavlov both argued that the environment plays a key role in determining behavior
d.	Wundt studied the structure of conscious thought

12. What is the main difference between Bandura's approach and other behavioral theories?
    a. Bandura emphasizes the influence of the environment on behavior.
    b. Bandura acknowledges the importance of cognitive processes.
    c. Bandura insists that behavior has to be measurable.
    d. Bandura rejects the notion that behavior should be observed.

a.   no that is the main notion in the behavioral theories
b.   THAT'S RIGHT; Bandura recognizes that thoughts influence the way the environment affects behavior
c.   no that's not a difference
d.   no; in fact Bandura would argue that behavior should be observed

13.   The _____ approach sees behavior as being influenced by the unconscious mind.
     a.   cognitive
     b.   humanistic
     c.   psychoanalytic
     d.   evolutionary

a.   the cognitive approach looks for the role of mental processes such as perception
b.   the humanistic approach asserts that people, not the unconscious mind, choose who they are
c.   RIGHT; the psychoanalytic approach also focuses on biological instincts
d.   the evolutionary approach focuses on the survival of the fittest

14.   Of the following, which best summarizes the humanistic approach?
     a.   People are influenced by their unconscious mind and the conflict between their biological instincts and society's demands.
     b.   Consciousness is understood by examining its basic elements.
     c.   Ethnicity, gender, and culture are the primary determinants of behavior.
     d.   People have the freedom to choose their own destiny.

a.   this summary describes the psychoanalytic approach
b.   this summary describes structuralism
c.   the sociocultural approach emphasizes ethnicity, gender, and culture
d.   YES; this view sees people as having the freedom and the capacity for self-understanding

15.   Which of the following best explains how Erik Erikson's views differ from Sigmund Freud's views of personality?
     a.   Erikson believes that personality develops before age 5.
     b.   Erikson believes sexual instincts are most important.
     c.   Erikson believes exploration of roles is not important.
     d.   Erikson believes culture plays a role in personality development.

a.   Erikson's theory considers the entire lifespan
b.   no; Erikson downplayed sexual instincts
c.   no; the exploration of roles is very important according to Erikson
d.   YEAH; Erikson argued that culture was important and that Freud shortchanged the role of culture in personality

16.   Which of the following would make the best title for a research paper on humanistic psychology?
     a.   Be all that you can be.
     b.   The human mind works like a computer.
     c.   Explore your unconscious and you will find yourself.
     d.   People are pawns of their environment.

a.   GOOD; the humanistic perspective stresses growth and self-actualization
b.   this sounds more like the cognitive approach
c.   the unconscious mind is the focus of the psychoanalytic approach
d.   this title would be best for the behavioral approach

17. Your professor says that memory, attention, problem-solving, and perception are key components of the _____ approach.
    a. cognitive
    b. sociocultural
    c. evolutionary
    d. functional

a.	THAT'S CORRECT; the cognitive approach focuses on mental processes
b.	the sociocultural view examines the role of ethnicity, culture, and gender
c.	this approach stresses natural selection
d.	the functional view examines how the mind adapts to the environment

18. Which of the following approaches emphasizes the brain and nervous system?
    a. cognitive
    b. behavioral neuroscience
    c. information processing
    d. behavioral

a.	the cognitive approach emphasizes mental processes
b.	YES; those in this approach examine how the physical structures of the brain and nervous system influence behavior, thoughts, and emotion
c.	the information processing focuses on attention, perception, and memory
d.	this approach examines the relationship between the environment and behavior

19. Chemical changes in the brain associated with anxiety would be of most interest to a(n)
    a. evolutionary psychologist.
    b. cognitive psychologist.
    c. cross-cultural psychologist.
    d. behavioral neuroscientist.

a.	probably not; because evolutionary psychology is more interested in how behavior allows organisms to adapt to the environment
b.	a cognitive psychologist examines the role of mental processes
c.	this psychologist would study the roles that culture, ethnicity, and gender play
d.	SOUNDS GOOD; behavioral neuroscience studies how the brain and nervous system are important to behavior, thought, and emotion

20. According to the evolutionary psychology approach, why does the mind have the capacity to achieve specific goals?
    a. the mind has evolved
    b. one's environment has shaped the mind
    c. the unconscious mind tends to create these goals
    d. because the person has so decided to achieve specific goals

a.	THAT'S RIGHT; it is theorized that the mind has evolved in ways that would have benefited hunters and gathers
b.	this option is best associated with the behavioral approach
c.	the psychoanalytic approach would suggest this role of the unconscious mind
d.	this best describes the humanistic approach

21. Dr. Cunningham is studying the impact of gender on behavior, thought, and emotion. What approach is she most likely to use?
    a. humanistic
    b. psychoanalytic
    c. cognitive
    d. sociocultural

a.	the humanistic approach would more likely examine self-understanding and choice
b.	the psychoanalytic approach examines the impact of the unconscious
c.	the cognitive approach studies mental processes
d.	CORRECT; the sociocultural approach looks at the roles that culture, ethnicity, and gender have on behavior, thought, and emotion

22. Which is the most appropriate conclusion we can draw about a research psychologist who employs different aspects of a number of psychological approaches in her work?
    a. She is using an eclectic approach.
    b. She is confused about the different approaches.
    c. She didn't specialize in any particular area of psychology.
    d. She will not be able to conduct effective research.

a.	YES; the eclectic approach allows one to select and use whatever is considered best in each approach
b.	no one approach can explain totally everything about behavior
c.	no; the eclectic approach is often seen in all specializations within psychology
d.	the eclectic approach acknowledges that no single approach is infallible

23. Marie and Tina are talking about the various approaches discussed in the textbook. Marie says that she is eclectic. What does Marie mean?
    a. Marie believes that the more traditional views such as structuralism are more valid.
    b. Marie believes that the more contemporary views such as the cognitive approach are more valid.
    c. It means that Marie is not willing to consider any other view besides her own.
    d. Marie selects and uses whatever is considered best in each approach.

a.	this is not the definition of eclectic
b.	this is not the definition of eclectic
c.	this is not the definition of eclectic
d.	YES; this is the definition of the eclectic approach

24. Which of the following was among those principles and themes discussed in the section on "What Matters"?
    a. environmental processes
    b. intelligence
    c. athleticism
    d. unconscious processes

a.	YES; environmental processes are among the ten principles and themes
b.	this is not among the ten principles and themes
c.	this is not among the ten principles and themes
d.	this is not among the ten principles and themes

25. Your text discusses ten major themes that are relevant to psychology. One of those themes is "science matters". What is the main benefit of the scientific approach to psychology?
    a.   objective knowledge
    b.   random observation
    c.   revolutionary discoveries
    d.   exchange of ideas

a.	THAT'S RIGHT; psychology, since it is a science, can provide objective knowledge
b.	no; this is not a benefit
c.	discoveries do happen in science, but first objective knowledge must be obtained
d.	while the exchange of ideas does occur in science, it is not the main benefit

26. Of the following, which is probably the most neglected cultural area of study in psychology?
    a.   objective knowledge and observation
    b.   religion
    c.   mental processes
    d.   controversies

a.	objective knowledge and observation are not considered to be culture
b.	THAT'S CORRECT; religion is a neglected cultural area of study
c.	mental processes are not considered to be cultural
d.	controversies play a large part in psychology

27. Critical thinking involves all of the following except which one?
    a.   thinking reflectively
    b.   thinking productively
    c.   thinking impulsively
    d.   evaluating evidence

a.	this is a component of critical thinking
b.	critical thinking involves thinking productively
c.	THAT'S RIGHT; critical thinking requires that we be reflective and not impulsive
d.	critical thinking requires that we evaluate evidence

28. What is the main difference between clinical psychologists and psychiatrists?
    a.   their education
    b.   their theoretical approach
    c.   their research interests
    d.   their number of publications

a.	YES; a psychiatrist holds a degree in medicine and a clinical psychologist does not
b.	both are interested in helping people
c.	both professionals help improve the lives of people and their research reflects this
d.	no; this is not important

29. Dr. Chen is a community psychologist. What does he do?
    a.   conducts basic research in the area of motivation
    b.   provides accessible care for people with psychological problems
    c.   prescribes medications to depressed patients
    d.   helps companies select the best workers for the job

a.	this describes an experimental psychologist
b.	YES; that is the focus of community psychology
c.	this sounds like a psychiatrist
d.	this describes the focus on an industrial/organizational psychologist

30. The most widely practiced specialization in psychology is
    a. experimental psychology
    b. physiological psychology
    c. forensic psychology
    d. clinical and counseling psychology

a.	no
b.	no
c.	no
d.	YES; clinical and counseling psychology is the most widely practiced specialization

31. If you want to be a forensic psychologist, you will probably take some classes on
    a. law
    b. medicine
    c. language
    d. engineering

a.	CORRECT; forensic psychology applies psychological principles to the legal system
b.	no
c.	no
d.	no

32. You are a psychologist and you study self-concept, aggression, and inner-directedness. You most likely specialize in
    a. school and educational psychology
    b. cross-cultural psychology
    c. personality psychology
    d. clinical psychology

a.	children's learning and adjustment in school take center stage in this specialization
b.	cross-cultural psychology examines the role of culture
c.	YES; these are examples of areas that a personality psychologist would study
d.	a clinical psychologist studies and treats psychological problems

33. The specialist who works at a secondary school and consults with teachers about children's school achievement problems is most likely in which field of specialization?
    a. learning and memory
    b. motivation and emotion
    c. school psychology
    d. biological psychology

a.	learning and memory are important in school, but this is not a field of specialization
b.	while important in school, motivation and emotion is not the name of a specialization
c.	CORRECT; school psychology is concerned about learning and adjustment in school
d.	biological psychology focuses on the relationships between brain and nervous and behavior, thought, and emotion.

34. Of the following, which is the newest specialty in psychology?
    a. sports psychology
    b. experimental psychology
    c. counseling psychology
    d. clinical psychology

a.	YES, THAT'S CORRECT; sports psychology is the one of the newest specialties	
b.	no	
c.	no	
d.	no	

Chapter 2 - Psychology's Scientific Methods

The Big Picture: Chapter Overview

Psychology is a science and, therefore, relies upon scientific research. In comparison to personal observations and experiences, scientific research is objective, systematic, and testable. Scientific research is a method for studying behavior and mental processes. An understanding of science helps us to evaluate the claims we see in the media.

Scientific research is based on the scientific method and involves conceptualizing a problem where the problem is operationally defined. Theories are often used in conceptualizing problems; theories also generate hypotheses. Another important feature of the scientific method is the collection of data. Research methods are used to collect data about the problem. In the scientific method, psychologists use mathematical (statistical) procedures to understand the meaning of the data they have collected. After this occurs, conclusions can be drawn. The final step in the scientific method is the revision of research conclusions or theory.

Psychologists often select a sample of subjects from the population. From this sample, the psychologist will draw conclusions that will apply to the larger population. The sample must be representative of the population to allow generalization to be accurate. One research method that psychologists use is observation, which must be made in some systematic way. Many of the observations that take place in psychology occur in the laboratory, which gives the psychologist much control over factors; however, there are several drawbacks of this method. In naturalistic observation, the psychologist observes behavior in real-world settings and makes no attempt to manipulate or control the situation. Another way to collect data is to ask people. An interview involves asking people questions to find out about their experiences and attitudes. One problem with interviewing people is social desirability, or the tendency to tell the interviewer what they think is socially acceptable or desirable. Questionnaires require subjects to read the questions and mark their answers on paper. Case studies provide an in-depth examination of a single individual. The results of case studies may not be easily generalized to other people. Some psychologists observe behavior and mental processes by administering standardized tests. Standardized tests provide information on individual differences among people. In physiological research, subjects' biological processes are assessed. Since it may not be possible to conduct some physiological research on humans, animals are sometimes used. The correlational approach describes how strongly two or more events or characteristics are related. It is important to note that correlation does not equal causation, but can allow us to make predictions.

Unlike correlational research, experimental research allows psychologists to determine behavior's causes. An experiment is conducted that involves one or more factors to be manipulated and all other factors are held constant. The independent variable refers to the manipulated factor. The behavior under study and being measured is called the dependent variable. The group whose experience is being manipulated is known as the experimental group, while the comparison group is called the control group. In experimental research, subjects are assigned to experimental and control groups by random assignment. One concern involves the experimenter's own bias influencing the outcome of the research; this is called experimenter bias. Another concern is research participant bias, where the research participants have beliefs about how they are expected to behave. Changes in behavior may be due to participants' expectations; this is referred to as the placebo effect. To control for these expectations, an experiment may be designed as a double-blind experiment.

Ethics and values are of great concern to psychologists. Values influence the types of questions psychological research poses. The Canadian Psychological Association has developed a code of ethics for researchers that calls for researchers to provide subjects with informed consent, confidentiality, debriefing, the careful use of deception, and protection from physical and mental harm. Current controversies surround the values of psychology and use of animals in research. In recent years, psychologists have shown increasing interest in and sensitivity toward gender, cultural, and ethnic bias in psychological research.

Learning to read journals can be of benefit regardless of one's career choice. Journal articles are often written with technical language and specialized terms since they are usually intended to be read by professionals in the field. Research articles typically consist of an abstract, introduction, methods, results, discussion, and references. Learning to be a wise consumer of information about psychology is very important. When reading information presented in the media, one needs to pay attention to overgeneralization based on a small sample It is also important to acknowledge that one study should not be taken as the final answer to a problem.

Learning Objectives

When you have studied the material in this chapter, you should be able to:

1.   describe the steps used in the scientific method. (pp. 35-37)
2.   devise operational definitions for given variables. (p. 35)
3.   distinguish between a theory and hypothesis. (p. 36)
4.   distinguish between a population and a sample. (p. 38)
5.   discuss the advantages and disadvantages of laboratory and naturalistic observation. (pp. 41-43)
6.   distinguish between survey, interview, and case study techniques in psychological research. (pp. 43-44)
7.   explain why social desirability is a shortcoming of some research methods. (p. 43)
8.   describe the characteristics of a standardized test. (p. 44)
9.   explain the role of physiological research and research with animals. (pp. 44-45)
10.   distinguish between correlational and experimental research strategies. (pp. 45-46)
11.   distinguish between the dependent and independent variable in an experiment. (p. 46)
12.   explain the purpose of random assignment and distinguish between the experimental group and the control group in an experiment. (p. 46)
13.   differentiate between experimenter and participant bias. (pp. 48-49)
14.   discuss the importance of ethical and value considerations in psychological research. (pp. 51-53)
15.   discuss the controversies surrounding research with animals. (p. 53-54)
16.   identify three key questions regarding gender, culture, and ethnicity that need consideration in psychological research. (pp. 54-55)
17.   differentiate between the six sections of a research article published in a journal. (p. 57)
18.   discuss the importance of being a wise consumer of psychological research. (pp. 57-59)
19.   From *Images of Psychology and Life* and *Explorations in Psychology*: examine differences between psychology-based thinking and the processes we commonly use to make judgments about behavior. (p. 33, p. 41, and p. 54)

Guided Review

Scientific Research and the Scientific Method

Science is not defined by the subject matter it studies, but by how it studies it. _Scientific research_ is objective, systematic, and testable. The _scientific method_ is an approach that can be used to discover accurate information and includes _conceptualizing_ a problem, collecting _data_, drawing conclusions, and revising research conclusions and theory. A(n) _operational definition_ consists of a precise description of a problem and how it is studied in terms of _observable_ events that can be _measured_. A theory is a coherent set of interrelated ideas that helps us to make predictions and _explain_ data. A theory generates _hypotheses_, which are assumptions or predictions that can be tested to determine their accuracy. Psychologists use _mathematical_ procedures to analyze the data that have been collected.

Science - p. 34	
Scientific research - p. 34	
scientific method - p. 35	
conceptualizing/data - p. 35	
operational definition - p. 35	
observable/measured - p. 35	
explain/hypotheses - p. 36	
mathematical (statistical) - p. 36	

Who Will the Participants Be?

A psychologist studying a group of subjects, will want to be able to draw _conclusions_ that will apply to a large group of people. A(n) _sample_ is a subset of a(n) _pop._. For the generalization to be accurate, the sample should be _repres_ of the population.

conclusions - p. 37	
sample/population - p. 38	
representative - p. 38	

Research Methods

In order for observations to be effective, they must be collected in a _systematic_ way. Much psychological research is conducted in a _lab_, a controlled setting that removes many complex "real world" factors. Laboratory research has several drawbacks: 1) _subjects_ are likely to know they are being studied; 2) the laboratory setting is _unnatural_; 3) participants in university laboratory research are unlikely to represent diverse _ethnic_ backgrounds; and 4) some aspects of psychology may be _difficult_ or _impos_ to study in a laboratory. A technique that allows psychologists to observe behavior in real-world settings is called _natur obs_. In this method, observers often have difficulty making presence _unobtrusive_.

In a(n) _interview_ a person is asked face-to-face questions about experiences and attitudes. A shortcoming of interviews, where participants are not willing to disclose socially unfavorable information about them, is called social _desirabl_. In (a) _questionnaire_ the respondents read the questions and make their answers on paper. An in-depth look at a single individual is called a _case_ study. This method is primarily used by _clinical_ psychologists. _Stand_ tests are another method used by psychologists; this method provides information about _individ_ differences among people. Standardized tests have been criticized since information obtained from these tests does not always predict behavior in _nontest_ situations. Other shortcomings are that tests may be _biased_ against minority groups and individuals from different _cultures_. _Physio_ research

systematic - p. 40	
laboratory - p. 41	
subjects - p. 41	
unnatural - p. 41	
cultural - p. 42	
difficult - p. 42	
impossible - p. 42	
naturalistic observation - p. 42	
unobtrusive - p. 43	
interview - p. 43	
desirability/questionnaire (survey) - p. 43	
case - p. 43	
clinical - p. 43; standardized - p. 44	
individual - p. 44	
nontest - p. 44	
biased - p. 44	
cultures/Physiological - p. 44	

examines the biological basis of behavior. The goal of correlational [correlational - p. 45] research is to describe how strongly two or more events or characteristics are related [related - p. 45]. It is important to remember that just because two events may be correlated, it does not prove that one event causes [causes p. 45] the other.

A technique that does allow psychologists to determine the causes of behavior is called experi [experimental - p. 46] research. In conducting an experiment, [experiment - p. 46] the researcher manipulates one variable to see the effect [effect/independent - p. 46] on behavior. The indep [independent - p. 46] variable is the manipulated factor. The dep. [dependent - p. 46] variable is the factor that is measured in an experiment and changes as the indep [independent - p. 46] variable is manipulated. Subjects, whose experience is manipulated by the experimenter are called the exp. [experimental - p. 46] group, while those who act as a comparison group are the control [control - p. 46] group. Subjects are assigned to groups by random assign [random assignment - p. 46] which means that assignments are made by chance. Exper [Experimenter - p. 48] bias may occur in an experiment if the experimenter's own expectations influence the outcome of the research. Research participants have beliefs about how they should behave; this is known as r.p.b. [research participant bias - p. 49]. Effects that are due to participants' expectations are called place [placebo effects - p. 49]. To control for the influence of expectations, d.b [double blind - p. 49] experiments are used where neither experimenter nor participant is aware of which participants are in which groups.

Research Challenges

Three important reasons for studying the importance of ethics and values in psychological research are 1) we are active members of society in the age of information and tech [technology - p. 51]; 2) we may be participate in psychological research, so we need to know about our rights [rights - p. 51]; and 3) students may themselves become exp [experimenters/CPA - p. 51/ p. 52]. The CPA has developed ethical guidelines for psychologists. One guideline requires telling the subject about their participation and any potential risks. Researchers are responsible for keeping all of the data gathered on individuals completely confidential [confidential - p. 52] and when possible completely anon [anonymous - p. 52]. Informing participants of the purpose and methods used in a study when the study is completed is called debrief [informed consent - p. 52]. Subjects must not be harmed and must be debriefed as soon as possible in cases of deception [deception - p. 53]. Regarding values, some psychologists believe that psychology should be value-free [value-free - p. 53] and morally neutral. For too long, the female experience was subsumed under the male experience; this illustrates gender [gender - p. 54] bias. The use of an ethnic label in a way that makes a group seem more homogeneous than it is in actuality is called ethnic bias [ethnic gloss - p. 56].

A journal article has several parts: abstract, introduction, method [method - p. 57], results, discussion, and references. Many times, when psychological research is reported by the media [media - p. 57], it is sensationalistic and dramatic. A wise consumer of psychological information will recognize the most research focuses on grou [groups - p. 58], not individuals. The wise consumer also is aware of the effect that sample _____ [size - p. 58] has on generalizing the results of a study to a larger population. In addition, it is important that one study is not the final [final - p. 59] authority on the issue.

Explorations in Psychology

To respond to the questions and exercises presented in this section, please write your thoughts, perspectives, and reactions on a separate piece of paper.

Explorations in Psychology: Hans, the Clever Horse

- As you were reading this section on Hans, the horse who could "do" math, but before Hans' secret was revealed, what was going through your mind as to his success?
- If you were Oskar von Pfungst, how would you approach Mr. von Osten with your proposal of more carefully testing Hans?
- How could Mr. von Osten be legitimately "angry at the horse and [feel] betrayed by him"? If you were Mr. von Osten, what would be your reaction?
- Oskar von Pfungst was a keen observer. What areas of your life would be improved if you could develop your observational skills?

Explorations in Psychology: Psychology and Values

- Prior to reading this article, did you think that science, and more specifically psychology, were value free?
- It is possible for psychology to be free of values?
- How have your values influenced the way you understand behavior?
- If you were a psychologist, what would you study? Is this area of study related to your values?

In Your Own Words

To respond to the questions and exercises presented in this section, please write your thoughts, perspectives, and reactions on a separate piece of paper.

✓ What comes to mind when you think of "science"?
✓ How would you operationally define love, test anxiety, and fun?
✓ Look carefully at the definitions of experimental and control groups and independent and dependent variables. Try to define these very important terms using pictures. Don't worry if you're not an artist.
✓ Do you like to sit someplace like the student's union, a library, or a park and just watch people? Describe what you typically see as you conduct your own naturalistic observation.
✓ A friend of yours is talking with you about psychology. She claims that psychology is not a real science, at least not like biology. What's is your reasoned response to her?
✓ Watch the popular media (e.g., television, radio, print) for the next couple of days. Keep a tally of the number of times there is a reference to research, particularly psychological research. How many times did you hear, "A major university study... " or something like that. Or, buy a copy of a supermarket tabloid. Scan it for references to research.
✓ List some ways that scientific research affects your daily life.

Correcting the Incorrect

Carefully read each statement. Determine if the statement is correct or incorrect. If the statement is incorrect, make the necessary changes to correct it. Then look directly under the statement for the correct statement and page reference in the textbook.

1.   Personal experience is objective, systematic, and testable. \
   ❑ *Personal experience is not objective, systematic, and testable. (p. 34)*
2.   Information based on personal experiences isn't always objective.
   ❑ *Information based on personal experiences isn't always objective. (p. 34)*
3.   Science is defined by what it investigates.
   ❑ *Science is defined by how it investigates. (p. 34)*

4. If a term is defined by the scientific method, it means it is defined precisely and in terms of observable events that can be measured.
   - ❑ *If a term is defined by an operational definition, it means it is defined precisely and in terms of observable events that can be measured. (p. 35)*
5. A hypothesis is a coherent set of interrelated ideas that helps to make predictions and explain data.
   - ❑ *A theory is a coherent set of interrelated ideas that helps to make predictions and explain data. (p. 36)*
6. Psychologists use research methods to collect data.
   - ❑ *Psychologists use research methods to collect data. (p. 36)*
7. Theories are typically never revised.
   - ❑ *Theories are typically revised. (p. 36)*
8. The population is the entire group of participants about which the researcher wants to draw conclusions.
   - ❑ *The population is the entire group of participants about which the researcher wants to draw conclusions. (p. 38)*
9. From the population, an experimental group is selected.
   - ❑ *From the population, a sample is selected. (p. 38)*
10. The sample should be representative of the population.
    - ❑ *The sample should be representative of the population. (p. 38)*
11. In the laboratory, all of the complex factors of the real world are removed.
    - ❑ *In the laboratory, many of the complex factors of the real world are removed. (p. 41)*
12. If a psychologist is conducting naturalistic observation, she is attempting to manipulate the behavior of the subjects.
    - ❑ *If a psychologist is conducting naturalistic observation, she is not attempting to manipulate the behavior of the subjects. (p. 42)*
13. One shortcoming of the interview is the placebo effect.
    - ❑ *One shortcoming of the interview is social desirability. (p. 43)*
14. The MMPI is an example of a questionnaire.
    - ❑ *The MMPI is an example of a standardized test. (p. 44)*
15. Correlation equals causation.
    - ❑ *Correlation does not equal causation. (p. 45)*
16. If a psychologist is interested in determining behavior's causes, experimental research is the most appropriate method.
    - ❑ *If a psychologist is interested in determining behavior's causes, experimental research is the most appropriate method. (p. 46)*
17. The independent variable is the factor that is measured in an experiment.
    - ❑ *The dependent variable is the factor that is measured in an experiment. (p. 46)*
18. The experimental group acts like a comparison group.
    - ❑ *The control group acts like a comparison group. (p. 46)*
19. The researcher assigns participants to experimental and control groups by chance.
    - ❑ *The researcher assigns participants to experimental and control groups by chance. (p. 46)*
20. Experiments should have experimental bias since it can improve the results.
    - ❑ *Experiment should avoid experimental bias since it can tarnish the results. (p. 48)*
21. A placebo effect occurs when the experimenter's expectations and not the experimental treatment produces a desired outcome.
    - ❑ *A placebo effect occurs when the participant's expectations and not the experimental treatment produces a desired outcome. (p. 49)*
22. In the double-blind experiment, the participant and the researcher both know which participants are in the experimental and placebo control groups.
    - ❑ *In the double-blind experiment, the participant and the researcher both do not know which participants are in the experimental and placebo control groups. (p. 49)*
23. When a study is about to begin, the researcher will inform the participants about the purpose and methods used in the study; this is called debriefing.

❑ When a study is about to begin, the researcher will inform the participants about the purpose and methods used in the study; this is called informed consent. (p. 52)

24. It is correct to magnify gender differences in psychological research.
   ❑ Gender differences in psychological research should not be exaggerated. (p. 55).
25. The term ethnic gloss means that an ethnic label has been used in a superficial way that makes an ethnic group more homogeneous than it really is.
   ❑ The term ethnic gloss means that an ethnic label has been used in a superficial way that makes an ethnic group more homogeneous than it really is. (p. 56)
26. Research articles published in journals include abstract, introduction, method, results, and discussion.
   ❑ Research articles published in journals include abstract, introduction, method, results, and discussion. (p. 57)
27. The introduction includes what the researcher found in the study.
   ❑ The results section includes what the researcher found in the study. (p. 57)
28. The media tends to focus on sensationalistic and dramatic psychological findings.
   ❑ The media tends to focus on sensationalistic and dramatic psychological findings. (p. 57)
29. As you read psychological information in the media, you should consider how the research affects you as an individual.
   ❑ As you read psychological information in the media, it is important to consider how the research affects you as an individual, keeping in mind that the study was done on groups. (p. 58)
30. One study is usually enough research on a particular topic or issue.
   ❑ One study is usually not enough research on a particular topic or issue. (p. 59)
31. Sample size is not important to know when reading media reports of psychological information.
   ❑ Sample size is important to know when reading media reports of psychological information. (p. 59)

Practice Test

1. Of the following, which best describes the role that the mass media plays in psychological research?
   a. The mass media tends to sensationalize psychological research.
   b. The mass media tends to accurately report most psychological research.
   c. Through its influence, the mass media determines what type of research is funded.
   d. The mass media has had a profound impact on making us more knowledgeable about science and psychology.

a.	CORRECT; the mass media tends to report only the sensational and dramatic
b.	reports in the media tend to be too brief as to leave out important details
c.	deciding what research is funded is not the role of the mass media
d.	actually, the mass media has made us less knowledgeable

2. _____ is objective, systematic, and testable.
   a. The scientific method
   b. The placebo effect
   c. Scientific research
   d. Experimenter bias

a.	the scientific method is a series of steps that serves as the basis for scientific research
b.	the placebo effect refers to changes in behavior that are due to expectations
c.	YES; scientific research reduces the chance that information will be based on personal beliefs, opinions, and emotions
d.	experimenter bias occurs when the experimenter has expectations that influence the outcome of the research

3. Juan is engaged in a process to discover accurate information. He has followed several steps: conceptualizing a problem, collecting data, drawing conclusions, and revising research conclusions and theory. Juan is using:
   a. an operational definition of the dependent variable
   b. a standardized test
   c. the scientific method
   d. a double-blind experiment

a.	operational definitions are a part of the scientific method, but do not have these steps described
b.	a standardized test may be used to collect data, but is not relevant to the other steps
c.	YES, THAT'S CORRECT; these steps describe the scientific method
d.	a double-blind experiment may be used by the experimenter to control for expectations during the data collection step

4. What is the first step of the scientific method?
   a. draw conclusions
   b. revise research conclusions
   c. collect data
   d. conceptualize a problem

a.	drawing conclusions is the third step
b.	no, this is the final step
c.	no, collecting data is the second step
d.	RIGHT; the first step in the scientific method is to conceptualize a problem

5. You have received feedback on your research proposal from your psych professor. He has written, "You need to state your definitions more precisely and in terms of observable events that can be measured." What is he talking about?
   a. He is referring to including more references in your study.
   b. His feedback is in regard to operational definitions.
   c. He is suggesting that readers will not understand what you mean by the placebo effect.
   d. You need to spell out in greater detail what statistical techniques you are proposing to use to analyze your data.

a.	the comment is not related at all to the references used in the study
b.	RIGHT; your variables are not defined by their operations
c.	readers will understand the term placebo effect
d.	the comment is really the definition of an operational definition and does not relate to statistical techniques

6. The number of correct answers given on a unit test in history would best serve as an operational measure for which concept?
   a. interest in history
   b. unit information that was learned
   c. dislike of history
   d. time spent studying for the test

a.	interest of history would not be operationally defined this way
b.	CORRECT; the information that was learned could be operationally defined as the number of correct answers
c.	dislike of history would not be operationally defined this way
d.	an operational definition of interest in history would not be the number correct on a history test

7. To help explain and make predictions about a condition such as schizophrenia or childhood autism, ideas would be formed into a(n)
    a. assumption.
    c. theory.
    b. inference.
    d. hypothesis.

a.	no	
b.	no	
c.	YES; a theory is a set of ideas that help us make predictions and explain data	
d.	a hypothesis is a specific assumption or prediction that can be tested	

8. A theory generates _____, which are specific assumptions or predictions that can be tested to determine their accuracy.
    a. validity
    b. informed consent
    c. ethnic gloss
    d. hypotheses

a.	validity does not refer to specific assumptions or predictions	
b.	informed consent is an ethical guideline	
c.	ethnic gloss refers to labels that make ethnic groups more homogeneous	
d.	TRUE; a hypothesis is a specific assumption or prediction that can be tested	

9. The statement, "children who watch a model being reinforced for being aggressive or be given no consequence will be more likely to imitate the model than when the model is punished for being aggressive" is an example of a(n):
    a. case study
    b. operational definition
    c. theory
    d. hypothesis

a.	a case study is an example of a research method involving one individual	
b.	operational definition refers to making terms precise and measurable	
c.	a theory is a coherent set of interrelated ideas	
d.	YES; this is a hypothesis since it consists of a specific prediction that can be tested	

10. The use of statistical procedures allows researchers to:
    a. conceptualize the problem
    b. collect data
    c. draw conclusions
    d. revise theories

a.	statistical procedures are not involved in conceptualizing research problems	
b.	collecting data is accomplished through research methods	
c.	THAT'S RIGHT; statistical methods help psychologists understand the meaning of data	
d.	revision of theories occurs after statistical procedures are used to draw conclusions	

11. A _____ is selected from the population.
    a.   sample
    b.   placebo
    c.   dependent variable
    d.   theory

a.	YES; a sample is a subset of the population	
b.	a placebo is an inert treatment that has no real effect	
c.	the dependent variable is the variable that is being measured	
d.	a theory is a set of interrelated ideas	

12. Each of the following is a drawback of laboratory research, except
    a.   participants know they are being studied
    b.   the laboratory setting might produce unnatural behavior
    c.   the participants are not likely to represent diverse cultural groups
    d.   laboratory settings do not permit control over complex real-world factors

a.	this is a drawback; participants will know they are being studied
b.	this is a drawback; being in a laboratory can cause participants to behave unnaturally
c.	this is a drawback
d.	CORRECT; the laboratory does in fact permit control over factors

13. What is the main disadvantage of laboratory observation?
    a.   The researcher cannot control the situation.
    b.   The setting is too unpredictable.
    c.   Subjects may not behave naturally because they know they are being observed.
    d.   The variables cannot be defined in operational terms.

a.	the researcher can control the situation in laboratory observation
b.	since the researcher can control the laboratory observation, the setting is predictable
c.	THAT'S RIGHT; subjects may change their behavior if they think they are being watched
d.	operationally defined variables are necessary in laboratory observation

14. Ali and Michael are conducting a study where they sit in the lobby of the student center and take notes on different students' hand gestures as they speak. What type of research method are Ali and Michael using?
    a.   case study
    b.   correlational study
    c.   naturalistic observation
    d.   experimental research

a.	a case study involves an in-depth examination of one person
b.	a correlational study examines the relationships of two or more events or characteristics
c.	YES; this is the method by which behavior is observed in real-world settings
d.	experimental research consists of the manipulation of variables and groups of subjects

15. A researcher recently asked Caleb questions about his attitudes toward politics. Caleb participated in a(n) _____. He later admitted that he gave answers that he thought were socially acceptable and this illustrates _____.
    a.   questionnaire; the placebo effect
    b.   interview; social desirability
    c.   experiment; experimenter bias
    d.   experiment; informed consent

a. a questionnaire consists of the participant writing down responses; the placebo effect refers to the participant's expectations affecting the research
b. THAT'S RIGHT; an interview involves the person being asked questions; some people may give only social desirable or acceptable answers
c. an experiment involves the manipulation of variables; experimenter bias refers to the experimenter holding expectations that influence the outcome of the study
d. an experiment involves the manipulation of variables; informed consent is an ethical guideline that requires researchers to inform their research participants

16. A research method typically used by clinical psychologists with unique individuals is called a(n)
   a. interview
   b. random sample
   c. experiment
   d. case study

   a. an interview is a face-to-face method where the participant is asked questions
   b. a random sample is a sample that is selected from the population at random
   c. an experiment involves the manipulation of variables and subject groups
   d. YES; a case study is an in-depth look at a single individual

17. A psychologist would most likely use the case study method to examine which of the following phenomena?
   a. a young child's problems with anger control and inappropriate emotional reactions due to a unique type of brain injury
   b. an elderly person's depression associated with the grieving over the death of a spouse of 55 years
   c. adolescents' reactions to peer pressure with respect to sexual behavior
   d. prisoners' compliance with prison rules in a maximum security facility

   a. GOOD; the child has experienced a unique type of brain injury and the case study method would allow an in-depth look at the individual
   b. probably not since the person's reaction is typical among those who are grieving
   c. the emphasis in this option is on a group of adolescents not individual adolescents
   d. the emphasis in this option is on a group of prisoners not individual prisoners

18. Participants' tendency to answer survey questions in a way that is intended to create a good impression, rather than to provide true information, is known as
   a. the halo effect.
   b. intentional falsification.
   c. social desirability.
   d. demand characteristic.

   a. no
   b. no
   c. NICE; this defines social desirability
   d. no

19. Standardized tests, like the MMPI and the Stanford-Binet Intelligence Test,
   a. give every member of the population an equal chance to be tested
   b. are only used by clinical psychologists
   c. provide information about individual differences among people
   d. involve making careful observations of people in real-world settings

a.	this option describes a random sample
b.	standardized tests are used by several different types of psychologists
c.	CORRECT; these tests provide information about individual differences
d.	standardized tests are not given in real-world settings

21. What is the main advantage of using standardized tests?
    a. They have very good external validity.
    b. They can determine cause and effect.
    c. They provide information about individual differences.
    d. They contain no biases.

a.	this may be true, but is not the main advantage
b.	only experimentation can determine cause and effect
c.	THAT'S RIGHT; standardized tests gives information about individual differences
d.	standardized tests can be biased against certain groups of people

22. An area of inquiry in which psychologists gather knowledge about the biological basis of behavior is called:
    a. physiological research
    b. correlational research
    c. methodological research
    d. laboratory research

a.	CORRECT; physiological research often involves using technological advances
b.	correlational research examines the relationship between two or more events or characteristics
c.	this is incorrect
d.	while physiological research may take place in a laboratory, the area of inquiry is still known as physiological research

23. Which of the following is an advantage of animal research?
    a. The life cycle of some animals can be tracked over a short time.
    b. No control groups are necessary with animal research.
    c. Naturalistic observation can be accomplished in the laboratory.
    d. There is no need to follow ethical guidelines.

a.	YEAH; because of this animals are important for genetics research
b.	even with animals, control groups are required
c.	no this is not an advantage
d.	there are very rigorous ethical guidelines regarding the use of animals in research

24. The strength of the relationship between two or more events can be determined by:
    a. experimental research
    b. case study
    c. physiological research
    d. correlational research

a.	experimental research consists of manipulation of variables and subject groups
b.	case studies provide an in-depth look at an individual
c.	physiological research studies the biological basis of behavior
d.	TRUE; correlational research examines relationships

25. The research method that measures how much one characteristic is associated with another is known as
    a. classic experimentation.
    b. naturalistic observation.
    c. correlational strategy.
    d. quasi-experimentation.

a.	the experiment determines cause and effect relationships
b.	no, since naturalistic observation does not attempt to control variables
c.	YES, THAT'S RIGHT; correlational research attempts to determine the relationship between variables
d.	this is incorrect

26. A researcher finds a strong correlation between work stress and high blood pressure. Which of the following might *possibly* be true?
    a. Work stress causes high blood pressure.
    b. High blood pressure causes people to perceive high levels of work stress.
    c. A third factor could be causing the correlation.
    d. all of the above

a.	maybe, but we don't know for sure
b.	maybe, but we can't say for sure
c.	this is a possibility
d.	YES: but we don't know for sure which one is the best explanation

27. Which of the following research strategies allows for most control and precision?
    a. correlational
    b. quasi-experimental
    c. experimental
    d. pseudoexperimental

a.	correlational research only determines relationships among variables
b.	no
c.	RIGHT; experimental research can determine cause and effect between events
d.	no

28. If you conduct research in which you manipulate a variable while holding others constant and randomly assign participants to groups, what research method are you using?
    a. case study
    b. interview
    c. correlational research
    d. experimental research

a.	a case study consists of an in-depth analysis of a single individual
b.	an interview is a face-to-face questioning of another person
c.	in correlational research, we examine the relationship between two or more events
d.	CORRECT; the experiment can help psychologists determine the causes of behavior

29. An experiment is being conducted to determine the effects of different teaching methods on student performance. The independent variable is _____, while the dependent variable is _____.
    a. different teaching methods; number of students taking the test
    b. student performance; grades on a test
    c. different teaching methods; student performance
    d. student performance; different teaching methods

a.	partially correct; the different teaching methods are the independent variable, but the dependent variable is not the number of students the taking test, which is irrelevant	
b.	partially correct; student performance is not the independent variable, but student performance could be measured by grades on a test	
c.	TOTALLY CORRECT; the different teaching methods are being manipulated (cause) and student performance is the dependent variable (effect), it is being measured	
d.	no, they are backwards	

30. In an experiment, the _____ variable is the "cause" and the _____ variable is the "effect."
   a. dependent; independent
   b. independent; dependent
   c. control; dependent
   d. dependent; experimental

a.	no; the dependent variable is being measured to detect change that the manipulation of the independent variable might have caused
b.	CORRECT; the cause is the independent variable and the effect is the dependent variable
c.	no; the control group acts as a comparison; the dependent variable is the effect that is being measured because of changes to it due to manipulation
d.	no; the dependent variable is being measured to detect change that the manipulation of the independent variable might have caused; the experimental group is the group that receives the manipulation

31. In an experiment testing the effect of amphetamine on learning in rats, the amphetamine is known as the
   a. dependent variable.
   b. experimental variable.
   c. independent variable.
   d. extraneous variable.

a.	the dependent variable is learning
b.	no
c.	YES; the amphetamine is the "cause" that is being manipulated
d.	no

32. Manipulated factor is to _____ as measured factor is to _____.
   a. experimental group; independent variable
   b. control group; independent variable
   c. dependent variable; experimental group
   d. independent variable; dependent variable

a.	the experimental group receives the manipulation; the measured factor is the dependent variable
b.	the control group acts as a comparison group; the measured factor is the dependent variable
c.	the manipulated factor is the independent variable; the experimental group receives the manipulation
d.	THAT'S RIGHT; the experimenter manipulates the independent variable and determines what, if any, changes occurred in the dependent variable

33. Experiments with people involve a comparison between at least two groups: a group that receives the special treatment and a group that receives a placebo or neutral treatment. This latter group is called the
    a. control group.
    b. representative sample.
    c. experimental group.
    d. random sample.

a.	RIGHT; this is the control group
b.	the sample that is selected from the population should be a representative sample
c.	the experimental group receives the special treatment
d.	both groups make up the random sample

34. Which of the following statements about psychological research methods is correct?
    a. Only clinical psychologists are allowed to conduct experiments.
    b. It would be inappropriate to combine observation and the correlational method.
    c. Experiments usually involve standardized tests.
    d. Psychological research studies often combine several research methods.

a.	psychologists from all specializations conduct experiments
b.	combining methods is something that is often done and is appropriate when required
c.	experiments involve the independent variable and the dependent variable
d.	THIS IS CORRECT

35. If you were a psychologist concerned about reducing gender bias in psychological inquiry, you would be least concerned about which of the following?
    a. gender stereotypes
    b. exaggeration of gender differences
    c. gender of consumers of psychological research
    d. selection of research topics

a.	no; this is a very important issue
b.	gender differences are often exaggerated
c.	YEAH; this is the least important
d.	research topics often reflect a male bias

36. Which section of a research article presents the author's conclusions?
    a. abstract
    b. results
    c. methods
    d. discussion

a.	the abstract is a summary of the research article
b.	the results contain statistical analyses
c.	no; the methods describes the procedures used
d.	CORRECT; the conclusions are presented in the discussion section

Chapter 3 - Biological Foundations and Neuroscience

The Big Picture: Chapter Overview

The message of inheritance is passed from generation to generation through heredity. The nucleus of each human cell contains 23 pairs of chromosomes that contain DNA. Genes, the units of hereditary information, are short segments of chromosomes. Genes combine with other genes to determine our characteristics. There are dominant and recessive genes. Genotype refers to the person's actual genetic material, while the phenotype is the way the genotype is expressed in observed and measurable characteristics. Darwin proposed the idea of natural selection, which suggests that the organisms that are best adapted to their environments are the ones most likely to survive and reproduce, thus passing on their genes. The evolutionary psychology approach is a contemporary perspective that emphasizes the importance of adaptation, reproduction, and natural selection in explaining behavior. However, most scientists believe that behavior is determined by the interaction of the environment and the organism's biological inheritance.

Neurons are the basic building blocks of the nervous system. The multidisciplinary field known as neuroscience studies the nervous system. The nervous system is divided into the peripheral and central nervous system. The central nervous system consists of the brain and spinal cord. The peripheral system connects the brain and spinal cord to the other parts of the body; it also consists of the somatic nervous system, which contains sensory and motor nerves, and the autonomic nervous system, which monitors the body's internal organs.

Cells that carry input to the brain are called afferent neurons and those that carry output from the brain are efferent neurons. Interneurons mediate sensory input and motor output. A neuron is made of a (1) cell body, which regulates the cell's growth and maintenance; (2) dendrites, which collect information for the neuron; and (3) an axon, which carries information away from the cell body to other cells. Most axons are covered with a layer of fat cells called the myelin sheath that insulates the axon and speeds up the impulse. Neurons send information down the axon in the form of waves of activation called the action potential. The action potential operates according to the all-or-none principle. The nerve impulse is carried across the synapse by chemical substances called neurotransmitters such as GABA, acetylcholine, norepinephrine, dopamine, serotonin, and endorphins. Neurotransmitters land on receptor sites on the next neuron where they may excite and/or inhibit that next neuron. Some drugs, called agonists, mimic or increase a neurotransmitter's effect; antagonists are drugs that block a neurotransmitter's effects. Glial cells provide support and nutritive functions for neurons.

The brain consists of the hindbrain, midbrain, and forebrain. The hindbrain is the lowest portion of the brain and consists of the medulla, cerebellum, and pons. The midbrain is an area where many nerve-fibers ascend and descend. The mid-brain relays information between the brain and the eyes and ears. An important structure of the midbrain is the reticular formation. The highest region of the brain is the forebrain. Its major structures include the limbic system, amygdala, hippocampus, thalamus, basal ganglia, hypothalamus, and neocortex. Each structure performs certain specialized functions involving emotion, memory, senses, movement, stress, and pleasure. The neocortex comprises the largest part of the brain and consists of two halves, each with four lobes. The neocortex consists of sensory areas, motor areas, and association areas. Two important areas in the neocortex involved in language are Broca's area and Wernicke's area. The Wernicke-Geschwind model describes how Broca's and Wernicke's areas function together when we hear words. The two hemispheres are connected by the corpus callosum. No complex function can be assigned to one single hemisphere or the other. There is interplay between the two hemispheres

Plasticity refers to the brain's capacity for modification and reorganization following damage. The amount of damage is a key factor in determining the degree of recovery. Collateral sprouting and substitution of functioning are repair mechanisms that can lead to the brain restoring some lost functions. Brain grafts and implants may help individuals with brain damage like that due to Parkinson's disease and Alzheimer's disease. Scientists have developed techniques to study the functioning of the living brain. These include EEGs, CAT scans, PET scans, and MRIs.

A number of important body reactions produced by the autonomic nervous system result from its action on the endocrine glands. These glands release hormones directly into the bloodstream. The pituitary gland is referred to as the master gland. The adrenal glands play an important role in mood, energy, and stress.

Learning Objectives

When you have studied the material in this chapter, you should be able to:

1. describe the relationship between chromosomes, DNA, and genes, and explain the dominant-recessive gene principle. (pp. 66-67)
2. explain the concept of natural selection and how it relates to evolutionary psychology. (pp. 68-70)
3. explain the effects of nature and nurture. (pp. 69-70)
4. distinguish between the central and peripheral nervous system. (p. 71)
5. name the functions of the somatic, autonomic, sympathetic, and parasympathetic nervous systems. (pp. 71-72)
6. distinguish between the functions of afferent neurons, efferent neurons, and interneurons. (pp. 72-73)
7. describe the structure of a neuron, including the cell body, the dendrite, the axon, and the myelin sheath. (p. 73)
8. describe the conduction of a nerve impulse, including the roles of synapses and neurotransmitters. (pp. 73-78)
9. list six common neurotransmitters and their functions. (p. 76)
10. describe the role of glial cells. (p. 78)
11. describe the hindbrain and its components: the medulla, the cerebellum, and the pons. (p. 80)
12. describe the midbrain and its component: the reticular formation. (p. 80-81)
13. describe the forebrain and its components: the limbic system, thalamus, basal ganglia, and the hypothalamus. (pp. 80-84)
14. identify the neocortex, and distinguish between the four lobes: occipital, temporal, frontal, and parietal. (p. 84)
15. explain the results of topographical mapping of the neocortex. (pp. 85-87)
16. identify the corpus callosum, explain its role in split-brain research, and discuss integration of function in the brain. (pp. 87-89)
17. describe the location and list the functions of Broca's and Wernicke's areas, and describe how they function together according to the Wernicke-Geschwind model. (p. 87)
18. discuss the brain's plasticity and describe techniques to repair damaged brains. (p. 93)
19. differentiate among the methods used to study the brain: EEG, CAT scan, PET scan, and MRI. (pp. 93-94)
20. describe the functions of the endocrine glands, including the pituitary gland and the adrenal glands. (pp. 95-96)
21. from *Explorations in Psychology*: discuss the significance of the Mankato Nun Studies and the potential contributions of the study to human brain research. (p. 92)

Guide Review

Biological Foundations

The nucleus of each human cell has 46 chromosomes. Chromosomes are composed of molecules called DNA. The units of hereditary information, found on DNA molecules, are called genes. Each person has two genes for each hereditary characteristic. According to the dominant-recessive genes principle, the dominant gene exerts its influence. A recessive gene exerts its influence only when the two genes of a pair are both recessive. A person's genotype refers to her actual genetic material inherited from her parents. The way the genotype is expressed in observed and measurable characteristics is called phenotype. For each genotype, a variety of phenotypes can be expressed. The task of the Human Chromosome Project is to construct a map of every human gene. Darwin believed that evolution favors genes that result in design features that are most likely to lead to survival and reproduction; this process is referred to as natural selection.

A contemporary view that emphasizes the importance of adaptation, reproduction, and the survival of the fittest in explaining behavior is called the evolutionary psychology approach. Scientists agree that it is difficult to separate the effects of genes and the effects of the the envir. An organism's environmental experiences are called nurture, while biological inheritance is called nature. The relative contributions of heredity and environment are not _____.

chromosomes - p. 66
DNA - p. 66

genes/two - p. 66

dominant - p. 66
recessive - p. 66
genotype - p. 67

phenotype - p. 67
range - p. 67
Human Genome - p. 67

survival - p. 68
natural selection - p. 68

evolutionary - p. 69

environment - p. 69
nurture/nature - p. 69
additive - p. 69

The Field of Neuroscience, the Nervous System, and Neurons

The body's electrochemical communication circuitry is known as the nervous system. The nerve cell, the basic unit of the nervous system, is called the neuron. Neuroscience is the multidisciplinary study of the nervous system.

The nervous system is divided into two parts: the central nervous system and the peripheral nervous system. The central nervous system consists of the brain and spinal cord; the peripheral nervous system connects the brain and spinal cord to other parts of the body. The peripheral nervous system consists of two major divisions: one, which contains both sensory nerves and motor nerves, is called the somatic nervous system. The other, which monitors breathing, heart rate, and digestion, is the autonomic nervous system. The autonomic nervous system is divided into the sympathetic nervous system, which helps arouse the body, and the parasympathetic nervous system, which helps calm the body. The cells that carry input to the brain are called afferent neurons; the cells that carry the output from the brain are referred to as efferent neurons. Most of the brain consists of cells called interneurons

When examining neurons, the nucleus can be found in the cell body. Information is collected for the neurons by the dendrites. Information is carried away from the cell body by the axons. Most axons are covered with a layer of insulating fat cells called the myelin sheath. Neurons create electrical signals as

nervous system - p. 70
neuron/Neuroscience - p. 71

peripheral - p. 71
spinal cord - p. 71

somatic - p. 71
autonomic - p. 72

sympathetic - p. 72
parasympathetic - p. 72
afferent - p. 72
efferent - p. 72
interneurons - p. 73

cell body - p. 73
dendrites - p. 73
axon - p. 73
myelin sheath - p. 73

electrically charged particles called _ions_ move back and forth through their membranes. _Resting Potential_ refers to the stable, negative charge of an inactive neuron. Neurons send messages by creating a brief wave of electrical charge; this is charge is called a(n) _neural impulse_. The action potential conforms to the _____ principle. As neural impulses reach the end of the axon, they face a gap between neurons called a _synapse_. Impulses are able to cross the synapse by acting on a group of chemical substances called _neurotransmitters_.

GABA is a neurotransmitter that _inhibits_ the firing of neurons. A neurotransmitter that produces contractions of skeletal muscles by acting on motor nerves is _____. Too little of the neurotransmitter norepinephrine is associated with _____, while an excess is linked to agitated, _____ states. An excess of the neurotransmitter dopamine is associated with _____ while low levels are associated with _____. A neurotransmitter that is involved in the regulation of sleep and depression is _____. Finally, neurotransmitters that seem to function as natural opiates are called _____. If you are taking a drug that mimics or increases a neurotransmitter's effects, you are taking a(n) _agonist_. An _antagonist_ is a drug that can block a neurotransmitter's effect. Non-neurons that provide support and nutritive functions to neurons are the _glial cells_.

Brain Structure and Function

During embryological development, the nervous system begins as a long, hollow _cord_. There are three major division of the brain: hindbrain, _mid_, and _forebrain_. The portion of the brain located at the rear of the skull is called the _hindbrain_. The hindbrain contains the _hipocampus_ which helps control breathing, and the _thalmus_, which is believed to help control movement. The _pons_ is a bridge in the hindbrain involved in sleep and arousal. The midbrain is involved in the relay of information between the brain and the _spine_ and _nerves_. A midbrain structure called the _basil ganglia_ is involved in stereotyped patterns of behavior. The highest region of the brain is called the _hypothalamus_. A forebrain structure that plays important roles in both memory and emotion is the _limbic_ system. One main part of the limbic system is the _____, which is important in the organism's survival and emotion. Another part of the limbic system, the _____, plays a role in the storage of memory. A forebrain structure that serves mainly as a relay station is called the _____. Another forebrain structure, essential to starting and stopping voluntary movement, is called the _____ _____. The forebrain structure that regulates eating, drinking, and sex is called the _hippocampus_. Olds and Milner's rat research in Montreal in the 1950s pointed to the existence of a _pleasure centre_ in the hypothalamus. Their research has important implications for _____ _____.

The largest region of the forebrain is the _____. The neocortex is divided into two halves, called _hemisphers_ and each is divided into four _lobe_. The occipital lobe is involved with vision ; hearing is associated with the temporal lobe; control of the voluntary muscles is associated with the frontal lobe; the parietal lobe is involved in body sensation. The research of Penfield and others has indicated that there is a point-to-point relation between a part of the body and a location on the brain . About 75 % of the neocortex is made up of the cerebral cortex . These regions are involved in our highest intellectual functions. The area of the cerebral cortex known as brocas area plays an important role in the production of speech. The _____ is involved in comprehending language. The Wernke Gershw model describes how these brain areas cooperate to understand speech.

The corpus callosum is a large bundle of axons and connects the two hemispheres. Speech and grammar are localized to the left hemisphere, which mainly controls the ability in most people, while understanding aspects of language such humor and metaphors, is localized in the right hemispher Researchers believe that complex thinking involves both sides of the brain.

Exploring the Brain

The brain's capacity to modify and reorganize following damage is called plasticity The human brain shows that most plasticity in young age . A process in which the axons of some healthy neurons adjacent to damaged cells grow new branches is called brain graft . When the function of a damaged region is taken over by other areas of the brain it is called _____ of functioning. Healthy tissue that is transplanted into damaged brains is referred to as a brain graft . Brain grafts have a higher success rate when young both brain tissue is used. Two diseases that have been the subjects of brain graft research are Alzheimer disease and Parkinson disease

The use of high-powered microscopes allows scientists to study the brain in great detail. The electrical activity of the brain is recorded by the EEG . A three-dimensional image of the brain is provided by computer-assisted axial topography, known as a CAT scan. The amount of glucose in various areas of the brain is measured by positron emmission tomography. Another technique, which uses radio waves to construct images of brain tissues and biochemical activity, is called magnetic _____ imaging (MRI).

Important body reactions result from the effect of the autonomic nervous system on the endocrine glands. Endocrine glands release their hormones directly into the bloodstream Among the important endocrine glands are (1) the gland that sits at the base of the skull, called the pituitary gland, and (2) the endocrine glands, which secrete epinephrine and _____, and which play an important role in our moods, our emotion level, and our ability to cope with stress .

Explorations In Psychology

To respond to the questions and exercises presented in this section, please write your thoughts, perspectives, and reactions on a separate piece of paper.

Explorations in Psychology: Left-Brain, Right-Brain Myths

- If you were writing a short science-fiction story, why would you be using both hemispheres?
- Ask five people to comment on which side of the brain controls creativity. Do your results reflect the left brain/right brain myth.
- What was Phil Bryden describing with the phrase *complementary specialization*?

Explorations in Psychology: The Brains of the Mankato Nuns

- Speculate on the type of intellectually challenging tasks that the Mankato Nuns engage in.
- What types of intellectually challenging tasks do you engage in?
- If you were an administrator of a retirement facility or nursing home, what steps would you take to ensure an intellectually challenging environment?
- Based upon what you've read in the section, what advice would you give people who fear aging?

In Your Own Words

To respond to the questions and exercises presented in this section, please write your thoughts, perspectives, and reactions on a separate piece of paper.

- ✓ Give some examples of what is meant by "nurture"?
- ✓ What did D.O. Hebb mean when he said, "The interaction of heredity and environment is so extensive that to ask which is more important, nature or nurture, is like asking which is more important to a rectangle, height or width"?
- ✓ What are some circumstances where your sympathetic nervous system is activated? In these circumstances, what advantage do you gain from the sympathetic nervous system being activated?
- ✓ Imagine that an evil scientist kidnaps you to study your brain. In his diabolical investigation, he must destroy one part of your brain. He asks you, "What part of the brain are you willing to give up for my diabolical investigation?" So, what part of the brain would you give up and why?
- ✓ Think of an activity that you have done in the last 24 hours. Describe the brain areas that were especially active as you performed the activity.
- ✓ Why study biology in a psychology course?

Correcting the Incorrect

Carefully read each statement. Determine if the statement is correct or incorrect. If the statement is incorrect, make the necessary changes to correct it. Then look directly under the statement for the correct statement and page reference in the textbook.

1. Chromosomes are made up of genes.
   - ❑ *Chromosomes are made up of DNA.* (p. 66).
2. The actual genetic material a person has is called the phenotype.
   - ❑ *The actual genetic material a person has is called the genotype.* (p. 67)
3. Natural selection is also known as the "survival of the fittest."
   - ❑ *Natural selection is also known as the "survival of the fittest."* (p. 68)
4. Nature refers to surrounding conditions and influences that affect the development of living things.
   - ❑ *Nurture refers to surrounding conditions and influences that affect the development of living things.* (p. 69)
5. Genetic heritage and environmental influences are additive.

  ❏ *Genetic heritage and environmental influences are not additive.* *(p. 69)*

6. Nerves are the basic unit of the nervous system.
  ❏ *Neurons are the basic unit of the nervous system.* *(p. 71)*

7. The two main parts of the nervous system are the central nervous system and autonomic nervous system.
  ❏ *The two main parts of the nervous system are the central nervous system and peripheral nervous system.* *(p. 71)*

8. The parasympathetic nervous system consists of the brain and spinal cord.
  ❏ *The central nervous system consists of the brain and spinal cord.* *(p. 71)*

9. Motor neurons are called afferent nerves.
  ❏ *Motor neurons are called efferent nerves.* *(p. 72)*

10. Interneurons carry sensory information to the brain.
  ❏ *Afferent neurons carry sensory information to the brain.* *(p. 72)*

11. The neuron consists of a cell body, dendrites, and an axon.
  ❏ *The neuron consists of a cell body, dendrites, and an axon.* *(p. 73)*

12. The wave of electricity within the axon is called the resting potential.
  ❏ *The wave of electricity within the axon is called the action potential.* *(p. 76)*

13. The gap between neurons is called the axon.
  ❏ *The gap between neurons is called the synapse.* *(p. 75)*

14. Neurotransmitters move across the synapse.
  ❏ *Neurotransmitters move across the synapse.* *(p. 76)*

15. GABA, dopamine, and serotonin are examples of endorphins.
  ❏ *GABA, dopamine, and serotonin are examples of neurotransmitters.* *(p. 76)*

16. A structure in the hindbrain is the reticular formation.
  ❏ *A structure in the hindbrain is the reticular formation.* *(p. 80)*

17. The medulla plays important roles in motor behavior.
  ❏ *The medulla plays important roles in breathing and reflexes.* *(p. 80).*

18. The thalamus plays an important role in memory and emotion.
  ❏ *The limbic system plays an important role in memory and emotion.* *(p. 81)*

19. A person suffering damage to the hippocampus would be unable to see.
  ❏ *A person suffering damage to the hippocampus would be unable to remember new memories.* *(p. 82).*

20. Starting and stopping voluntary movement are governed by the hypothalamus.
  ❏ *Starting and stopping voluntary movement are governed by the basal ganglia.* *(p. 82).*

21. The Olds studies have important implications for research on Alzheimer's disease.
  ❏ *The Olds studies have important implications for research on drug addiction.* *(p. 84).*

22. The occipital lobe is involved in hearing.
  ❏ *The temporal lobe is involved in hearing.* *(p. 84)*

23. The parietal lobe is involved in bodily sensation.
  ❏ *The parietal lobe is involved in bodily sensation.* *(p. 84)*

24. More than 75 % of the neocortex is made up of sensory cortex.
  ❏ *More than 75 % of the neocortex is made up of association cortex.* *(p. 86)*

25. The large bundle of axons that connects the brain's two hemispheres is called the corpus callosum.
  ❏ *The large bundle of axons that connects the brain's two hemispheres is called the corpus callosum.* *(p. 87)*

26. Language comprehension is carried out in Broca' area.
  ❏ *Language comprehension is carried out in Wernicke's area.* *(p. 87).*

27. Plasticity describes the nerve impulse.
  ❏ *Plasticity describes the brain's capacity to modify and reorganize itself following damage.* *(p. 91).*

28. PET scans and CAT scans are techniques to study the brain.
  ❏ *PET scans and CAT scans are techniques to study the brain.* *(p. 94)*

29. Endocrine glands release their chemicals directly into the brain.
  ❏ *Endocrine glands release their chemicals directly into the bloodstream.* *(p. 95)*

30. The master gland is the cerebellum gland.
  ❏ *The master gland is the pituitary gland.* *(p. 96)*

Practice Test

1. Genes are short segments of _____ that are composed of _____.
    - a.   genotype; phenotype
    - b.   chromosomes; dopamine
    - (c.) chromosomes; DNA
    - d.   DNA; chromosomes

a.	genotype refers to the genetic material and phenotype to how the genotype is expressed
b.	no; dopamine is a neurotransmitter
c.	CORRECT
d.	it is the other way around

2. The dominant-recessive genes principle states all of the following except which one?
    - a.   A recessive gene exerts its influence only if both genes of a pair are recessive.
    - b.   Dominant genes override the effects of recessive genes.
    - c.   If one gene of a pair is dominant and one is recessive, the dominant gene exerts its effect.
    - (d.) If both genes of a pair are dominant, the effect converts into a recessive trait.

a.	no; this statement is correct
b.	this statement is correct
c.	no; this statement is correct
d.	YOU BET; this statement is incorrect

3. Allen is tall and lean. These characteristics best describe his
    - a.   genotype.
    - b.   recessive genes.
    - c.   dominant genes.
    - (d.) phenotype.

a.	a person's genotype is the inherited genetic material
b.	we don't know if his tallness and leanness are caused by recessive genes
c.	we don't know if his tallness and leanness are caused by dominant genes
d.	RIGHT; the phenotype refers to how the genotype is expressed in an individual

4. Dr. Beenken is working on one of the largest scientific projects ever carried out. Her responsibility is to map out the 19th chromosome pair. She is working on:
    - a.   the evolutionary perspective.
    - b.   the Mankato Nun study.
    - c.   split-brain research.
    - (d.) the Human Genome Project.

a.	this is not related to mapping out human genes
b.	this study has nothing to do with mapping out human genes
c.	split-brain research would not map out human genes
d.	RIGHT; the Human Genome Project hopes to map out every human gene

5. According to evolutionary psychology, fears and phobias are related to
    a. the inheritance of recessive genes.
    b. the inheritance of dominant genes.
    c. successful survival and reproduction.
    d. low rates of survival and reproduction.

a.	no	
b.	no	
c.	RIGHT; the evolutionary perspective focuses on natural selection, survival, and reproduction	
d.	fears and phobias are seen as being adaptive leading to successful survival and reproduction	

6. Most psychologists believe that intelligence is determined.
    a. primarily by nature.
    b. primarily by nurture.
    c. primarily by one's environment.
    d. by the interaction of nature and nurture.

a.	no	
b.	no	
c.	the term "nurture" means the same as environment	
d.	CORRECT ANSWER; both the environment and one's genetic inheritance interact to determine intelligence	

7. The brain and the spinal cord comprise the
    a. central nervous system (CNS).
    b. peripheral nervous system (PNS).
    c. autonomic nervous system.
    d. sympathetic nervous system.

a.	THAT'S RIGHT; the CNS is made up of the brain and spinal cord	
b.	the PNS is made up of somatic nervous system and autonomic nervous system	
c.	this is part of the PNS	
d.	the sympathetic nervous system is part of the autonomic system	

8. When you accidentally touch a hot burner on a stove, which part of your nervous system carries the pain message from your skin to your brain?
    a. the autonomic nervous system
    b. the sympathetic nervous system
    c. the parasympathetic nervous system
    d. the somatic nervous system

a.	the autonomic nervous system regulates internal organs	
b.	the sympathetic nervous system arouses the body	
c.	the parasympathetic nervous system calms the body	
d.	YES; the somatic nervous system contains sensory neurons	

9. The physiological arousal that you feel as you enter a classroom to take an exam is produced by the _____ nervous system.
    a. parasympathetic
    b. sympathetic
    c. somatic
    d. central

a.	the parasympathetic nervous system calms the body	
b.	THAT'S RIGHT; during stressful situations, the sympathetic increases the body's arousal	
c.	the somatic nervous system provides sensory information to the CNS	
d.	the central nervous system is made up of the brain and spinal cord	

10. Which of the following types of neurons carries input to the brain?
   a. afferent neurons
   b. efferent neurons
   c. interneurons
   d. intraneurons

a.	YES; afferent neurons carry sensory information to the brain
b.	efferent neurons carry motor messages from the brain
c.	interneurons mediate sensory input and motor output
d.	no

11. The majority of the brain consists of which type of neurons?
   a. afferent neurons
   b. efferent neurons
   c. interneurons
   d. axons.

a.	afferent neurons carry information to the brain
b.	efferent neurons carry the brain's output
c.	YES; most of the brain is comprised of interneurons
d.	no; an axon is a part of a neuron

12. Messages from other neurons are collected by the _____ of the receiving neuron.
   a. axon.
   b. synapse.
   c. cell body.
   d. dendrite.

a.	the axon carries information away from the cell body to other cells
b.	the synapse is the space between neurons
c.	no; the cell body contains the nucleus
d.	YES; the dendrites collect information

13. The part of the neuron that carries messages away from the soma and toward the terminal buttons is called the
   a. nucleus.
   b. axon.
   c. dendrite.
   d. cell body.

a.	the nucleus is part of the cell body
b.	CORRECT
c.	the dendrites receives information
d.	the cell body is responsible for the growth and maintenance of the neuron

14. The _____ is the brief wave of electrical change that races down the axon.
    a. action potential
    b. resting potential
    c. all-or-none principle
    d. ions

a.	YES, THAT'S RIGHT; the action potential is caused by the exchange of ions across the neuron's membrane
b.	the resting potential refers to the stable, negative charge of an inactive neuron
c.	the all-or-none principle describes the action potential
d.	ions are electrically charged particles that create the action potential

15. The function of synaptic vesicles is to
    a. break down neurotransmitters.
    b. restore the electrical balance of the cell after an action potential has occurred.
    c. receive information from other cells and store it for later use.
    d. store neurotransmitter molecules.

a.	no
b.	no
c.	no
d.	GOOD JOB; the vesicles store molecules of neurotransmitters

16. A neurotransmitter associated with schizophrenia is
    a. GABA.
    b. acetylcholine.
    c. dopamine.
    d. norepinephrine.

a.	GABA is related to anxiety
b.	acetylcholine is associated with learning and memory
c.	THAT'S RIGHT; high levels of dopamine are linked to schizophrenia
d.	norepinephrine is implicated in depression and manic states

17. If a person has a low level of dopamine, this would most likely cause which problem?
    a. The person would have difficulty with walking.
    b. The person would suffer from anxiety.
    c. The person would suffer from depression.
    d. The person would have sleep problems.

a.	YES; dopamine is involved in voluntary movement
b.	the neurotransmitter GABA is involved with anxiety
c.	depression and serotonin and norepinephrine are related
d.	sleep problems are associated with serotonin

18. Glial cells
    a. are fewer in number than neurons.
    b. have dendrites just like neurons.
    c. provide supportive and nutritive functions in the brain.
    d. are specialized to send and receive information.

a.	there are more glial cells than neurons
b.	glial cells do not have dendrites or axons
c.	YES; these are the functions of glial cells
d.	glial cells do not send and receive information

19. The hindbrain structure that helps to control our breathing is called the _____.
   a. pons.
   b. reticular formation.
   c. medulla.
   d. cerebellum.

a.	the pons is a structure in the hindbrain that is involved in sleep and arousal
b.	the reticular formation is involved in stereotyped behaviors
c.	YEAH: the medulla controls breathing and other reflexes
d.	the cerebellum plays a role in motor behavior

20. A blow to the back of the head can be dangerous because the
   a. thalamus is there.
   b. medulla, which regulates breathing, is there.
   c. substantia nigra, which regulates movement, is there.
   d. memories are stored there.

a.	the thalamus is located in the forebrain and plays a role in sensation and perception
b.	YES; the medulla is located in the hindbrain and is very important
c.	no
d.	memories are not stored in this area

21. The _____ is forebrain structure that monitors eating, drinking, and sexual behavior is called the
   a. thalamus
   b. hypothalamus
   c. neocortex
   d. cerebellum

a.	the thalamus is not involved in these behavior
b.	CORRECT; the hypothalamus monitors eating, drinking, and sexual behavior
c.	no; the neocortex is a large portion of the forebrain
d.	the cerebellum is involved in motor behavior and is in the hindbrain

22. The hypothalamus can be described best as a(n)
   a. screen.
   b. subordinate.
   c. regulator.
   d. advisor.

a.	no
b.	no
c.	YES; the hypothalamus regulates several behaviors by its interaction with the pituitary gland
d.	no

23.   A forebrain structure that plays an important role in the storage of memories is the
  - a. hippocampus.
  - b. amygdala.
  - c. thalamus.
  - d. limbic system.

a.	RIGHT; this structure plays a role in the storage of memories
b.	the amygdala plays a role in emotion
c.	the thalamus serves as a rely station-like function for sensory information
d.	the limbic system is a network of structures

24.   Which of the following is not one of the lobes of the neocortex?
  - a. occipital
  - b. frontal
  - c. temporal
  - d. posterior

a.	no
b.	no
c.	no
d.	CORRECT; there is no posterior lobe in the neocortex

25.   Research about various brain areas indicates that higher mental processes like thinking and problem solving are located within the
  - a. association area.
  - b. parietal sulcus.
  - c. limbic system.
  - d. thalamic nuclei.

a.	YES; association areas are involved in the highest intellectual functions
b.	no
c.	no
d.	no

26.   The two hemispheres are connected by which structure?
  - a. corpus callosum
  - b. thalamus
  - c. hypothalamus
  - d. reticular formation

a.	CORRECT; the corpus callosum, a large bundle of fibers, connects the hemispheres
b.	no; the thalamus serves to relay sensory information
c.	the hypothalamus is involved in eating, drinking, and sex
d.	the reticular formation plays a role in stereotyped behaviors

27. Which of the following individuals would have the best chance to recover from damage to Broca's area?
   a. Tonya, a forty-year-old high school teacher
   b. Sean, a twenty-five-year-old university student
   c. Tara, a fifteen-year-old high school student
   d. Rodney, a four-year-old preschooler

a.	no	
b.	no	
c.	no	
d.	YES; the brain shows the most plasticity in young children	

28. The process by which the axons of healthy neurons adjacent to damaged cells grow new branches is called
   a. implanting.
   b. collateral sprouting.
   c. substitution of function.
   d. brain grafting.

a.	implanting refers to the procedure of grafting brain tissue
b.	CORRECT
c.	this is when damaged area's function is taken over by another area of the brain
d.	brain grafting is implanting healthy brain tissue

29. A technique for studying the brain that measures the amount of glucose in various areas of the brain is called
   a. PET scan.
   b. CAT scan.
   c. MRI.
   d. electroencephalography.

a.	YES; a PET scan measures the amount of glucose used in various parts of the brain
b.	a CAT scan involves passing X rays through the brain
c.	a MRI scan creates a magnetic field around the brain
d.	this measures the electrical activity of the brain

30. _____ is the brain's capacity to modify and reorganize itself following damage.
   a. Implanting
   b. Collateral sprouting
   c. Imprinting
   d. Plasticity

a.	implanting refers to the procedure of grafting brain tissue
b.	no; this is where health neurons grow new branches
c.	no
d.	YES; there is more plasticity in young children

Chapter 4 - Sensation and Perception

The Big Picture: Chapter Overview

Sensation is the process of detecting and encoding stimulus energy in the world by our sense organs. Perception refers to the process of organizing and interpreting sensory information to give it meaning. Psychophysics studies the links between the physical properties of stimuli and a person's experience of them. In psychophysics, two important thresholds are absolute threshold, which is the minimum amount of energy that we can detect, and difference threshold, which is the smallest difference in stimulation required to discriminate one stimulus from another 50 % of the time. In determining the difference threshold, Weber's law must be considered. Signal detection theory holds that criterion, our willingness to report that we have detected a stimulus, also influences threshold. Factors such as motivation, expectancy, and urgency of the moment influence sensitivity to sensory stimuli.

In regard to the visual system, light is a form of electromagnetic energy that can be described in terms of wavelength, which refers to the distance from the peak of one wave to the peak of the next wave. The main external structures of the eye included the sclera, iris, pupil, and cornea. Within the eye, the lens focuses light rays on the retina by the process called accommodation. The retina is made up of light-sensitive receptors called rods and cones. The rods and cones perform transduction, which is the conversion of energy into neural impulses. The fovea is the most important part of the retina. The blind spot lacks receptors since it is where neural impulses exit the eye on the optic nerve. The optic nerve fibers cross and divide at the optic chiasm. In the brain, features detectors in the visual cortex process visual information. Sensory adaptation refers to the change in the responsiveness of a sensory system based on average level of surrounding stimulation. Objects have color because they reflect only certain wavelengths of light. Three important characteristics of color are hue, saturation, and brightness. Two major theories of color vision are the trichromatic theory and the opponent-process theory.

Sound waves vary from each other in frequency, amplitude, and complexity. The ear is made up of the outer ear, middle ear, and inner ear. The middle ear consists of the eardrum, hammer, anvil, and stirrup. The inner ear is made up of the oval window, cochlea, and the organ of Corti. The basilar membrane and organ of Corti are located within the cochlea and are involved in changing vibrations into neural impulses. Three theories that explain auditory processing in the cochlea are place theory, frequency theory, and volley theory. Information travels from the cochlea to the brain stem by the auditory nerve.

The skin senses include touch, temperature, and pain. Melzack and Wall proposed gate control theory to explain pain perception and acupuncture. The chemical senses are taste and smell, since they react to chemicals rather than to energy. Taste buds respond to sweet, sour, bitter, and salty qualities. The olfactory epithelium contains the receptor cells for smell. The kinesthetic sense provides information to the brain about movement, posture, and orientation, while the vestibular system provides information about balance and movement from the semicircular canals.

Selective attention refers to focusing on a specific aspect of experience and plays an important role in perception. The Stroop effect illustrates automatic perception. The principles of perception include those involving shape perception, depth perception, motion perception, and perceptual constancy. The world is full of shapes and our perception of them is influenced by contour and figure-group relationship. Gestalt psychology describes how we tend to perceive according to certain patterns, and a main principle is that the whole is not equal to the sum of its parts. Depth perception allows us to perceive objects three dimensionally and involves binocular cues (e.g., disparity) and monocular cues (e.g., aerial perspective). In studying motor perception, psychologists examine apparent movement, stroboscopic motion, and movement aftereffects. Perceptual constancy includes size constancy, shape constancy, and brightness constancy. Visual illusions occur when the same retinal image is produced by two objects, but is perceived as different images. Well-known visual illusions include the Müller-Lyer illusion, Ponzo illusion, and the moon illusion.

Two major approaches that address the way we perceive the world are the information processing approach and the ecological approach. Research with infants, individuals who have recovered from blindness, and cross-cultural studies, have all addressed the same issue regarding whether perception is innate or learned.

Extrasensory perception is perception that occurs without the use of any known sensory process. The forms of ESP include telepathy, precognition, clairvoyance, and psychokinesis. Many demonstrations of ESP are actually magic tricks and other claims have not held up to scientific testing.

Learning Objectives

When you have studied the material in this chapter, you should be able to:

1.   define sensation and perception. (p. 102-103)
2.   explain the concept of absolute threshold and the effect of noise. (pp. 102-103)
3.   explain the relationship between Weber's Law and the difference threshold. (pp. 103,105)
4.   discuss signal detection theory, distinguishing between sensitivity and criterion. (p. 105)
5.   describe the properties of light waves. (p. 106)
6.   describe the functions of the components of the eye: sclera, iris, pupil, lens, and retina. (pp. 107-108)
7.   differentiate between the functions of the rods and the cones. (pp. 108, p. 110)
8.   trace nerve conduction by identifying the route from the retina to the visual cortex. (pp. 110-111)
9.   define what a feature detector is and describe the role of feature detectors in visual perception. (p. 110)
10.   discuss the process of sensory adaptation. (pp. 110-111)
11.   define the basic components of color: hue, saturation, and brightness. (pp. 111-112)
12.   compare and contrast the trichromatic and opponent-process theories of color vision. (pp. 112-115)
13.   match the basic components of sound waves (frequency, amplitude, and wave complexity) to the psychological perceptions of loudness, pitch, and timbre. (pp. 116-117)
14.   identify the structures of the outer, middle, and inner ear and their respective functions. (p. 118)
15.   explain how transduction is accomplished in the ear. (pp. 118-119)
16.   contrast place, frequency, and volley theories of hearing. (pp. 119-120)
17.   describe the process whereby skin senses touch and pressure. (pp. 120-121)
18.   summarize issues relevant to pain: pain threshold, Melzack and Wall's gate control theory, and acupuncture. (pp. 121-122)
19.   identify the types of receptors involved in taste and smell. (pp. 122-124)
20.   describe the kinesthetic and vestibular senses. (pp. 125-126)
21.   identify variables that influence selective attention. (pp. 128-129)
22.   explain the relationship between Gestalt psychology and shape perception. (pp. 129-130)
23.   distinguish between binocular and monocular depth perception cues. (pp. 130-136)
24.   define the monocular cues: aerial perspective, familiar size, height in the visual field, overlap, linear perspective, shadowing, size in the field of view, and texture gradient. (pp. 131-133)
25.   discuss the concepts of motion perception, perceptual constancy, and visual illusions. (pp. 136-139)
26.   explain and give an example of how culture might influence perception. (p. 141)
27.   define extrasensory perception and its associated phenomena: telepathy, precognition, clairvoyance, and psychokinesis. (pp. 141-143)
28.   from *Explorations in Psychology*, summarize the information refuting both the power of subliminal perception and extrasensory perception. (p. 104, p.143)

Guided Review

Detecting and Perceiving the World

The process of detecting and encoding stimulus energy is called _____. The process of organizing and interpreting sensory information to give it meaning is referred to as _____. Most contemporary psychologists refer to these processes as a unified _____ system. A psychologist who studies the relationship between the physical properties of stimuli and a person's experience of them is studying _____. The minimum amount of a stimulus an individual can detect 50 percent of the time is called _____ _____. The term given to irrelevant and competing stimuli is _____. The difference threshold, or _____ _____, is the point at which a person detects the difference between two stimuli 50 percent of the time. _____ law states that, regardless of their magnitude, two stimuli must differ by a constant proportion to be detected. According to _____ _____ theory, one's sensitivity to sensory stimuli depends on factors other than the intensity of the stimulus.

sensation - p. 102
perception - p. 102

information-processing - p. 102

psychophysics - p. 102
absolute threshold - p. 102

noise - p. 103/jnd - p. 105

Weber's - p. 105

signal detection - p. 105

The Visual System

Light is a form of _____ energy that can be described in terms of _____. The distance from the peak of one wave of light to the next is a _____. The white part of the eye, which helps maintain the shape of the eye and protects it from injury, is called the _____. The colored part of the eye, which can range in color from light blue to dark brown, is the _____. The opening in the center of the iris is called the _____. The clear membrane just in front of the eye is called the _____. The transparent and flexible ball-like structure is called the _____. When the lens increases its curvature in order to help focus, the process is called _____. The light-sensitive surface in the back of the eye is the _____. The retina contains two kinds of light receptors, called _____ and _____. Rods and cones turn light energy into energy that can be processed by the nervous system in a process called _____. Rods are active in _____ vision but are not useful for color vision. Cones are the receptors used for _____ vision. In the center of the retina, where vision is the sharpest, is an area called the _____. As a result of the placement of the rods on the retina, we are able to detect fainter spots of light in the _____ than at the fovea. Information is carried out of the eye toward the brain by the _____ _____. The place on retina where the optic nerve leaves the eye is the _____ _____. After the optic nerve leaves the eye, most of its fibers divide and cross over to the other side at the _____ _____. Therefore, what we see on the left side of our visual field ends up on the _____ side of the brain. Visual information is processed in the _____ cortex, located in the _____ lobe. _____ _____ are neurons in the brain's visual system that respond to particular lines or other features of a stimulus.

electromagnetic - p. 106
wavelengths - p. 106
wavelength - p. 106

sclera - p. 107
iris - p. 107
pupil - p. 107
cornea - p. 107
lens - p. 107
accommodation - p. 108
retina - p. 108
rods - p. 108
cones - p. 108
transduction - p. 108
night - p. 108
color - p. 108
fovea - p. 109

periphery - p. 109

optic nerve - p. 110
blind spot - p. 109

optic chiasm - p. 110, p. 111
right - p. 110, p. 111
visual - p. 110
occipital/Feature detectors - p. 110

The change in responsiveness of the sensory system based on the average level of surrounding stimulation is called _____ adaptation. Objects appear colored because they reflect certain _____ of light to our eyes. Three important properties of color are hue, _____, and brightness. A theory of color vision that suggests that the retina responds to only one of three colors-red, blue, and green-is the _____ theory. Although the trichromatic theory helps explain color blindness, it cannot adequately explain _____. The phenomenon of afterimages led Hering to propose that the visual system treats colors as _____ pairs. The theory that cells in the retina respond to pairs of color is called the _____ theory. There are three kinds of cones; they each respond best to the colors _____, green and _____.

sensory - p. 111

wavelengths - p. 111
saturation - p. 111

trichromatic - p. 112
afterimages - p. 113

complementary - p. 113
opponent-process - p. 114

red/blue - p. 114

The Auditory System

Sound, or sound waves, are _____ in the air that are processed by our auditory system. One way in which sound waves differ from each other is in _____. The ear detects the frequency of a sound wave as _____. Sound waves also vary in _____, which is the change of pressure created by sound waves. The amplitude of a sound wave is measured in _____. The perception of a sound wave's amplitude is referred to as _____. The blending of numerous sound waves results in _____ _____. We experienced the different qualities of sound as _____.

The outer ear is made up of the _____, which helps us localize sounds, and the external auditory canal, which funnels sound to the _____ _____. In the middle ear, the first structure touched by sound is the _____. The eardrum's vibrations then touch the three tiny bone structures, the hammer, the _____, and the stirrup. In the inner ear, sound waves travel from the oval window to the _____, a structure that contains the organ of Corti. Sensory receptors in the organ of Corti are stimulated by vibrations of the _____ _____. These vibrations generate neural impulses.

How does the inner ear register the frequency of sound? According to place theory, each frequency produces vibrations at a particular place on the _____ membrane. Another theory suggests that the perception of sound is due to how often the _____ _____ fires. This is called _____ theory. Another theory of hearing argues that neural cells can fire impulses in _____ succession and this is called the volley principle. Information travels from the cochlea to the lower portion of the brain by means of the _____ nerve. Ultimately, auditory information is stored and integrated in the _____ lobe of the neocortex.

vibrations - p. 116

frequency - p. 116
pitch/amplitude - p. 116

decibels - p. 116
loudness - p. 117
complex sounds - p. 117
timbre - p. 117
pinna - p. 118

middle ear - p. 118
eardrum - p. 118
anvil - p. 118

cochlea - p. 118

hairlike cells - p. 118

basilar - p. 119
auditory nerve – p. 120
frequency - p. 120
rapid - p. 120

auditory - p. 120
temporal - p. 120

Other Senses

Our largest sensory system is the _____. The skin contains receptors for touch, _____, and pain. Receptors located under the skin that respond to increases and decreases in temperature are called _____. The sensation that warns us that damage is

skin - p. 120
temperature - p. 120

thermocreceptors - p. 121

occurring to our bodies is _____. Pain is affected by motivation as well as cultural and ethnic _____. Melzack and Wall's theory of pain, suggesting that neural "gates" determine whether or not we experience pain, is called the _____-_____ theory. A technique for relieving pain that involves the insertion of thin needles into the body is called _____. The senses of taste and smell differ from other senses because they react to _____ stimulation rather than energy. Taste buds are found in the tongue on the _____. Taste buds respond to four main qualities: sweet, _____, bitter, and _____. Located at the top of the nasal cavity is a sheet of receptor cells called the _____ _____. Information about movement, posture, and orientation is provided to the brain by the _____ _____. Information about balance and movement is provided by the _____ sense. The kinesthetic senses are located in the cells of our muscles and _____. An important part of the vestibular sense is the semicircular canals, which lie in the _____ ear.

Perception

The process of organizing and interpreting information is called _____. The ability that we have to focus on a specific aspect of experience while ignoring others is called _____ _____. An example of automatic perception is the _____ effect. We are able to perceive shapes because they are marked off from the rest of what we see by _____. The principle that organizes our perceptual field into stimuli that stand out and those that do not stand out is called the _____-_____ relationship. An area of psychology that studies how people organize their perceptions is called _____ psychology. In addition to figure-ground, other Gestalt principles include closure, _____, and similarity.

The ability to perceive objects three-dimensionally is called _____ _____. The cues that we use for depth perception are both _____ and _____. When an individual perceives a single scene, even though the two images on the eyes are slightly different; this is called _____. People with vision in only one eye still see a world of depth because of _____ cues. An example of a monocular cue is _____ where one object partially blocks another object. Monocular cues are sometimes called _____ cues. When an object is stationary but is perceived to be moving, this is referred to as _____ movement. Two forms of apparent movement are _____ motion and movement _____.

We perceive three types of perceptual constancy: the recognition that an object remains the same size even though the retinal image changes is called _____ constancy. The perception that an object is the same even though its orientation to us changes is called _____ constancy. The recognition that an object retains the same degree of brightness even though different amounts of light fall on it is called _____ constancy. When two objects produce exactly the same retinal image but are perceived as being different images, a _____ _____ occurs.

Is perception _____ or learned? One approach argues that perception is a process of representing information from the world internally; this is the _____-_____ approach. Perception is an active process where the person explores and moves about the environment and this is the _____ approach. Researchers have attempted to answer these questions through: (1) experiments with infants, using a structure called a _____ _____; (2) studies of individuals who recover from _____; and (3) _____ studies. the influence of cultural experiences on perception is illustrated by the _____-_____ hypothesis.

innate - p. 139

information-processing - p. 139

ecological - p. 139

visual cliff - p. 139-140
blindness/cultural - p. 140, p. 141
carpentered-world - p. 141

Perception that does not occur through normal sensory processes is called _____ _____. One type of ESP, the transfer of thought from one person to another, is called _____. The perception of events before they occur is called _____. The ability to perceive remote events is _____. The ability to move objects without touching them is called _____. Many ESP phenomena have not been _____ when rigorous experimental standards have been applied.

extrasensory perception - p. 141
telepathy - p. 142
precognition - p. 142
clairvoyance - p. 142
psychokinesis - p. 142
replicated - p. 143

Explorations in Psychology

To respond to the questions and exercises presented in this section, please write your thoughts, perspectives, and reactions on a separate piece of paper.

Explorations in Psychology: Analyzing Subliminal Perception

- Before you read this section, what was your view on subliminal messages in rock music? Do they exist and if so, do they affect people?
- Ignoring the question of the subliminal effects of music, does music affect us in ways that are within our awareness?
- What would you say to someone who purchases a tape with subliminal messages to stop smoking and then actually quits? How could you explain this change in behavior, given what the textbook says about subliminal perception?

Explorations in Psychology: The Perceptual Worlds of Art

- Does state of mind influence an artist's art?
- If you are talking with someone on the phone or listening to a boring lecture, do you draw doodles? If so, what depth cues did you use?
- React to this statement: Art is artist, observer, and communication.

Explorations in Psychology: Debunking Psychics' Claims

- Has your view of the claims of psychics changed after reading this section?
- Have you ever witnessed first hand a psychic claim? How would people like Jim Alcock and the Amazing Randi most likely explain it? How would you?
- In your view does the lady who claimed to psychically will the fish to swim really believe that "her mind could not penetrate the brown paper," or was she consciously trying to escape criticism?

In Your Own Words

To respond to the questions and exercises presented in this section, please write your thoughts, perspectives, and reactions on a separate piece of paper.

✓ Put the definitions of sensation and perception in your own words and give an example of each.

✓ What did the Gestalt psychologists mean when they said, "the whole is not equal to the sum of its parts"?

✓ On a separate piece of paper, draw a landscape that includes objects such as a house, road, and trees. Give your drawing depth. See if you can use all the monocular cues described in the textbook.

✓ If culture influences perception, list some ways that your culture has influenced your perception of clothing, behavior, music, or food.

✓ Give an example of selective attention that you have recently experienced.

✓ Do the Gestalt principles of perception support or question the assumption that perception is innate?

✓ If you were creating a robot and could also "create" any new sense for it, what would you create and why?

✓ How would your life change if you lost your ability to experience the sense of pain?

Correcting the Incorrect

Carefully read each statement. Determine if the statement is correct or incorrect. If the statement is incorrect, make the necessary changes to correct it. Then look directly under the statement for the correct statement and page reference in the textbook.

1. Perception refers to the process of detecting and encoding stimulus energy in the world.
    ❑ *Sensation refers to the process of detecting and encoding stimulus energy in the world. (p. 102)*
2. Perception involves transduction.
    ❑ *Sensation involves transduction. (pp. 104, 110)*
3. The minimum amount of energy that can be detected is called the difference threshold.
    ❑ *The minimum amount of energy that can be detected is called the absolute threshold. (p. 102)*
4. Signal is the term given to irrelevant and competing stimuli.
    ❑ *Noise is the term given to irrelevant and competing stimuli. (p. 103)*
5. Weber's law says that sensitivity to sensory stimuli depend on factors other than the physical intensity of the stimulus.
    ❑ *Signal detection theory says that sensitivity to sensory stimuli depend on factors other than the physical intensity of the stimulus. (p. 105)*
6. The pupil contains the rods and cones.
    ❑ *The retina contains the rods and cones. (p. 108)*
7. The visual receptors are the rods and cones.
    ❑ *The visual receptors are the rods and cones. (p. 108)*
8. Rods provide color vision.
    ❑ *Cones provide color vision. (p. 108)*
9. Perceptual constancy is the change in the sensory system's responsiveness based on the average level of surrounding stimulation.
    ❑ *Sensory adaptation is the change in the sensory system's responsiveness based on the average level of surrounding stimulation. (p. 110)*
10. A color's hue is based on its wavelength.
    ❑ *A color's hue is based on its wavelength. (p. 111)*
11. A color's brightness is based on its purity.
    ❑ *A color's brightness is based on its intensity. (p. 112)*
12. The three different cones are red, white, and yellow.

❑ *The three different cones are green, red, and blue. (p. 114)*

13. The opponent-process theory of color vision states that there are three types of receptors that are maximally sensitive to different but overlapping ranges of wavelengths.
❑ *The trichromatic theory of color vision states that there are three types of receptors that are maximally sensitive to different but overlapping ranges of wavelengths. (p. 112)*

14. The trichromatic and opponent-process theory are both correct.
❑ *The trichromatic and opponent-process theory are both correct. (p. 114)*

15. We experience frequency as loudness.
❑ *We experience frequency as pitch. (p. 116)*

16. The organ of Corti is found in the middle ear.
❑ *The organ of Corti is found in the inner ear. (p. 118)*

17. The place theory of hearing adequately explains high-frequency sounds.
❑ *The place theory of hearing adequately explains high-frequency sounds. (p. 118-119)*

18. The auditory nerve carries neural impulses to the brain's auditory areas.
❑ *The auditory nerve carries neural impulses to the brain's auditory areas. (p. 120)*

19. Gate-control theory proposes that acupuncture opens pain gates.
❑ *Gate-control theory proposes that acupuncture closes pain gates. (p. 122)*

20. Smell, taste, and vision are our chemical senses.
❑ *Smell and taste are our chemical senses. (p. 122)*

21. The taste qualities include sweet, sour, bitter, and salty.
❑ *The taste qualities include sweet, sour, bitter, and salty. (p. 124)*

22. The sense that provides information about balance and movement is the kinesthetic sense.
❑ *The sense that provides information about balance and movement is the vestibular sense. (p. 125)*

23. The kinesthetic and vestibular senses are supplemented by information from hearing.
❑ *The kinesthetic and vestibular senses are supplemented by information from sight. (p. 126)*

24. Selective attention allows us to focus on some aspects of the environment while ignoring others.
❑ *Selective attention allows us to focus on some aspects of the environment while ignoring others. (p. 128)*

25. Gestalt means learned.
❑ *Gestalt means configuration or form. (p. 130)*

26. Figure-ground relationship is a principle that explains depth perception.
❑ *Figure-ground relationship is a principle that explains shape perception. (p. 129)*

27. Monocular cues provide us information about shape perception.
❑ *Monocular cues provide us information about depth perception. (p. 133)*

28. A binocular cue is overlap.
❑ *A monocular cue is overlap. (p. 130)*

29. If a person sees an object moving that is not actually moving, apparent movement is said to have occurred.
❑ *If a person sees an object moving that is not actually moving, apparent movement is said to have occurred. (p. 136)*

30. The Ponzo illusion illustrates perceptual constancy.
❑ *The Ponzo illusion illustrates size constancy. (p. 138)*

31. The carpentered-world hypothesis explains why ESP cannot possibly be a valid phenomenon.
❑ *The carpentered-world hypothesis explains how culture affects perception. (p. 141)*

32. Telepathy is the type of ESP where remote events can be perceived.
❑ *Telepathy is the type of ESP where remote events can be perceived. (p. 142)*

33. ESP claims have been scientifically tested and found valid.
❑ *ESP claims have been scientifically tested and found invalid. (p. 143)*

Practice Test

1. The process of detecting and encoding stimuli is _____.
   a. sensation
   b. perception
   c. Gestalt psychology
   d. accommodation

a.	RIGHT; this is sensation
b.	no; perception refers to organizing and interpreting sensory information
c.	Gestalt psychology refers to the notion that perception follows certain patterns
d.	accommodation is the lens changing its curvature

2. The eye is to sensation as the brain is to
   a. feeling.
   b. perception.
   c. impression.
   d. hearing.

a.	no
b.	RIGHT; perception refers to the brain's process of organizing and interpreting sensory information
c.	no
d.	no

3. The minimum amount of energy that we can detect is called
   a. the absolute threshold.
   b. minimal threshold.
   c. the difference threshold.
   d. Weber's law.

a.	YEAH
b.	no
c.	the different threshold refers to the smallest difference in required to discriminate two stimuli
d.	Weber's law is the principle that two stimuli must differ by a constant proportion

4. A painter who is able to tell the difference between two similar shades of paint is demonstrating
   a. the absolute threshold.
   b. the difference threshold.
   c. Weber's law.
   d. sensory adaptation.

a.	this is the minimum amount of energy that can be detected
b.	CORRECT; the different threshold refers to the smallest difference in required to discriminate two stimuli, in this case two shades of paint
c.	no
d.	sensory adaptation is the change of responsiveness to stimulation

5. Psychologists call the presence of competing and irrelevant stimuli
   a. noise.
   b. accommodation.
   c. saturation.
   d. disparity.

a.	THAT'S RIGHT
b.	accommodation refers to the ability of the lens to change its curvature
c.	saturation is based on the color's purity
d.	disparity refers to the difference in retinal image of the two eyes

6. Dr. Richardson says, "There is no such thing as an absolute threshold because stimulus detection depends on a number of factors beside the physical intensity of a stimulus and the sensory abilities of the observer." Dr. Richardson is most likely an advocate of which theory?
    a. subliminal perception theory
    b. signal detection theory
    c. adaptation theory
    d. opponent-process theory

a.	no
b.	YES; signal detection theory recognizes that such things as fatigue influences sensitivity to sensory stimuli
c.	no
d.	no

7. Wavelength is defined as the distance between
    a. peak and valley of a light wave.
    b. peak and peak of a light wave.
    c. valley and amplitude of a light wave.
    d. amplitude and peak of a light wave.

a.	no this is not the correct definition
b.	CORRECT
c.	no
d.	no

8. In order to do its job, the pupil depends most on which other part of the eye?
    a. lens
    b. iris
    c. cornea
    d. retina

a.	the lens focuses
b.	RIGHT; the iris as a muscle controls the size of the pupil
c.	the cornea is clear membrane in front of the eye
d.	the retina contains the rods and cones and is located in the back of the eye

9. The rods and cones are found in what part of the eye?
    a. the sclera
    b. the retina
    c. the cornea
    d. the fovea

a.	no; the sclera is outer white part of the eye
b.	YES; the rods and cones are found in the retina
c.	no; the cornea is the clear membrane in the front of the eye
d.	the fovea is the area of the retina where vision is the most sensitive

10. Why is vision sharpest in the fovea?
   a. because it contains only cones
   b. because it contains more cones than rods
   c. because it contains both rods and cones
   d. because it is located in the center of the retina

a.	YES; cones are the receptors that provide us with fine detail	
b.	no; it only contains cones	
c.	no; the fovea only contains cones	
d.	while the fovea is located in the center of the retina, the presence of cones is responsible for the sharp vision	

11. After information passes the optic chiasm, images from the left side of our visual field end up
   a. being reflected back to the blind spot.
   b. being reflected back to the optic nerve.
   c. on the right side of the brain.
   d. on the left side of the brain.

a.	no	
b.	no	
c.	RIGHT. information crosses over to the other side	
d.	no, information crosses over to the other side	

12. The visual cortex, which is responsible for processing visual information, is located in the _____ lobe.
   a. occipital
   b. parietal
   c. temporal
   d. frontal

a.	YES; the occipital lobe contains the visual cortex	
b.	no	
c.	no	
d.	no	

13. A color's intensity is based on its
   a. vividness.
   b. brightness.
   c. color
   d. hue.

a.	no	
b.	THAT'S RIGHT	
c.	color is determined by wavelengths	
d.	hue is based on the color's wavelength	

14. A change in the wavelength of light would result in a change in our perception of
   a. hue.
   b. saturation.
   c. brightness.
   d. timbre.

a.	YEAH; hue is based on the color's wavelength	
b.	saturation is based on the color's purity	
c.	brightness refers to the intensity of light	
d.	timbre the perceptual quality of sound	

15. Which theory of color vision does the best job of explaining afterimages?
   a. trichromatic theory
   b. the opponent-process theory
   c. the additive-subtractive theory
   d. No theory currently explains afterimages.

a.	no; the trichromatic theory says that there are three types of color receptors
b.	YES; the opponent-process theory suggests that if one member of the pair fatigues, the other member rebounds and gives an afterimage
c.	no
d.	no

16. Your text states that the term *color blindness* is misleading. Which of the following terms would be the most appropriate replacement?
   a. color vision deficit
   b. green blindness
   c. blue blindness
   d. visually impaired

a.	CORRECT; the old term suggest that a person cannot see color at all
b.	no
c.	no
d.	no

17. Pitch is to frequency as loudness is to
   a. amplitude.
   b. Hertz.
   c. wavelength.
   d. pulsation

a.	EXACTLY; loudness is determined by the sound's amplitude
b.	Hertz is a measurement of sound
c.	wavelength refers to the physical characteristic of sound
d.	no

18. Which structures comprise the inner ear?
   a. eardrum, oval window, and stirrup
   b. pinna, external auditory canal, and eardrum
   c. hammer, anvil, stirrup
   d. oval window, cochlea, and organ of Corti

a.	no
b.	no
c.	no; these structures make up middle ear
d.	CORRECT; the inner is made up of these structures

19. Which part of the ear is most important in the transduction of sound?
   a.   the auditory nerve
   b.   the outer ear
   c.   the middle ear
   d.   the inner ear

a.	this is important, but not in the actual transduction of sound
b.	no
c.	no
d.	RIGHT; the inner ear contains the organ of Corti

20. Which theory of hearing suggests that high frequency tones are explained by cells firing in rapid succession?
   a.   place theory
   b.   frequency theory
   c.   volley theory
   d.   similarity theory

a.	no; each frequency stimulates cells at particular places on the basilar membrane
b.	frequency theory says that how often cells fire is important
c.	YES, THAT'S RIGHT; the volley theory says that neural cells produce a volley of impulses
d.	no

21. What is the main difference between touch receptors and thermoreceptors?
   a.   sensitivity and speed
   b.   location and function
   c.   number and location
   d.   function and speed

a.	no
b.	CORRECT
c.	no
d.	no

22. The semicircular canals are found in
   a.   Venice.
   b.   the inner ear.
   c.   the outer ear.
   d.   the middle ear.

a.	no
b.	no
c.	no
d.	YES

23. What do the sense of taste and the sense of smell have in common?
   a.   They are both mechanical senses.
   b.   They are both chemical senses.
   c.   They are both electromagnetic senses.
   d.   They are both electric senses.

a.	no	
b.	THAT'S CORRECT; taste and smell	
c.	no	
d.	no	

24. What allows you to focus on this question while ignoring all the other stimulation in your environment?
  a. perception
  b. hue
  c. selective attention
  d. selective adaptation

a.	while you are perceiving this question, it does not allow you to focus on the question
b.	no
c.	THIS IS CORRECT; selective attention allows you to attend to one thing while ignoring other things
d.	no

25. You want to design a poster to advertise your company's new product. In order to entice people to pay attention to your poster and its message, you would design which of the following?
  a. a large poster with much small print and a few standard graphics
  b. a small poster with black and white text only
  c. a medium sized poster with unique graphics and small print
  d. a large poster with vivid colors, large print, and unique graphics

a.	no
b.	no
c.	no
d.	YES; size and color and novel objects influence our attention

26. The principle by which we organize perception into those stimuli that stand out and those that are left over is called
  a. figure-ground
  b. closure.
  c. similarity.
  d. proximity.

a.	THAT'S RIGHT
b.	no; closure refers to seeing incomplete figures as complete
c.	no; we tend to perceive objects together that are similar to each other
d.	no; we tend to group objects together that are near each other

27. The tendency to mentally "fill in the spaces" in order to see figures as complete refers to the Gestalt principle of
  a. closure.
  b. figure-ground.
  c. proximity.
  d. similarity.

a.	YEAH;
b.	no; figure-ground illustrates how we divide our visual world into
c.	no; we tend to group objects together that are near each other
d.	no; we tend to perceive objects together that are similar to each other

28. An object that partially conceals another object is perceived as being closer, according to the monocular cue of
   a. shadowing
   b. overlap
   c. texture gradient
   d. linear perspective

a.	no; the shadow of the objects provides information to its depth
b.	GOOD
c.	no; texture gradient refers to how the texture changes as distance changes
d.	no; linear perspective is when two parallel lines appear to converge in the distance

29. Pollution and water vapor in the air help give distant objects a hazy appearance according to the monocular cue called
   a. linear perspective.
   b. texture gradient.
   c. aerial perspective.
   d. overlap.

a.	no; linear perspective is when two parallel lines appear to converge in the distance
b.	no; texture gradient refers to how the texture changes as distance changes
c.	THAT'S RIGHT
d.	no; this refers to one object is partially blocking another object

30. Research on individuals who recover from blindness
   a. conclusively proves that perception is innate.
   b. conclusively proves that perception is learned.
   c. has conclusively demonstrated the interaction of learning and innate perception.
   d. is inconclusive regarding the issue of whether perception is innate or learned.

a.	no
b.	no
c.	no
d.	THAT IS CORRECT; some perceptual abilities may be innate and others may be learned

31. Claire believes she can predict events before they actually occur. Which type of ESP does Claire believe she possesses?
   a. clairvoyance
   b. precognition
   c. psychokinesis
   d. telepathy

a.	no; clairvoyance is the ability to perceive remote events that are not in sight
b.	YES; precognition involves knowing before something has happened
c.	no; psychokinesis is mind-over-matter
d.	no; telepathy is the transfer of thought from one person to another

Chapter 5 - States of Consciousness

The Big Picture: Chapter Overview

At one time consciousness was not considered for study in psychology. Consciousness is awareness of both internal and external stimuli or events. Consciousness can be described as a continuous flow of changing sensations, images, thoughts, and feelings. The study of consciousness includes unconscious thought, controlled processes, automatic processes, daydreaming, sleep and dreaming, and altered states of consciousness produced by hypnosis and psychoactive drugs.

One theory that explains why we sleep is called repair theory, which suggests that sleep restores and replenishes our bodies. Ecological theory states that sleep keeps us from wasting energy and risking harm during those times to which we have not adapted. The 24-hour human sleep/awake cycle is referred to as a circadian rhythm. This rhythm can become desynchronized by long air travel or changing work shifts. In Canada, long winter nights can lead to seasonal affective disorder. Without cues like sunlight or clocks, the natural circadian rhythm changes to a 25-to 26-hour rhythm. Most people are sleep deprived and sleep deprivation can have serious effects. The stages of sleep correspond to electrophysiological changes that can be measured using the EEG, a measure of the brain's electrical activity. During a relaxed or drowsy state, the EEG pattern is alpha waves. When we sleep, we pass through four stages, from light sleep in stage 1 to deep sleep in stages 3 and 4. Most dreaming occurs in REM sleep. We complete several sleep cycles nightly. The amount of REM sleep changes over the life span which raise questions about the function of REM sleep, such as memory. During REM sleep, the brain carries out complex processes. Sleep disorders include insomnia, sleepwalking, sleeptalking, nightmares and night terrors, narcolepsy, and sleep apnea.

Dreams have long been of interest and several theories have been proposed to explain them. According to Freud's view, dreams reflect wish fulfillment of unmet needs and have manifest content and latent content. The cognitive view holds that dreams are related to information processing, memory, and problem solving. According to the activation-synthesis view, dreams are the brain's way of making sense out of neural activity. Questions which have been asked about dreams include whether we dream in color, whether animals dream, whether men's and women's dreams are different, and why our recall of dreams is often poor. Lucid dreams are those in which the dreamer is aware that a dream is taking place.

Hypnosis is a psychological state of altered attention in which the individual is very receptive to suggestion. In the eighteenth century, Mesmer credited his success in curing his patients' problems to animal magnetism. The special process theory of hypnosis views hypnotic behavior as being qualitatively different than nonhypnosis behavior. Ernest Hilgard has used this approach in his hidden observer demonstrations. Nicholas Spanos' nonstate view holds that hypnosis is similar to other forms of social behavior; the individual who has become hypnotized is under the social influence of the hypnotist. Hypnosis has been applied in psychotherapy, medicine, dentistry, criminal investigations, and sports.

Psychoactive drugs are drugs that alter consciousness. Users of psychoactive drugs may develop tolerance, physical dependence, or psychological dependence. The three main types of psychoactive drugs are depressants, stimulants, and hallucinogens. Alcohol is an extremely powerful drug and is a depressant. The most widely used drug in our society is alcohol. Alcoholism and binge drinking are two problems associated with alcohol. Research suggests that both genetic and environmental factors play roles in alcoholism. Barbiturates (e.g., sleeping pills), tranquilizers (e.g., Valium), and opiates (e.g., morphine; heroin) are other depressants that are abused. Stimulants are drugs that increase activity in the CNS such as caffeine. A group of widely prescribed stimulants is amphetamines. Cocaine is also classified as a stimulant and is associated with a rush of euphoria; crack is an intensified form of cocaine and is usually smoked. Another stimulant, caffeine, is the most widely used psychoactive drug in the world. Hallucinogens are drugs that modify an individual's perceptual experiences. Marijuana, which produces its effect by disrupting neurons and neurotransmitters, and LSD are examples of hallucinogens.

Addiction is characterized by an overwhelming involvement with using a drug and securing its supply. Addiction can be explained by two views of addiction. The disease model describes addiction as a lifelong disease characterized by loss of control and a requirement of treatment for recovery. The life-process model of addiction suggestions that addiction is a habitual response and source of gratification or security that must be understood in the context of social relationships and experiences. Drug abuse programs are implemented at the primary, secondary, and tertiary levels.

Learning Objectives

When you have studied the material in this chapter, you should be able to:

1. define consciousness. (p. 150)
2. distinguish between controlled and automatic processing. (pp. 150-151)
3. define altered state of consciousness. (p. 151)
4. contrast repair and ecological theory as explanations for why we sleep. (p. 154)
5. explain the concept of circadian rhythms and their relationship to sleep. (pp. 154-156)
6. list and describe the stages of sleep. (pp. 156-158)
7. illustrate the sleep cycle for a typical night's sleep. (p. 158)
8. discuss the neurological basis for REM and non-REM sleep. (p. 159)
9. describe the following sleep disorders: insomnia, sleepwalking and sleeptalking, nightmares and night terrors, narcolepsy, and sleep apnea. (pp. 161-163)
10. explain the following dream theories: Freudian theory, cognitive theory, and activation-synthesis theory. (pp. 164-166)
11. define hypnosis and list four features of the hypnotic state. (pp. 167-168)
12. contrast the special process and nonstate theories of hypnosis. (pp. 168-170)
13. explain why psychoactive drugs induce altered states. (pp. 170-171)
14. differentiate between tolerance, physical dependence, and psychological dependence. (p. 172)
15. explain how depressants act on the central nervous system and give examples of depressants. (pp. 172-175)
16. explain how stimulants act on the central nervous system and give example of stimulants. (p. 174)
17. explain how hallucinogens act on the central nervous system and give examples of hallucinogens. (p. 175)
18. define addiction and distinguish between the disease and life process models of addiction. (pp. 175-178)
19. list and describe the levels of drug abuse prevention: primary, secondary, and tertiary. (pp. 178-179)
20. list four factors critical to recovery from drug abuse or addiction. (p. 179)
21. summarize the material from *Explorations in Psychology: Altered States of Consciousness and the World's Great Religions*. (p. 153)
22. summarize and relate the material from *Explorations in Psychology: Is Hypnosis a Window to Forgotten Events?* to theories of hypnosis. (p. 169)

Guided Review

What is Consciousness?

When individuals experience a sudden arousal from sleep and an intense fear, this is referred to as a _night terror_. The awareness of both external and internal stimuli or events is called _conscious_ William James described consciousness as a continuous flow called a _stream_ of _conscious_ Freud believed that most of our thoughts are contained in a reservoir of unacceptable wishes; he referred to this as _____ _____. Consciousness comes in different forms and levels. The most alert state of consciousness, in which individuals are actively focused on a goal, is referred to as _____ _____. Activities that require minimal attention are called _____ processes. Another form of consciousness that involves a low level of conscious effort is called _____. A mental state that is noticeably different from normal awareness, produced by drugs, meditation, trauma, fatigue, hypnosis, or sensory deprivation, is called an _____ _____ of consciousness.

night terror - p. 162

consciousness - p. 150
stream/consciousness - p. 150

unconscious thought - p. 150

controlled processes - p. 150
automatic - p. 151

daydreaming - p. 151

altered state - p. 151

Sleep

On the average, sleep takes up about _____ of our lives. Two theories exist about why we sleep. One, which states that sleep restores or replenishes our brains and bodies, is called _____ _____. The other theory, which says that sleep helps keep us from wasting energy and from risking harm during those times for which we are not adapted, is called _____ _____.
A _____ rhythm is a daily behavioral or physiological cycle. These rhythms may become _____ when we fly cross-country, change our working hours, or experience very long winter nights. To help shift workers, _____ _____ at work has been used. When all time and light cues are removed, the natural circadian rhythm averages _____ hours. Most individuals have difficulty staying awake between 3:00 and _____ AM. About _____ percent of the North American population is sleep deprived.
The _____ allows researchers to measure changes in the brain's electrical activity. When we are awake but in a relaxed state, we produce an EEG pattern called _____ waves. As we fall asleep, we begin to produce slow brain waves; these are characteristic of _____ sleep. During Stage 2 sleep, we periodically produce brief bursts of high-frequency waves called _____ _____. During Stage 3 and Stage 4 sleep we produce large, slow EEG waves called _____ waves. After 90 minutes of sleep, the sleeper enters _____ sleep when dreams often occur. REM stands for _____ _____ _____. The amount of deep (Stage 4) sleep is greater in the _____ half of a night's sleep, whereas the majority of REM sleep takes place during the _____ half of a night's sleep. The amount of REM sleep _____ over the life span. REM sleep may _____ the brain and may play a role in brain _____. Non-REM sleep involves neurons in both the forebrain and _____; REM sleep also involves several brain systems.

one-third - p. 154

repair theory - p. 154

ecological theory - p. 154
circadian - p. 154
desynchronized - p. 154

artificial illumination - p. 155

25-26 - p. 156
6:00/50 - p. 156

electroencephalograph - p. 157

alpha - p. 157

Stage 1 - p. 157
sleep spindles - p. 157
delta - p. 157
REM - p. 157
rapid eye movement - p. 157
first - p. 158

second - p. 158
decreases/stimulate - p. 158
growth - p. 158
medulla - p. 159

62

A common sleep disorder, characterized by the inability to fall asleep, is _____. The hormone _____ may play a role in sleep disorders. A sleep disorder in which individuals walk in their sleep is called _____. A frightening dream that awakens a sleeper from REM sleep is called a _____. When individuals experience a sudden arousal from sleep and an intense fear, this is called a _____ _____. Nightmares occur more often than night terrors. Some individuals have a sleep disorder in which they experience an overpowering urge to sleep; this is called _____. Some individuals may have a sleep disorder in which they stop breathing while they are asleep; this is called _____ _____.

insomnia/melatonin - p. 161

somnambulism - p. 161
nightmare - p. 162
night terror - p. 162

narcolepsy - p. 162

sleep apnea - p. 162

Dreams

Throughout history, dreams have had historical, personal, and religious significance. According to psychoanalysts, the sexual and aggressive content of dreams represents _____ _____. The _____ content is the dreams surface content, while the _____ content is the dream's hidden meaning. Freud suggested that we disguise our wish fulfillment through the use of _____. Some researchers believe that dreams allow us to solve problems and to think _____. A different view of dreaming that suggests that dreams have no inherent meaning is the _____ _____ view. This view holds that dreams are the way in which the brain tries to make sense out of _____ activity. Although some people claim they dream in black-and-white, virtually everyone's dreams contain _____. The dreams of _____ are more likely that those of _____ to contain aggression and sexuality.

wish fulfillment - p. 164
manifest/latent - p. 164

symbols - p. 164

creatively - p. 165
activation synthesis - p. 166

neural - p. 166
color - p. 166
males/females - p. 166

Hypnosis

A psychological state of altered attention in which the individual is very receptive to suggestions is called _____. In the eighteenth century, physician Anton Mesmer credited his success in curing problems to "_____ _____"; we sometimes refer to a hypnotized person as being "_____."

hypnosis - p. 167

animal magnetism - p. 168
mesmerized - p. 168

Four elements of the hypnotic state include: (1) the subject is made to feel comfortable; (2) the subject is told to _____ on one specific thing; (3) the subject is told what to expect; (4) they hypnotist suggests that certain events are to occur. Individuals vary widely in their ability to be _____.

concentrate - p. 168

hypnotized - p. 168

Two general theories try to explain how hypnosis works. One theory advanced by Hilgard views hypnosis as being different that nonhypnotic behavior; this is the _____ _____ _____. In this view, a _____ _____ remains fully aware of what is happening. A different perspective suggested by Spanos is that hypnosis is similar to other forms of social behavior; this is referred to as the _____ theory. Psychotherapy, medicine, dentistry, criminal investigations, and sports have all made use of hypnosis. The least effective, but most common application has been to help people _____ _____ and stop _____.

special process theory - p. 168
hidden observer - p. 168

nonstate - p. 170

lose weight/ smoking - p. 170

Psychoactive Drugs

Drugs that act on the nervous system to alter our state of consciousness, modify our perceptions, and alter our moods are called _____ drugs. The users of many psychoactive drugs find that they need increasing amounts of the drug for its effect to be produced; they have developed _____. The physical need for a drug that is accompanied by unpleasant withdrawal symptoms is called _____ _____. The psychological need to take a drug is called psychological _____.

The three main types of psychoactive drugs are _____, _____, and hallucinogens. The most widely used drug in our society is _____. A special concern among university students is _____ drinking. A disorder involving long-term, repeated, compulsive, and extensive use of alcohol is called _____. Family studies of alcoholism find a _____ frequency of the disorder in first-degree relatives of alcoholics. Two types of depressants that are widely used are _____ and _____. Depressant drugs that consist of opium and its derivatives are _____. When opium addicts share needles, they are at increased risk for contracting _____. Drugs that increase activity in the CNS are referred to as _____. A group of widely prescribed stimulants are _____. A stimulant derived from the coca plant is _____. A highly addictive, intensified form of cocaine is called _____. Treating cocaine addiction has been relatively _____. An often overlooked drug is _____ and is found in soft drinks and chocolate. Caffeine activates the _____ _____ of the brain. Psychoactive drugs that modify a person's perceptual experiences and produce visual images that are not real are called _____. One hallucinogen that produces striking perceptual changes, even in low doses, is _____. LSD acts primarily on the neurotransmitter _____, though it can affect dopamine as well. Marijuana produces its effects by disrupting the membranes of neurons and affecting the functioning of a variety of _____. and hormones Physically, marijuana produces increases in _____ rate and blood _____, reddening of the eye, coughing and _____ of the mouth. Psychological effects include excitation, _____, and mild hallucination. _____ is a pattern of behavior characterized by an overwhelming involvement with using a drug and securing its supply. A view of addictions that sees them as biologically-based, life-long diseases is called the _____ model of addiction. A criticism of this view is that it _____ people with labels. The view of addictions as habitual responses and sources of gratification that must be understood in the social context is the _____-_____ model of addiction. Drug abuse prevention programs aimed at discouraging people from starting to take drugs are called _____ prevention programs. Programs that attempt to minimize the harm caused by drug use with a high-risk population are called _____ prevention programs. Those programs that provide treatment for people who have been afflicted with drug abuse are called _____ programs. Research has found that the best approach is to use _____ drug treatment programs. In a long-term study of 700 individuals, Vaillant has found the _____ rule.

Explorations in Psychology

To respond to the questions and exercises presented in this section, please write your thoughts, perspectives, and reactions on a separate piece of paper.

Explorations in Psychology: Altered States of Consciousness and the World's Great Religions

- Why do you suppose altered states of consciousness play an important role in the world's great religions?
- What role do altered states of consciousness play in your own religious traditions?

Explorations in Psychology: Can We Learn While We Are Asleep?

- Why does sleep learning seem to be ineffective?
- Explain why someone might think we could learn while sleeping?
- What role does REM sleep have in learning?

Explorations in Psychology: Is Hypnosis a Window to Forgotten Events?

- Why should hypnotic testimony in the courtroom be banned?
- What is a pesudomemory and do hypnotic witnesses strongly believe them?

In Your Own Words

To respond to the questions and exercises presented in this section, please write your thoughts, perspectives, and reactions on a separate piece of paper.

- ✓ Look at the definition of consciousness. Give some examples of external and internal stimuli or events of which you are now aware. Next consider what controlled processes you have performed in the last hour? What automatic processes have you performed in the last hour?
- ✓ List some questions you have about sleep and dreams. After you are done reading the chapter, determine if these questions have been answered.
- ✓ Complete the questionnaire in the section on *Adventures for the Mind: Do You Get Enough Sleep*. How did you do? If you are sleep deprived, what effects of deprivation have you experienced? What steps can you take to increase your sleep?
- ✓ Take one of your dreams and describe it in terms of manifest content and latent content.
- ✓ How do you know that you are aware?
- ✓ Most people are very fascinated by sleep and dreams. Why do you think that is so?
- ✓ Imagine that you are a consultant who specializes in sleep and circadian rhythms. You have been hired by a large manufacturing company to guide them as they overhaul their shiftwork schedule. What pieces of advice do you give?
- ✓ Should marijuana be legalized?

Correcting the Incorrect

Carefully read each statement. Determine if the statement is correct or incorrect. If the statement is incorrect, make the necessary changes to correct it. Then look directly under the statement for the correct statement and page reference in the textbook.

1. Consciousness is awareness of both external and internal stimuli or events.
    - ❑ *Consciousness is awareness of both external and internal stimuli or events. (p. 150)*
2. An unconscious thought is what the individual experiences while in an altered state of consciousness.
    - ❑ *Unconscious thought refers to a reservoir of unacceptable wishes, feelings, and thoughts. (p. 150)*
3. If you are doing a task that requires minimal attention, then you are experiencing a controlled process.
    - ❑ *If you are doing a task that requires minimal attention, then you are experiencing an automatic process. (p. 151)*

4. Drugs, meditation, fatigue, and hypnosis can produce daydreaming.
   - ❑ *Drugs, meditation, fatigue, and hypnosis can produce altered states of consciousness. (p. 151)*
5. The purpose of sleep is to prevent animals from wasting their energy according to the activation-synthesis theory.
   - ❑ *The purpose of sleep is to prevent animals from wasting their energy according to the ecological theory. (p. 154)*
6. A 24-hour behavioral or physiological cycle is called an alpha rhythm.
   - ❑ *A 24-hour behavioral or physiological cycle is called a circadian rhythm. (p. 154)*
7. When deprived of all time and light cues, the circadian rhythm is about 28 to 29 hours.
   - ❑ *When deprived of all time and light cues, the circadian rhythm is about 25 to 26 hours. (p. 156)*
8. Sleep spindles occur in Stage 1 sleep.
   - ❑ *Sleep spindles occur in Stage 2 sleep. (p. 157)*
9. REM sleep is a stage of sleep during which dreaming occurs.
   - ❑ *REM sleep is a stage of sleep during which dreaming occurs. (p. 157)*
10. The hormone dopamine may be effective in reducing insomnia.
    - ❑ *The hormone melatonin may be effective in reducing insomnia. (p. 161)*
11. Sleep apnea is the formal term for sleepwalking.
    - ❑ *Somnambulism is the formal term for sleepwalking. (p. 161)*
12. Night terrors occur in REM and are really just bad dreams.
    - ❑ *Nightmares occur in REM and are really just bad dreams. (p. 162)*
13. The overpowering urge to fall sleep is called sleep apnea.
    - ❑ *The overpowering urge to fall sleep is called narcolepsy. (p. 162)*
14. A dream's true meaning is called the manifest content.
    - ❑ *A dream's true meaning is called the latent content. (p. 164)*
15. The activation-synthesis theory of dreaming suggests that dreaming may allow us to solve problems.
    - ❑ *The cognitive theory of dreaming suggests that dreaming may allow us to solve problems. (p. 165)*
16. Dreams reflect the brain's efforts to make sense out neural activity that takes placed during sleep according to the activation-synthesis theory.
    - ❑ *Dreams reflect the brain's efforts to make sense out neural activity that takes place during sleep according to the activation-synthesis theory (p. 166)*
17. About 80% of dreams include negative emotions.
    - ❑ *About 80% of dreams include negative emotions. (p. 166)*
18. Mesmer cured his patients using psychoactive drugs.
    - ❑ *Mesmer cured his patients using hypnosis. (p. 168)*
19. In the special process theory, the hypnotized individual is under the social influence of the hypnotist.
    - ❑ *In the nonstate theory, the hypnotized individual is under the social influence of the hypnotist. (p. 170)*
20. Psychoactive drugs do not produce tolerance.
    - ❑ *Psychoactive drugs do produce tolerance. (p. 172)*
21. The strong desire and craving to repeat the use of a drug is called psychological dependence.
    - ❑ *The strong desire and craving to repeat the use of a drug is called psychological dependence. (p. 172)*
22. Alcohol is a stimulant.
    - ❑ *Alcohol is a depressant. (p. 172)*
23. Barbiturates are depressant drugs that are used medically to induce sleep.
    - ❑ *Barbiturates are depressant drugs that are used medically to induce sleep. (p. 173)*
24. Tranquilizers include morphine and heroin.
    - ❑ *Opiates include morphine and heroin. (p. 173)*
25. Crack is an intensified form of caffeine.
    - ❑ *Crack is an intensified form of cocaine. (p. 174)*
26. Cocaine increases the amount of dopamine in the nervous system.
    - ❑ *Cocaine decreases the amount of dopamine in the nervous system (p. 174)*
27. The activate ingredient in marijuana is THC.
    - ❑ *The activate ingredient in marijuana is THC. (p. 175)*

28. According to the disease model of addiction, you can rid yourself of the diseases of addiction through treatment.
   ❏ *According to the disease model of addiction, you cannot rid yourself of the diseases of addiction through treatment.* (p. 178)
29. If a university has a program to stop students from ever starting to use drugs, then secondary prevention is being used.
   ❏ *If a university has a program to stop students from ever starting to use drugs, then primary prevention is being used.* (p. 178)
30. Tertiary prevention consists of treatment for people who abuse drugs.
   ❏ *Tertiary prevention consists of treatment for people who abuse drugs.* (p. 179)

Practice Test

1. If you are aware of both external and internal stimuli, you are in a(n)
   - a. altered state.
   - b. conscious state.
   - c. REM state.
   - d. narcoleptic state.

a.	no; this state refers to a state that is noticeable different from normal awareness
b.	YES; this is the definition of consciousness
c.	no; REM is rapid eye movement that occurs in sleep
d.	no

2. At the beginning of his lecture class, Mike, a student, finds that he is alert, attentive, and focused on the lecture. In which state of consciousness is Mike?
   - a. controlled processes
   - b. automatic processes
   - c. hypnotized
   - d. stream of consciousness

a.	THAT'S RIGHT; Mike is experiencing a controlled processes with attention
b.	no; automatic processes require minimal attention
c.	no; hypnosis involves a heighten suggestibility
d.	no; this refers to the continuous flow of sensations and thoughts

3. A form of consciousness that requires minimal attention is
   - a. controlled processes.
   - b. automatic processes.
   - c. stream of consciousness.
   - d. unconscious thought.

a.	no; controlled processes require much attention and focus
b.	CORRECT; automatic processes require minimal attention
c.	no; this refers to the continuous flow of sensations and thoughts
d.	no; unconscious thought refers to the reservoir of unconscious wishes and feelings

4. You can talk, eat a Big Mac, or listen to music while driving an automobile because
   - a. driving an automobile has become an automatic process.
   - b. you have developed an altered state of consciousness.
   - c. you have the special ability to be able to concentrate on several things at one time.
   - d. driving an automobile has become a controlled process.

a.	YES; driving requires minimal attention and doesn't interfere with ongoing activities	
b.	no; altered states refer to a state that differs from normal awareness	
c.	no; this is not a special ability	
d.	no; driving is not a controlled since it doesn't interfere with ongoing activities	

5. Which of the following would be **least likely** to induce an altered state of consciousness?
   - a. meditation
   - b. hypnosis
   - c. caffeine
   - d. cocaine

a.	no; this is very likely to cause an altered state of consciousness
b.	no; this is very likely to cause an altered state of consciousness
c.	YES; caffeine is a stimulant and will not likely induce an altered state
d.	no; this is very likely to cause an altered state of consciousness

6. Which theory suggests that sleep is necessary to restore and replenish our bodies?
   - a. ecological theory
   - b. repair theory
   - c. neural theory
   - d. circadian theory

a.	no; the ecological theory states that sleep prevents energy waste
b.	YES; this is the definition of repair theory
c.	no
d.	no

7. Which theory of sleep would provide the best explanation for why an individual becomes irritable after missing a couple of nights of sleep?
   - a. repair theory
   - b. activation-synthesis theory
   - c. ecological theory
   - d. special process theory

a.	CORRECT; the repair theory says that sleep restores us
b.	no; this is a theory of dreaming
c.	no; the ecological theory states that sleep prevents energy waste
d.	no

8. Which theory suggests that sleep helps prevent animals from wasting energy and harming themselves during those periods for which they are not adapted?
   - a. ecological theory
   - b. repair theory
   - c. neural theory
   - d. circadian theory

a.	RIGHT; the ecological theory states that sleep prevents energy waste
b.	no; the repair theory says that sleep restores us
c.	no
d.	no

9.   Circadian rhythm refers to
      a.   a popular Latin dance.
      b.   a daily cycle.
      c.   the brain's level of activity when taking a psychoactive drug.
      d.   an abnormal biological rhythm associated with jet lag

a.	no; not even close	
b.	YES; a circadian rhythm is a daily behavioral or physiological cycle	
c.	no; circadian rhythm is not related to drug use	
d.	no; jet lag is the result of rhythms being out of sync	

10.   Which of the following is a circadian rhythm?'
      a.   the stream of consciousness
      b.   the four stages of sleep
      c.   hypnosis
      d.   the sleep/wake cycle

a.	no; the stream refers to the ever-changing thoughts, sensations, and images	
b.	no; the four stages of sleep are not necessarily a daily cycle	
c.	no; hypnosis is a change in consciousness	
d.	YES; this is an example of a circadian rhythm	

11.   Which of the following air travelers would require the most time to recover from jet lag?
      a.   Michael, who is traveling east from Chicago to Paris.
      b.   Carla, who is traveling west from Paris to Chicago.
      c.   Karen, who is traveling north from Lima to Toronto.
      d.   Benjamin, who is traveling south from Toronto to Lima.

a.	THAT'S RIGHT; Michael is travel east and this direction is difficult to adjust to	
b.	no; traveling west is easy on our sleep/wake cycle	
c.	no; traveling north is easy on our sleep/wake cycle	
d.	no; traveling south is easy on our sleep/wake cycle	

12.   Delta waves are produced in which stage of sleep?
      a.   REM sleep
      b.   Stage 1 sleep
      c.   Stage 2 sleep
      d.   Stage 4 sleep

a.	no; in REM we experience fast waves	
b.	no	
c.	no; in stage 2 sleep there are sleep spindles	
d.	YES	

13.   While your father is napping on the couch, you notice his eyes moving around under his closed eyelids. If you wake your father up at this time, he is likely to
      a.   claim that he was really awake.
      b.   report that he was dreaming.
      c.   describe the presence of a "hidden observer."
      d.   report seeing slow-wave movement.

a.	no; this is not likely	
b.	CORRECT; dad is experiencing REM where dreaming occurs	
c.	no; the idea of the "hidden observer" is used in explaining hypnosis	
d.	no; slow-wave movement cannot be seen	

14. A person's who usually sleeps eight hours completes an average of how many sleep cycles per night?
   a. 2
   b. 3
   c. 4
   d. 5

a.	no	
b.	no	
c.	no	
d.	RIGHT; the cycles of sleep last about 90 minutes	

15. What is the **main** difference between REM sleep and non-REM sleep?
   a. number of times a person wakes up
   b. hypnagogic level
   c. degree of brain activity
   d. number of sleep stages included

a.	no; this is not relevant
b.	no; this is not a difference
c.	THAT'S CORRECT; the stages of sleep correspond to changes in brain activity
d.	no; while this is a difference, it is not a main difference

16. Joe was upset when his date kept suddenly falling asleep, until she explained that she is
   a. circadian.
   b. bored.
   c. somnambulistic.
   d. narcoleptic.

a.	no
b.	no; at least probably not
c.	no; somnambulism refers to sleepwalking
d.	YES; she has narcolepsy and experiences the overpowering urge to sleep

17. Another name for somnambulism is
   a. sleepwalking.
   b. hallucination.
   c. insomnia.
   d. bed-wetting.

a.	CORRECT; somnambulism is the formal term for sleepwalking
b.	no
c.	no
d.	no

18. Bethany, a two-year old, experiences sudden arousal from sleep and intense fear. She experiences
   a. night terrors
   b. insomnia
   c. sleep apnea
   d. narcolepsy

a.	YES; Bethany has night terrors that occur in non-REM sleep
b.	no; insomnia is the inability to sleep
c.	no; sleep apnea is a condition where the person stops breathing while sleeping
d.	no; narcolepsy is the overpowering urge to sleep

19. The cognitive view of dreaming asserts that dreams
    a. help dissipate problematic sexual and aggressive energy.
    b. are the conscious equivalent of innate instincts.
    c. are the conscious interpretation of relatively random neural activity.
    d. are used to review daily events and orient toward future goals.

a.	no; this option sounds Freudian
b.	no
c.	no; this answer summarizes the activiation-synthesis theory
d.	YES; it focuses on information processing, memory and problem solving

20 According to the activation-synthesis view
    a. dreams represent wish fulfillment.
    b. dreams have no inherent meaning.
    c. dreams are a way to solve problems and think creatively.
    d. dreams have manifest and latent content

a.	no; Freud would argue this option
b.	YUP; dreams are the brain's effort to make sense of neural activity
c.	no; the cognitive theory is consistent with this option
d.	no; Freud's theory includes manifest and latent content

21. When Maria dreams, she knows she is dreaming. This illustrates
    a. sleep spindles
    b. latent content.
    c. lucid dreaming.
    d. the nonstate theory.

a.	no; sleep spindles are bursts of brain activity in stage 2 of sleep
b.	no; latent content is the dream's underlying meaning
c.	YES: Maria is having a lucid dream
d.	no; the nonstate theory is a theory of hypnosis

22. The standard hypnosis session involves a hypnotist swinging a pocket watch or a pendulum in front
    of the subject to be hypnotized. The hypnotist does this because she wants the subject to
    a. concentrate.
    b. fall asleep.
    c. lose control.
    d. hallucinate.

a.	RIGHT; concentration is an important element in hypnosis
b.	no; falling asleep does not occur in hypnosis
c.	no; the subject does not lose control, but only becomes more suggestible
d.	no; using a pocket watch or pendulum does not lead to hallucinations

23. When hypnosis is induced, the hypnotist
    a. tries to keep the subject distracted.
    b. discourages the subject from concentrating on anything specific.
    c. suggests to the subject what will be experienced in the hypnotic state.
    d. is careful to prevent posthypnotic amnesia.

a.	no; in fact, concentration and focus is very important
b.	no; concentrating and focusing on something specific is very important
c.	CORRECT; when the experience occurs, the person will believe it was suggested
d.	no; the hypnotist may actually desire posthypnotic amnesia to occur

24. According to Spanos' nonstate view of hypnosis
    a. hypnotic behavior involves a hidden observer.
    b. hypnotic behavior can be explained without resorting to special processes.
    c. hypnosis is a special cognitive state
    d. is very different from nonhypnotic behavior

a.	no; this option describes the special process theory	
b.	YES, CORRECT; the nonstate view asserts that social influence is very important	
c.	no; this option describes the special process theory	
d.	no; this option describes the special process theory	

25. Which of the following statements about hypnosis is **correct**?
    a. Hypnosis is an unconscious state of awareness.
    b. The majority of the population can be easily hypnotized.
    c. Hypnosis tends to enhance people's memory.
    d. Some people are more easily hypnotized than others.

a.	no; the person remains very conscious and aware during hypnosis	
b.	no; only about 10 to 20 percent are very susceptible to hypnosis	
c.	no; hypnosis does not dramatically improve accuracy of memory	
d.	RIGHT; people differ in their susceptibility to hypnosis	

26. When he first started using drugs, Ben needed only a small amount to feel euphoric. Now, 6 months later, he requires almost three times as much to have the same feeling. Ben
    a. is addicted.
    b. has developed psychological dependence.
    c. has developed tolerance.
    d. is a narcoleptic.

a.	no; the description does not imply addiction	
b.	no; psychological dependence is the strong desire and craving to use a drug	
c.	YES; tolerance occurs when more of the drug is needed to produce an effect	
d.	no; this refers to narcolepsy, which is a sleep disorder	

27. People are attracted to psychoactive drugs because they believe the drugs
    a. help people adapt.
    b. help people feel at ease socially.
    c. can provide unique and profound experiences.
    d. all of the above

a.	no; although this is partially correct	
b.	no; although this is partially correct	
c.	no; although this is partially correct	
d.	YES; this is the best answer	

28. What do caffeine and cocaine have in common?
    a. They are stimulants.
    b. They are depressants.
    c. They are hallucinogens.
    d. They are opiates.

a.	YES, THAT'S RIGHT; both caffeine and cocaine are stimulants	
b.	no	
c.	no	
d.	no	

29. Which of the following is a stimulant?
   a.   marijuana
   b.   alcohol
   c.   cocaine
   d.   LSD

a.	no; marijuana is a hallucinogenic drug	
b.	no; alcohol is a depressant	
c.	YES; cocaine is classified as a stimulant	
d.	no; LSD is a hallucinogenic drug	

30. Which of the following would develop the **strongest** psychological addiction?
   a.   someone who smokes cocaine frequently
   b.   someone who occasionally takes tranquilizers
   c.   someone who regularly takes LSD
   d.   someone who occasionally drinks alcohol at parties

a.	YES; cocaine, when smoked is called crack and is very addictive
b.	no; tranquilizers are less addictive than cocaine
c.	no; LSD is less addictive than cocaine
d.	no; alcohol is less addictive than cocaine

31. Each of the following is a criticism of the disease model of addiction except
   a.   It discourages people from developing self-control.
   b.   It stigmatizes people with labels.
   c.   It is not consistent with the approach taken by the medical profession
   d.   It prescribes a rigid program of therapy.

a.	no; the model does discourage people from developing self-control
b.	no; the labels are "addict" and "alcoholics"
c.	YES; the approach is consistent with the medical profession
d.	no; programs are very rigid and not flexible

32. The life-process model of addiction views addictions as being
   a.   lifelong.
   b.   biologically based.
   c.   understandable only in the context of social relationships.
   d.   either inherited or bred into a person early in life.

a.	no; this is not a characteristics of the life-process model
b.	no; addiction is seen as a habitual response
c.	YES: this model says that the entire person's life be must be examined
d.	no; addiction is seen as a source of gratification

Chapter 6 - Learning

The Big Picture: Chapter Overview

According to Shepard Siegel, the principles of classical conditioning can even be used to explain some deaths due to drug overdoses. Learning is a relatively permanent change in behavior due to experience. This chapter presents the forms of learning known as classical conditioning, operant conditioning, and observational learning. Pavlov discovered the principle of classical conditioning as he was investigating digestion. He found that his dogs were conditioned to salivate to various stimuli in anticipation of eating meat powder. In this type of learning, an organism learns an association between an unconditioned stimulus (US) and a conditioned stimulus (CS). The US automatically produces an unconditioned response (UR). After conditioning, the CS can also elicit a conditioned response (CR). Classical conditioning is a form of associative learning. In classical conditioning, the organism is learning that the occurrence of one stimulus predicts the presence of another. Extinction, spontaneous recovery, generalization, and discrimination are involved in classical conditioning. Pavlov's explanation for classical conditioning was that the CS substitutes for the US, a process he called stimulus substitution. A more contemporary view of classical conditioning, which focuses on the information individuals receive from the situation, is called information theory. Many psychologists believe that, in humans, phobias and certain physical complaints are explained by classical conditioning. The case of little Albert illustrates how a fear of rats could be conditioned. Counterconditioning is a procedure for weakening a classically conditioned CR.

In operant conditioning, the consequences of behavior produce changes in the probability of its occurrence. It is called operant conditioning because the behavior operates on the environment and then, the environment operates back to the behavior. Operant conditioning is also an example of associative learning; but the contingency is between an organism's response and its consequences. Thorndike's law of effect illustrates how S-R associations can weaken or strengthen behavior. Behavior learned in this manner is called operant conditioning. Reinforcement strengthens a response. Consequences that increase the probability of a behavior's occurrence are called positive reinforcements. Negative reinforcement occurs when the frequency of a response increases because it either removes an unpleasant stimulus or allows the individual to avoid the stimulus. Skinner studied animals in the laboratory in the belief that the principles of learning apply to all species. He developed the Skinner box, an apparatus for studying animals. He even worked to train pigeons to guide missiles during World War II. Other important concepts in operant conditioning are time interval, shaping, primary and second reinforcement, and schedules of reinforcement (i.e., fixed-ratio, variable-ratio, fixed-interval, variable-interval). Like classical conditioning, the principles of operant conditioning also include extinction, generalization, and discrimination. Punishment refers to a consequence that decreases the probability of a behavior occurring since it weakens the behavior. Positive punishment refers to a consequence that is an unpleasant stimulus, whereas in negative punishment a pleasant stimulus is removed. The procedure called time out is an example of a technique that uses negative punishment. For a variety of reasons, reinforcement is usually recommended over punishment to change behavior. In applied behavior analysis (or behavior modification), the principles of operant conditioning are used to change behavior.

Observational learning is also called imitation or modeling. According to Bandura, the following processes influence an observer's behavior after viewing a model: attention, retention, motor reproduction, and reinforcement. According to Bandura, observational learning is an information-processing activity.

Many contemporary psychologists believe that learning involves more than stimulus-response connections and that cognitive factors play a role in learning. Tolman is associated with the concepts of expectancy and cognitive map. Kohler studied insight learning and argued that organisms develop sudden insight or understanding of a problem's solution. There are also biological influences on learning, such as instinctive drift, preparedness, and taste aversion. Culture can influence the degree to which learning processes occur and often determines the content of learning.

Learning Objectives

When you have studied the material in this chapter, you should be able to:

1. define learning. (p. 186)
2. define classical conditioning and explain the processes involved in classically conditioning a response. (pp. 186-188)
3. identify the US, CS, UCR, and CR in examples of classical conditioning. (pp. 187-188)
4. provide examples of the following: stimulus generalization, stimulus discrimination, extinction, and spontaneous recovery. (pp. 188-191)
5. distinguish between Pavlov's theory of stimulus substitution and modern information theory as explanations of classical conditioning. (p. 191)
6. explain the role of classical conditioning and counterconditioning in phobias. (pp. 191-193)
7. contrast Thorndike's law of effect and Skinner's operant conditioning. (pp. 195-196)
8. define operant conditioning. (p. 195)
9. distinguish between and give examples of positive reinforcement, negative reinforcement, and punishment. (pp. 196-197 and pp. 201-203)
10. define shaping. (p. 198)
11. distinguish between primary and secondary reinforcers. (pp. 198-199)
12. list and provide examples of each of the four reinforcement schedules. (pp. 199-201)
13. identify and provide examples of extinction, generalization, and discrimination in operant conditioning. (p. 201)
14. define applied behavioral analysis. (pp. 203-204)
15. define observational learning. (p. 207)
16. list the four elements essential to observational learning. (p. 207-209)
17. discuss the cognitive factors involved in cognitive maps. (pp. 208-209)
18. explain insight learning. (p. 209)
19. discuss the importance of preparedness and instinct drift in learning. (p. 210)
20. give an example of taste aversion. (p. 210)
21. explain why culture determines both the degree to which learning principles are used and the content of learning. pp. 211-212)
22. From *Explorations in Psychology: Using Behavior Modification to Improve Self-Control*, design a self-control program using the five steps. (p. 205)
23. From *Explorations in Psychology: The Role of Immediate and Delayed Consequences in Developing Self-Control*, summarize the principles of immediate and delayed reinforcement. (p. 200)

Guided Review

What is Learning?

Learning is a relatively permanent change in _____ that occurs through _____.

behavior - p. 186
experience - p. 186

Classical Conditioning

Ivan Pavlov described the principle of _____ _____. Classical conditioning consists of the following components: the _____ _____ is a stimulus that produces a response without prior learning; an unlearned response, called the _____ response; a previously neutral stimulus that eventually elicits the conditioned response, called the _____ stimulus; and a learned response called a _____ response. The time interval between the CS and the US is important because it helps define the degree of association, or _____, of the stimulus. When a new stimulus similar to the CS produces a similar CR, this is called _____. When an organism is conditioned to respond to one stimulus and not another, this is called _____. A weakening of the CR in the absence of the US is called _____. When a CR recurs without further conditioning, this is called _____ _____. Pavlov's explanation for classical conditioning was that the CS substitutes for the US, a process he termed _____ _____. A more contemporary view of classical conditioning, which focuses on the information individuals receive from the situation, is called _____ theory. Many psychologists believe that, in humans, irrational fears, or _____, are caused by classical conditioning. A procedure for weakening a classically conditioned fear response is called _____. Behaviors associated with health problems or mental disturbances can involve _____ conditioning. Classical conditioning views the organism as _____ in the environment.

classical conditioning - p. 187

unconditioned stimulus - p. 187
unconditioned response - p. 187
conditioned - p. 188
conditioned - p. 188

contiguity - p. 188
generalization - p. 190

discrimination - p. 190
extinction - p. 188
spontaneous recovery - p. 188
stimulus substitution - p. 191

information - p. 191
phobias - p. 192

counterconditioning - p. 192
classical - p. 192
active - p. 193

Operant Conditioning

A form of learning in which the consequences of behavior lead to changes in the probability of the behavior's occurrence is called _____ conditioning. Operant conditioning generally does a better job than classical conditioning of explaining _____ behavior. In classical conditioning, the association is made between two _____. In operant conditioning, the association is between a _____ and its _____. The concept of operant conditioning was developed by _____. According to Thorndike, behavior followed by positive outcomes is _____ and behavior followed by negative outcomes is _____. Thorndike referred to these concepts as the _____ _____ _____. The stimuli that govern classically conditioned behavior _____ the behavior, but in operant conditioning the stimuli that govern behavior _____ the behavior. Skinner used the term _____ to describe the behavior of the organism. According to Skinner, consequences that increase the probability that a behavior will occur are called _____; consequences that decrease a behavior's probability are labeled _____. When the

operant - p. 195
voluntary - p. 195

stimuli - p. 195
response/consequences - p. 195
Thorndike - p. 195
strengthened - p. 196
weakened - p. 196
Law of Effect - p. 196
precede - p. 196
follow - p. 196
operant - p. 196

reinforcement - p. 196
punishment - p. 202

frequency of a behavior increases because it is followed by a rewarding stimulus, it is a _____ reinforcement. Negative reinforcement increases the frequency of a response by _____ an unpleasant stimulus. Skinner has extensively studied animals in the laboratory, in the belief that the principles of learning are the same for all _____.

positive - p. 196
removing - p. 197

species - p. 197

Skinner's ideas for a utopian society are spelled out in his novel _____ _____. Skinner developed an apparatus for studying animals that has become known as the _____ _____. Several factors impact the effectiveness of operant conditioning; for example, learning is more efficient under _____ rather than delayed consequences. Also, behaviors are learned more rapidly if approximations to the desired behavior are rewarded; this is called _____. Positive reinforcements that are innately rewarding are called _____ reinforcements; those reinforcements that acquire their positive value through experience are called _____ reinforcements. Money and other objects that can be exchanged for another reinforcer eventually acquire reinforcing value themselves; these are referred to as _____ reinforcers.

Walden Two - p. 198
Skinner box - p. 198

immediate - p. 198

shaping - p. 198
primary - p. 198
secondary - p. 198

token - p. 199

Often, reinforcements do not follow every occurrence of a response. This is called _____ reinforcement and occurs in four different _____ of reinforcement. Generally, behaviors are learned most rapidly on _____ reinforcement schedules. When a behavior must occur a set number of times before it is rewarded, it is referred to as a _____-_____ schedule. On the other hand, slot machines give out rewards on a _____-_____ schedule. Behaviors that are rewarded after the passage of a fixed amount of time are on _____-_____ schedules, whereas behaviors that are rewarded after differing amounts of time are referred to as _____-_____ schedules. The interval schedules produce behavior at a _____ rate than the ratio schedules. In operant conditioning, a decrease in the tendency to perform a response that is brought about by no longer reinforcing the response is called _____. Giving the same response to similar stimuli is called _____. Discriminative stimuli signal that a response will be _____.

partial - p. 199
schedules - p. 199
continuous - p. 199

fixed-ratio - p. 199
variable-ratio - p. 199

fixed-interval - p. 199
variable-interval - p. 201

slower – p.201

extinction - p. 201
generalization - p. 201
reinforced (punished) - p. 201

In _____, a consequence that decreases the likelihood a behavior will occur is presented. In _____ punishment, a behavior decreases when it is followed by an unpleasant stimulus. In _____ punishment, a behavior decreases when a positive stimulus is removed from it. Applying the principles of operant conditioning to changing human behavior is called applied _____ _____. The principles of behavior modification have been applied to the computer field through the development of computer _____ _____.

punishment - p. 202
positive - p. 202

negative - p. 202

behavior analysis - p. 203

assisted instruction - p. 204

Observational Learning

When an individual learns by imitation or modeling, psychologists refer to this as _____ _____. Observational learning allows us to learn without having to go through _____-_____-_____. Bandura believes that the following processes influence an observer's behavior after being exposed to a model: (1) _____, (2) retention, (3) _____ reproduction, and (4) reinforcement or

observational learning - p. 207
trial-and-error - p. 207

attention - p. 207
motor - p. 207

_____ conditions. Bandura views observational learning as an
_____-_____ activity.

| | incentive - p. 207 |
| | information-processing - p. 208 |

Cognitive Factors in Learning
According to Tolman, when classical and operant conditioning are occurring, the organism acquires _____. Tolman wrote that individuals select information from the environment and develop a ____ _____ of their world. Wolfgang Kohler's work with apes led him to conclude that humans and other animals engage in _____ _____.

	expectations - p. 208
	cognitive map - p. 208
	insight learning - p. 209

Biological and Cultural Factors
When animals are being trained, they tend to revert to instinctive behavior, a concept called _____ _____. Organisms also bring a biological background to the learning context. An example of this is called _____, which refers to why some animals learn readily in one situation but have great difficulty in others. Culture can influence the _____ to which learning processes occur and the _____ of learning.

	instinctive drift - p. 210
	preparedness - p. 210
	degree - p. 211
	content - p. 211

Explorations in Psychology

To respond to the questions and exercises presented in this section, please write your thoughts, perspectives, and reactions on a separate piece of paper.

Explorations in Psychology: The Role of Immediate and Delayed Consequences in Developing Self-Control

- Think about your self-control and problem areas in your life (e.g., studying, eating, drinking). Analyze your behaviors with regard to the role of immediate and delayed consequences. Are those behaviors that you should cease, controlled by immediate reinforcers? Are the behaviors that you should engage in more, controlled by delayed reinforcers?

Explorations in Psychology: Using Behavior Modification to Improve Self-Control

- Develop a self-control program to assist you in establishing and maintaining self-control in your life. See page 205 for the five steps.

In Your Own Words

To respond to the questions and exercises presented in this section, please write your thoughts, perspectives, and reactions on a separate piece of paper.
- ✓ As you first started to read this chapter on learning, what were your first impressions of the material? Were you intimated by the terminology? Now, after spending some time with the material, what are your current impressions?
- ✓ Focus on what the words actually mean in US, UR, CS, CR. What are these terms' literal meanings?
- ✓ Have you ever been classically conditioned? Try analyzing the experience by identifying the US, UR, CS, and CR.
- ✓ How would you classically condition a six-year-old child to be afraid of the song, "Row, row, row your boat"? Make sure you indicate the US, UR, CS, and CR.
- ✓ Can you give an example of generalization and discrimination that Pavlov's dogs might have experienced?
- ✓ List a couple of examples of positive reinforcement and negative reinforcement in your life.

✓ As you think back to the things that you've done that were reinforced in the last 24 hours, what were the schedules under which reinforcement was given?

✓ How has observational learning impacted your behavior? Create examples of behaviors that you have acquired through observational learning. Include adaptive, positive behaviors and maladaptive, negative behaviors.

Correcting the Incorrect

Carefully read each statement. Determine if the statement is correct or incorrect. If the statement is incorrect, make the necessary changes to correct it. Then look directly under the statement for the correct statement and page reference in the textbook.

1. Learning is relatively permanent change in behavior that occurs through maturation.
   - ❑ *Learning is relatively permanent change in behavior that occurs through experience. (p. 186)*
2. Skinner is most remembered for his work in classical conditioning.
   - ❑ *Pavlov is most remembered for his work in classical conditioning. (p. 187)*
3. In classical conditioning, a US becomes associated with a meaningful stimulus and acquires the capacity to elicit a similar response.
   - ❑ *In classical conditioning, a CS becomes associated with a meaningful stimulus and acquires the capacity to elicit a similar response. (p. 188)*
4. Reflexes play a role in operant conditioning.
   - ❑ *Reflexes play a role in classical conditioning. (p. 187)*
5. A US is a stimulus that produces a response only after prior learning.
   - ❑ *A CS is a stimulus that produces a response only after prior learning. (p. 188)*
6. The CS elicits the UR.
   - ❑ *The US elicits the UR. (p. 188)*
7. In classical conditioning, the learned association is between the CS and US.
   - ❑ *In classical conditioning, the learned association is between the CS and US. (p. 188)*
8. The CR elicits the CS.
   - ❑ *The CS elicits the CR. (p. 188)*
9. Classical conditioning is a form of operant conditioning.
   - ❑ *Classical conditioning is a form of associative conditioning. (p. 188)*
10. After a period of extinction, contingency recovery may occur.
    - ❑ *After a period of extinction, spontaneous recovery may occur. (p. 188)*
11. If an organism shows discrimination after being classically conditioned, it will respond to certain stimuli and not to others.
    - ❑ *If an organism shows discrimination after being classically conditioned, it will respond to certain stimuli and not to others. (p. 190)*
12. According to the information theory of classical conditioning, the organism is gathering information.
    - ❑ *According to the information theory of classical conditioning, the organism is gathering information. (p. 191)*
13. Little Albert was conditioned to fear a rat
    - ❑ *Little Albert was conditioned to fear a rat (p. 191)*
14. In counterconditioning, the CS is weakened.
    - ❑ *In counterconditioning, the CR is weakened. (p. 192)*
15. In operant conditioning, the CS and the CR are paired.
    - ❑ *In operant conditioning, a response and its consequences are paired. (p. 195)*
16. Thorndke developed the law of effect.
    - ❑ *Thorndke developed the law of effect. (p. 196)*
17. In positive reinforcement, the frequency of a response is increased because it is followed by a reward stimulus.
    - ❑ *In positive reinforcement, the frequency of a response is increased because it is followed by a reward stimulus. (p. 196)*

18. In negative reinforcement, the behavior is punished.
   - ❏ *In negative reinforcement, the behavior is reinforced.* (p. 197)
19. Skinner thought that the principles of operant conditioning could be used to train pigeons to guide missiles.
   - ❏ *Skinner thought that the principles of operant conditioning could be used to train pigeons to guide missiles.* (p. 197)
20. Through the process of generalization, approximations of the desired behavior are reinforced.
   - ❏ *Through the process of shaping, approximations of the desired behavior are reinforced.* (p. 198)
21. Primary reinforcers are learned reinforcers.
   - ❏ *Secondary reinforcers are learned reinforcers.* (p. 198)
22. A fixed-ratio schedule is a timetable in which reinforcement is given after a certain amount of time has passed.
   - ❏ *A fixed-interval schedule is a timetable in which reinforcement is given after a certain amount of time has passed.* (p. 199)
23. A variable-interval schedule is a timetable in which reinforcement is given after a variable amount of time has passed.
   - ❏ *A variable-interval schedule is a timetable in which reinforcement is given after a variable amount of time has passed.* (p. 199)
24. In positive punishment, a behavior decreases when a positive stimulus is removed from it.
   - ❏ *In negative punishment, a behavior decreases when a positive stimulus is removed from it.* (p. 202)
25. Punishment decreases the likelihood that behavior will be repeated.
   - ❏ *Punishment decreases the likelihood that behavior will be repeated.* (p. 202)
26. Observational learning is also called imitation or modeling.
   - ❏ *Observational learning is also called imitation or modeling.* (p. 207)
27. The four processes involved in observational learning are extinction, discrimination, generalization, and discrimination.
   - ❏ *The four processes involved in observational learning are attention, retention, motor reproduction, and reinforcement.* (p. 207)
28. Kohler found that apes show insight learning.
   - ❏ *Kohler found that apes show insight learning.* (209)
29. In instinctive drift, animals tend to revert to instinctive behavior.
   - ❏ *In instinctive drift, animals tend to revert to instinctive behavior.* (p. 210)
30. Discrimination refers to species-specific biological predispositions to learn in certain ways but not others.
   - ❏ *Preparedness refers to species-specific biological predispositions to learn in certain ways but not others.* (p. 210)

Practice Test

1. Each of the following is a part of the definition of learning except
   - a. relatively permanent.
   - b. change in behavior.
   - c. maturation.
   - d. experience.

a.	no; this is part of the definition of learning
b.	no; this is part of the definition of learning
c.	YES; the change in observable behavior is due to experience not maturation
d.	no; this is part of the definition of learning

2. As the term has been used in traditional psychology, learning refers to
    a.   any relatively permanent change in behavior brought about by experience.
    b.   changes in behavior, including those associated with fatigue and maturation.
    c.   most changes in behavior, except those caused by brain damage.
    d.   all permanent changes in behavior, including those caused by heredity.

a.	CORRECT; this is the definition of learning
b.	no; in fact changes in behavior due fatigue and maturation is not learning
c.	no; this is not the definition of learning
d.	no; the behavior change is relatively permanent and is due to experience

3. Sandra had a bad car accident a few months ago. Now, every time she has to pass the location where the accident occurred, she gets very anxious. The best explanation for Sandra's anxiousness is
    a.   classical conditioning.
    b.   extinction.
    c.   exhibition of an unconditioned stimulus.
    d.   generalization.

a.	YES; her anxiousness is associated with the location
b.	no; extinction refers to the weakening of an association
c.	no
d.	no; generalization refers to the tendency of a new similar stimulus to elicit a CR

4. In Pavlov's experiment, the bell was a previously neutral stimulus that became a(n)
    a.   conditioned stimulus.
    b.   conditioned response.
    c.   unconditioned response.
    d.   unconditioned stimulus

a.	CORRECT; the neutral stimulus becomes the conditioned stimulus since it can elicit the conditioned response
b.	no; a stimulus never becomes a response
c.	no; a stimulus never becomes a response
d.	no; a US is never a previously neutral stimulus

5. Jennifer is desperately afraid of snakes. Her psychologist believes that her fear of snakes may have been classically conditioned. If her psychologist is correct, Jennifer's fear is the
    a.   UCS.
    b.   UCR.
    c.   CS.
    d.   CR.

a.	no; fear is a response not a stimulus
b.	no; a UCR is unlearned response - Jennifer's fear is learned or conditioned
c.	no; her fear is a response, not a stimulus
d.	RIGHT; since the fear is classically conditioned, it is a CR

6. You volunteer to participate in an experiment in classical conditioning and the experimenter conditions your eye-blink reflex to the sound of a bell. The next day, you notice that you blink whenever the phone rings. You are not upset because you know that
    a.   this UR will extinguish soon.
    b.   discrimination will readily develop.
    c.   spontaneous recovery is not dangerous or long-lasting.
    d.   without the US, extinction will naturally occur.

a.	no; your eye blink is not a UR
b.	no; discrimination occurs when you eye blink to only specific stimuli
c.	no; you are not showing any spontaneous recovery
d.	YES; over time your eye blink will disappear or extinguish

7. The classical conditioning process by which little Albert learned to fear a rabbit, a dog, and a sealskin coat is called
   - a. extinction.
   - b. generalization.
   - c. spontaneous recovery.
   - d. discrimination.

a.	no; extinction would not lead to the development of fear
b.	RIGHT; little Albert's fear generalized to stimuli similar to the original stimulus
c.	no; spontaneous recovery occurs after extinction
d.	no; just the opposite since little Albert showed generalization

8. In Watson and Rayner's study, little Albert was conditioned to fear a white rat. Later, Albert showed a fear of similar objects, such as a white rabbit, balls of cotton, and a white stuffed animal. This is an example of stimulus
   - a. generalization.
   - b. substitution.
   - c. discrimination.
   - d. inhibition.

a.	GOOD; his fear was generalized from a white rate to other similar objects
b.	no; the CS is not substituting for the US
c.	no; in discrimination the response is seen only for specific stimuli
d.	no

9. Information theory views the organism as
   - a. being logical.
   - b. having preconceptions.
   - c. receiving information from stimuli.
   - d. all of the above

a.	no
b.	no
c.	CORRECT; the organism is receiving information about what to expect
d.	no

10. What do stimulus substitution theory and information theory have in common?
   - a. They agree on the role of the conditioned stimulus.
   - b. They attempt to explain how and why classical conditioning works.
   - c. They agree on the relationship between CS and US.
   - d. They attempt to explain how and why operant conditioning works.

a.	no; the CS is a substitute for the US and the CS provides an expectation
b.	AYE; both theories are explanation for classical conditioning
c.	no; one focuses on the CS as a substitute and the other CS provides expectancy
d.	no; these theories are explanations for classical conditioning

11. The term counterconditioning best describes which of the following procedures?
    a.   presenting the conditioned stimulus by itself
    b.   reintroducing the conditioned stimulus after extinction has occurred
    c.   pairing a fear-provoking stimulus with a new response incompatible with fear
    d.   reinforcing successive approximations of the goal response

a.	no; this would cause extinction, but the CS is associated with fear
b.	no; this would have little effect on the fear
c.	GOOD; the CS is paired with a new response that is pleasant
d.	no; this describes shaping

12. Which approach to learning represents the view that people learn from the consequences of their actions?
    a.   response cost theory
    b.   operant conditioning
    c.   stimulus substitution theory
    d.   classical conditioning

a.	no
b.	CORRECT; consequences that follow behavior affect the probability of it repeating
c.	no; this is an explanation of classical conditioning
d.	no; two stimuli are paired in classical conditioning

13. In operant conditioning, the conditioning is between a _____ and its _____.
    a.   reinforcer; stimulus
    b.   behavior; response
    c.   consequence; punisher
    d.   response; consequences

a.	no; although a reinforcer could be a consequence
b.	no; these terms refer to the same thing
c.	no; these terms refer to the same thing
d.	RIGHT; response is behavior. consequence maybe reinforcement or punishment

14. According to Thorndike's law of effect,
    a.   a conditioned stimulus ultimately produces a conditioned response.
    b.   behaviors followed by positive outcomes are strengthened.
    c.   behavior learned on variable-interval schedules is difficult to extinguish.
    d.   reinforcers should be given immediately after a desired response.

a.	no; this option refers to classical conditioning
b.	YES: the law of effect includes this option
c.	no; while the law of effect does involve behavior, it does not involve schedules
d.	no; the law of effect does not refer to timing of consequences

15. Lisa was very shy and would not play with her fellow first-graders. If the teacher praised her only when Lisa was interacting with her classmates, the teacher would be attempting to use
    a.   positive reinforcement.
    b.   shaping.
    c.   negative reinforcement.
    d.   extinction.

a.	RIGHT; the teacher was presenting something pleasant (i.e., praise)
b.	no; there is nothing in the question that refers to rewarding approximations
c.	no; negative reinforcement refers to withdrawing something unpleasant
d.	no; in extinction a previously reinforced behavior is longer reinforced

16. Which of the following illustrates negative reinforcement?
    a. teaching a dog to "shake hands" by giving him a biscuit every time he does so
    b. punishing a 3-year-old child for writing on the wall with crayons
    c. getting home early form a date to avoid getting yelled at by your parents
    d. developing a phobic response to anyone who looks like your mean third-grade teacher

a.	no; this is positive reinforcement where a pleasant stimulus is presented
b.	no; this option describes an example of punishment
c.	YES; the response (getting home early) removed the unpleasant stimulus (yelling)
d.	no; this sounds more like an example of classical conditioning

17. Shaping is defined as the process of
    a. reinforcing every avoidance response an organism makes.
    b. reinforcing successive approximations of the target behavior.
    c. directing an organism toward a specific stimulus target.
    d. changing a primary reinforcer into a secondary reinforcer.

a.	no
b.	YES, THAT'S CORRECT; this is the definition of shaping
c.	no
d.	no

18. Which reinforcement schedule helps explain the popularity of gambling?
    a. fixed-ratio
    b. variable-ratio
    c. fixed-interval
    d. variable-interval

a.	no; this refers to an unchanging number of responses to get reinforced
b.	YES; the number of responses necessary to obtain reinforcement keeps changing
c.	no; this refers to reinforcement given after passage of unchanging amount of time
d.	no; this refers to reinforcement given after passage of changing amount of time

19. According to the text, which schedule of reinforcement is most resistant to extinction?
    a. fixed-interval
    b. fixed-ratio
    c. variable-ratio
    d. variable-interval

a.	no; when the reward is given is unpredictable
b.	no; when the reward is given is unpredictable
c.	YES; when the reward is given is unpredictable
d.	no; behavior is slow and consistent

20. If you wanted to encourage a child to work hard in order to get good grades, which would be your best choice of reinforcement schedule?
   a. variable-interval
   b. variable-ratio
   c. fixed-interval
   d. fixed-ratio

a.	no; this schedule leads to behavior that is less resistant to extinction	
b.	RIGHT; variable-ratio schedule results in behavior that is very resistant to extinction	
c.	no; this schedule leads to behavior that is less resistant to extinction	
d.	no; this schedule leads to behavior that is less resistant to extinction	

21. Which of the following sets of terms best describes the difference between secondary and primary reinforcers?
   a. learned; unlearned
   b. hidden; observable
   c. positive; negative
   d. psychological; physical

a.	YEA; primary reinforcers are unlearned and secondary reinforcers are learned
b.	no
c.	no; reinforcers are considered to be positive (or pleasant)
d.	no; both primary and secondary can be psychological or physical

22. The frequency of little Johnny's temper tantrums decreased sharply after his parents began to ignore the behavior. In the language of operant conditioning, Johnny's behavior was undergoing
   a. generalization.
   b. extinction.
   c. discrimination.
   d. all of the above

a.	no; there is no response is being made to similar stimuli
b.	YES; the previously reinforced behavior is no longer reinforced
c.	no; Johnny is not responding to a stimuli that signals availability of reinforcement
d.	no

23. When an animal responds only to stimuli associated with reinforcement, it shows that it has the ability to
   a. discriminate.
   b. extinguish.
   c. generalize.
   d. modify.

a.	RIGHT; this occurs when there is response to stimuli that signal reinforcement
b.	no; this is not extinction
c.	no; there is no responding to a similar stimulus
d.	no

24. Little Noelle has learned to throw a temper tantrum in front of Dad (who often gives in). Jennifer has learned, however, that this same behavior is not effective with Mom. Noelle has demonstrated
   a. discrimination.
   b. instinctive drift.
   c. generalization.
   d. superstitious behavior.

a.	YES; she has learned that Dad reinforces her behavior, while Mom does not
b.	no; this refers to the biological influences on learning
c.	no; this means that the same response is given to similar stimuli
d.	no

25. Keller and Marion Breland found that training animals to perform behaviors at fairs was limited by
   a. taste aversion.
   b. physical characteristics.
   c. preparedness.
   d. instinctive drift.

a.	no
b.	no
c.	no; this refers to species-specific biological predispositions to learn in certain ways
d.	YES; this refers to an animal's tendency to revert to instinctive behavior

26. Scott is 6 years old. His parents received a note from his teacher complaining about Scott's use of some inappropriate language in the classroom. Scott's parents are puzzled and wonder how to deal with this situation. Given your knowledge about observational learning principles, what advice would you give Scott's parents?
   a. They should ignore the teacher's note; boys will be boys.
   b. They should closely examine the language they use when Scott is around.
   c. They should punish Scott by taking away his favorite activity.
   d. They should take Scott to see a psychologist.

a.	no
b.	YES; this option underscores learning by imitation
c.	no; this would still leave Scott hearing inappropriate language
d.	no

27. Observational learning can occur
   a. in less time than operant conditioning.
   b. whether or not a model is reinforced.
   c. only if a model is reinforced.
   d. only with young children.

a.	no
b.	YES; the model does not have to be reinforced for observational learning to occur
c.	no; the model does not have to be reinforced for observational learning to occur
d.	no; observational learning takes place in people of different ages

28. If you wanted a group of kids to learn from your example, you would first have to make sure of which of the following?
   a. that they can imitate the behavior
   b. that they remember what I tell them
   c. that they are paying attention
   d. that they get reinforced

a.	no; important, but not of primary importance
b.	no; important, but not of primary importance
c.	CORRECT; the first step in observational learning is for the model to pay attention
d.	no; important, but not of primary importance

29. Wolfgang Kohler is closely associated with experiments having to do with
    a.   classical conditioning.
    b.   insight learning.
    c.   latent learning.
    d.   learned helplessness.

a.	no	
b.	YES; Kohler used the stick problem and box problem to study insight learning	
c.	no	
d.	no	

30. How can culture influence learning?
    a.   Classical and operant conditioning are not used in some cultures.
    b.   Culture can influence the degree to which operant and classical conditioning are used.
    c.   Culture often determines the content of learning.
    d.   both "b" and "c"

a.	no; classical and operant conditioning are universal
b.	no; but you are half right
c.	no; but you are half right
d.	YES; both degree and content of learning are influenced by culture

Chapter 7 - Memory

The Big Picture: Chapter Overview

Memory refers to the retention of information over time. We tend not to think about how smoothly our memory systems work, except when our memory fails. Memory involves several aspects: encoding, storage, and retrieval. Encoding involves how information gets into memory. Storage consists of retention of information over time, and retrieval occurs when this information is taken out of storage. There are several examples of encoding processes that require effort. Rehearsal is the conscious repetition of information that increases the length of time that information stays in memory. Craik and Lockhart's levels of processing theory describes memory as being on a continuum from shallow to deep processing. Elaboration is the extensiveness of processing at any given depth in memory; self-reference is an effective way to elaborate information. Alan Paivio showed that the use of imagery can improve memory. Organization is another way to improve memory; we remember information better when we organize it hierarchically or use chunking. Rehearsal and deep processing are examples of encoding processes that require effort.

According to the Atkinson-Shiffrin theory, we can store information in three main stores that vary according to time: sensory memory, working memory, and long-term memory. Information is stored very briefly in the sensory memory. Visual sensory memory is called iconic memory, whereas auditory sensory memory is referred to as echoic memory. Working memory has a limited capacity of 7 ± 2 items, which can be illustrated by memory span; this capacity can be expanded by chunking. Working memory has a duration of up to 30 seconds; this can be expanded by maintenance rehearsal. Another proposed theory consists of a general executive and two subsystems called the visuospatial scratchpad and the articulatory loop. Long-term memory can retain enormous amounts of information up to a lifetime, and we can efficiently retrieve information from long-term memory.

Information in long-term memory that can be verbally communicated is called declarative memory or explicit memory. Nondeclarative memory, also called implicit memory, refers to memory in which behavior is affected by prior experience without that experience being consciously recollected. Endel Tulving distinguished between episodic and semantic memory. Episodic memory is the retention of information about the where and when of life's happenings; semantic memory is a person's knowledge about the world. Two theories explain the representation of knowledge in memory. Contemporary network theories stress the role of meaningful nodes in the surrounding network. New material is placed in the network by connecting it to appropriate nodes. Schema theory suggests that our memories are not precise and that we reconstruct our past. A schema is a concept or framework that already exists in a person's mind that organizes and interprets information. A script is a schema for an event. Much investigation has focused on the neurobiological basis of memory. A major issue is whether memory is localized or distributed. Neuroscientists are studying the chemicals in the brain and specific brain structures that are involved in memory (e.g., hippocampus, amygdala, cerebellum).

Retrieval is the process of getting information out of memory. Much of the interest in retrieval has focused on long-term memory. Research on the tip-of-the-tongue phenomenon suggests that good retrieval cues are helpful in retrieving information from memory. The serial position effect refers to how recall is superior for items at the beginning (i.e., primacy effect) and at the end of the list (i.e., recency effect). The serial position effect is explained by working memory. Retrieval is influenced by the presence of cues and the nature of the task. Recall is a memory measure where information must be retrieved from previously learned information, whereas in recognition one only has to identify learned items. The encoding specificity principle states that associations formed at the time of encoding or learning tend to be effective retrieval cues. Retrieval also is influenced by priming, which involves activating particular connections or associations in memory. Autobiographical memory consists of a person's recollections of life experiences. Memories of life experiences may be flashbulb memories, which are memories of emotionally significant events that people often recall with more accuracy and vivid imagery than everyday events. Many people have flashbulb memories of personal events and their accuracy is far more durable and accurate than memories of everyday events. Memory for traumatic events is usually more accurate than memory for ordinary events. Another aspect of emotional memories is mood-congruent memory. This refers to the tendency to remember information better when mood is similar at encoding and retrieval.

Forgetting may occur because of interference and decay. Proactive interference occurs when material learned earlier interferes with the recall of material learned later. Retroactive interference occurs when material learned later interferes with material learned earlier. Decay theory suggests that a memory trace, formed when something new is learned, can disintegrate with the passage of time. Anterograde amnesia affects memory for new information, whereas retrograde amnesia is memory loss for a segment of the past.

There are several strategies to improve memory: pay attention and minimize distraction, understand the material rather than memorizing it by rote, organize what you put into memory, and use mnemonics. Mnemonics are techniques for improving memory and include the method of loci, acronyms, and the keyword method. In improving memory for understanding, important strategies include asking yourself questions about what you're trying to learn, spreading out and consolidating your learning, engaging in cognitive monitoring, managing time effectively, and planning effectively. Taking good notes can be improved by summarizing, outlining, concept maps, the Cornell Method, and reviewing your notes. One technique that can assist in studying is the PQ4R Method.

Learning Objectives

When you have studied the material in this chapter, you should be able to:

1.   define memory. (p. 218)
2.   distinguish between encoding, storage, and retrieval. (p. 219)
3.   describe and give examples of the following methods of encoding: rehearsal, depth of processing, elaboration, imagery, and organization. (pp. 219-223)
4.   give an example of chunking. (p. 222)
5.   illustrate the Atkinson and Shiffrin model of memory. (p. 224)
6.   define sensory memory and identify its limits. (pp. 224-225)
7.   distinguish between iconic and echoic memory. (p. 225)
8.   define short-term or working memory and define its limits. (pp. 225-226)
9.   describe the hierarchical organization of long-term memory, including declarative and nondeclarative memory, and episodic and semantic memory. (pp. 227-228)
10.   summarize and compare the two theories that describe the representation of knowledge in memory: network theory and schema theory. (pp. 229-232)
11.   list and analyze five studies describing a neurological basis for memory. (pp. 233-236)
12.   describe the tip-of-the-tongue phenomenon and the serial position effect. (pp. 236-237)
13.   distinguish between the recency and primacy effect. (p. 237)
14.   define the encoding-specificity principle and relate the principle to retrieval cues. (pp. 237-238)
15.   contrast the processes of recall and recognition and relate those processes to retrieval cues. (p. 238)
16.   discuss the relationship between emotion and flashbulb, repressed, and mood congruent memories. (pp. 240-243)
17.   compare and contrast interference and decay theory. (pp. 243-244)
18.   define amnesia and distinguish between anterograde and retrograde amnesia. (p. 244)
19.   list and discuss 10 strategies for improving study skills. (p. 246-248)
20.   summarize and relate the material from *Explorations in Psychology: Repressed Memories, Child Abuse, and Reality, and Memory Construction and Eyewitness Testimony* to the material discussing how memories are reconstructed. (p. 242 and p. 232)
21.   from *Images of Psychology and Life: M. K. and the Russian, S.*, draw inferences as to how these memory anomalies might impact daily life. (p. 217)

Guided Review

The Nature of Memory

Memory is the retention of _____ over _____ . Psychologists study how information is _____ into memory, how it is stored, and how it is later _____ .

information/time - p. 218
encoded (placed) - p. 218
retrieved (found) - p. 218

Memory Encoding

Getting information into memory is called _____ . The conscious repetition of information is called _____ and it increases the length of time that information stays in memory. Craik and Lockhart's view that memory takes place on a continuum of depth is referred to as _____ _____ _____ theory. In this view, the physical or sensory features of information are analyzed at the _____ level, the stimulus is recognized and objects are labeled at the _____ level, and information is processed semantically at the _____ level. Memory improves as it is processed more extensively. This process is called _____ . Researchers have found that memory can also be improved through the use of _____ . According to Alan Paivio's _____ code hypothesis, memory for images is better since it is stored as both in an image code and as a _____ code. A distinctive feature of memory is its _____ ; when information is organized from general to specific classes, it is organized _____ . Organization of information can be improved by grouping information into higher-order units, a technique called _____ .

encoding - p. 219
rehearsal - p. 219

levels of processing - p. 220

shallow - p. 220
intermediate - p. 220
deepest - p. 220
elaboration - p. 220

imagery/dual - p. 221

verbal - p. 221
organization - p. 222
hierarchically - p. 222

chunking - p. 222

Memory Storage

In the Atkinson and Shiffrin model, memory involves a sequence of three stages: _____ memory, short-term memory, and _____-_____ memory. _____ memory holds information from our senses. Visual sensory memory is called _____ memory and is retained for about 1/4 second. The "What-did-you-say-Oh-never-mind" phenomenon involves _____ memory. Working memory, sometimes called _____-_____ memory, has a limited capacity. George Miller wrote that the capacity of working memory was _____ items, plus or minus _____ . The most widely cited example of the 7 $\pm$2 phenomenon involves _____ span. The conscious repetition of information, which increases the length of time it stays in working memory, is called _____ . Some people have _____ imagery, or a photographic memory. A contemporary view of working memory views it as a _____ to manipulate and assemble information. One model suggests that working memory contains an executive and two sub systems: (1) the _____ loop, which is specialized to process language, and 2) the _____ scratchpad, which processes spatial imagery information. Working memory can help to understand the influence of brain damage on _____ skills.

The relatively permanent memory system that holds information for long periods of time is called _____-_____ memory. Information in long-term memory that can be verbally

sensory - p. 224
long-term/Sensory - p. 224

iconic - p. 225
echoic - p. 225
short-term - p. 225

seven/two - p. 226

memory - p. 226

rehearsal/eidetic - p. 226

workbench - p. 226

articulatory - p. 226
visuospatial - p. 226

cognitive - p. 226

long-term - p. 226

communicated is call _____ memory. Information that cannot be verbalized or consciously recollected, is called _____ or implicit memory. One type of declarative memory that focuses on the where and when of events and episodes is called _____ memory; another type, which reflects our general knowledge about the world, is called _____ memory. Semantic memory appears to be independent of the individual's personal recall of the _____.

declarative - p. 227
nondeclarative - p. 227

episodic - p. 228

semantic - p. 228
past - p. 228

     Two approaches have been advanced to explain the representation of knowledge in memory: network theories and schema theories. Network theories view memory as a network of _____. A schema is information, and schema theory suggests that our long-term memory search is not very exact and we _____ the past. A schema for an event is called a _____.

nodes - p. 229
reconstruct - p. 230
script - p. 230

     The past several decades have seen extensive investigation of the biological basis of memory. Many neuroscientists believe that memory is located in discrete sets of _____ of neurons. Although _____ neurons are involved in memory, neurons must work together. Research on the sea slug has demonstrated the importance of _____ in memory. Some neuroscientists have focused on specific _____ structures that appear to be responsible for memory. For example, the _____ and the _____ are involved in declarative memory, while the cerebellum is involved in implicit memory used in doing various skills.

circuits - p. 233
single - p. 233

chemicals - p. 234
brain - p. 241
hippocampus/thalamus - p. 234

Memory Retrieval and Forgetting

     The process we use to get information out of memory storage is called _____. In some cases, we are confident we know something, but we can't quite "pull" it out of memory. This is called the _____-_____-_____-_____ phenomenon. One of the most important aspects of retrieval is the use of good _____. The superior recall for items at the beginning of a list is called the _____ effect, whereas the superior recall at the end of the list is called the _____ effect. Generally, items in the middle of a list produce a _____ level of recall. Collectively, this pattern is called the _____ _____ effect. Two important factors involved in retrieval are (1) the _____ of the cues and (2) the retrieval _____ required. A memory measure that requires retrieval of previously learned information is called _____. By contrast, a memory measure that requires only identification is called _____.

retrieval – p. 236

tip-of-the-tongue - p. 236
cues - p. 237

primacy - p. 237
recency - p. 237
low - p. 237
serial position - p. 237
nature – p. 237
task - p. 237
recall - p. 238
recognition - p. 238

     Associations formed at encoding tend to be effective retrieval cues according to the _____ _____ principle. Activating particular connections or associations in memory is called _____. Autobiographical memory is a form of _____ memory and can exist on _____ different levels. Memories of emotionally significant events that are often recalled more accurately and more vividly are known as _____ _____. From a psychoanalytic view, _____ makes threatening memories more difficult to retrieve. When a dramatic event occurs and the mind pushes the event into the unconscious mind, the process is called _____. We tend to remember information between when our mood is similar at encoding and retrieval and this is called _____-_____ memory.

encoding specificity - p. 238
priming - p. 238
episodic - p. 239
three - p. 239

flashbulb memories - p. 240
repression - p. 242

repression - p. 242

mood-congruent - p. 243

     Ebbinghaus used _____ _____ to study forgetting.

nonsense syllables - p. 243

Two kinds of _____ are proactive and retroactive. When material that has been learned earlier interferes with the recall of material learned later, this is called _____ interference; when material learned later interferes with material learned earlier, it is termed _____ interference. Decay theory suggests that, when something is learned, a _____ _____ is formed. With the passage of time, however, the memory trace _____. The loss of memory is referred to as _____. A type of amnesia that affects the retention of new information is called _____ amnesia. A type of amnesia involving memory loss for a segment of the past but not for new events is called _____ amnesia.

interference - p. 243

proactive - p. 243

retroactive - p. 243
memory trace - p. 243
disintegrates - p. 244
amnesia - p. 244
anterograde - p. 244

retrograde - p. 244

Memory and Study Strategies
Specific techniques designed to make memory efficient are called _____. Two techniques that make use of imagery are the method of _____ and the _____ method. If you assess your progress in studying, you are using _____ _____. The _____ method helps students remember information they are studying and involves several steps including Preview and Review.

mnemonics - p. 244
loci/keyword - p. 244
cognitive monitoring - p. 247
PQ4R - p. 248

Explorations in Psychology

To respond to the questions and exercises presented in this section, please write your thoughts, perspectives, and reactions on a separate piece of paper.

Explorations in Psychology: Memory Construction and Eyewitness Testimony

- Can people tell when their memories of an event are influenced by memory construction?
- Speculate on why people of one ethnic group are less likely to recognize people of other ethnic groups.
- If you were a lawyer prosecuting a case that hinged on eyewitness testimony, what steps would you take to insure its accuracy?
- According to John Yuille, why does the eyewitness testimony of children pose special problems?

Explorations in Psychology: Repressed Memories, Child Abuse, and Reality

- Why should we be concerned about repressed memories?
- If you were a judge trying a case in which a women who alleged abuse by her father 30 years ago experienced repressed memories of the abuse, what safeguards would you take to lessen the chance of an innocent man going to jail?
- Knowing what you know now about repressed memories, would you be in favor of prohibiting the use of evidence obtained from repressed memories more than 20 years old? Why? Give your reactions on a separate piece of paper.

In Your Own Words

To respond to the questions and exercises presented in this section, please write your thoughts, perspectives, and reactions on a separate piece of paper.
- ✓ The textbook describes rehearsal as the conscious repetition of information. What pieces of knowledge have you acquired through rehearsal? What classes have you had that encouraged rehearsal in order to do well on the exams?
- ✓ List some examples of how business and organizations use chunking in their 1-800 numbers.
- ✓ What declarative memories have you retrieved in the last hour? What nondeclarative memories have you retrieved in the last hour?

✓ Describe a flashbulb memory you have. Is it emotional? Why are emotional memories easier to remember? Now look at Figure 7.18. Do you have any flashbulb memories of any of these events? How about of the events pictured on p. 240?

✓ List some acronyms (e.g., musical scale--FACE; the Great Lakes--HOMES) that you have used as mnemonic devices.

✓ Is memory more than just remembering?

Correcting the Incorrect

Carefully read each statement. Determine if the statement is correct or incorrect. If the statement is incorrect, make the necessary changes to correct it. Then look directly under the statement for the correct statement and page reference in the textbook.

1. Memory is defined as remembering declarative and nondeclarative information.
    ❑ *Memory is defined as remembering the retention of information over time. (p. 218)*
2. The three processes of memory include encoding, retrieval, and remembering
    ❑ *The three processes of memory include encoding, storage, and retrieval. (p. 218-219)*
3. If you repeat information over and over again, you are using deep processing.
    ❑ *If you repeat information over and over again, you are using rehearsal. (p. 219).*
4. Remembering information over the long term, works when we repeat it many times.
    ❑ *Remembering information over the long term, works when we add meaning to it. (p. 220)*
5. If you focus on the meaning of a word, you are processing it at a deep level.
    ❑ *If you focus on the meaning of a word, you are processing it at a deep level. (p. 220)*
6. As you think of examples of the concepts you are learning, you are practicing elaboration.
    ❑ *As you think of examples of the concepts you are learning, you are practicing elaboration. (p. 220-221)*
7. Elaboration is helpful because it adds to the primacy of the information.
    ❑ *Elaboration is helpful because it adds to the distinctiveness of the information. (p. 221)*
8. According to Paivio's dual code hypothesis, memories encoded as verbal codes are better remembered.
    ❑ *According to Paivio's dual code hypothesis, memories encoded as verbal and imaginal codes are better remembered. (p. 221)*
9. Chunking involves taking information and packaging it into higher-order units that can be remembered as single units.
    ❑ *Chunking involves taking information and packaging it into higher-order units that can be remembered as single units. (p. 220)*
10. The three memory stores are sensory, iconic, and long-term memory.
    ❑ *The three memory stores are sensory, short-term, and long-term memory. (p. 223)*
11. Echoic memory refers to information from the visual sense in sensory memory.
    ❑ *Echoic memory refers to information from the auditory sense in sensory memory. (p. 225)*
12. Information can last as long as 30 seconds in sensory memory.
    ❑ *Information can last as long as 30 seconds in short-term memory. (p. 226)*
13. Capacity in short-term memory is about 12 items.
    ❑ *Capacity in short-term memory is about 7±2 items. (p. 226)*
14. The capacity of long-term is about 16 gigabytes.
    ❑ *The capacity of long-term is virtually unlimited. (p. 227)*
15. Declarative memory is the conscious recollection of information.
    ❑ *Declarative memory is the conscious recollection of information. (p. 227)*
16. Semantic memory refers to the retention of information about the where and when of life's happenings.
    ❑ *Episodic memory refers to the retention of information about the where and when of life's happenings. (p. 228)*
17. According to network theory, we add new material by relating it to appropriate nodes.
    ❑ *According to network theory, we add new material by relating it to appropriate nodes. (p. 230)*

18. A schema is a concept or framework that already exists in a person's mind that organizes and interprets information.
   - ❑ *A schema is a concept or framework that already exists in a person's mind that organizes and interprets information. (p. 230)*

19. There are no specific memory centers in the brain.
   - ❑ *There are specific memory centers in the brain. (p. 233)*

20. Memory seems to be written in chemicals in the spinal cord.
   - ❑ *Memory seems to be written in chemicals in the brain. (p. 234)*

21. In the serial position effect, we tend to remember items in the middle of a list of items.
   - ❑ *In the serial position effect, we tend to remember items at the beginning and end of a list of items. (p. 237)*

22. In recall, the individual has to identify only learned items, such as in a multiple choice exam.
   - ❑ *In recognition, the individual has to identify only learned items, such as in a multiple choice exam. (p. 238)*

23. The associations made at the time of encoding tend to be effective retrieval cues.
   - ❑ *The associations made at the time of encoding tend to be effective retrieval cues. (p. 238)*

24. Flashbulb memories are typically inaccurate.
   - ❑ *Flashbulb memories are typically accurate. (p. 240)*

25. Memory for traumatic events is usually less accurate than memory for ordinary events.
   - ❑ *Memory for traumatic events is usually more accurate than memory for ordinary events. (p. 241)*

26. Repression's main function is to protect the person from harm.
   - ❑ *Repression's main function is to protect the person from harm. (p. 242)*

27. According to mood-congruent memory, you are more likely to remember information between when your mood is similar at encoding and retrieval.
   - ❑ *According to mood-congruent memory, you are more likely to remember information between when your mood is similar at encoding and retrieval. (p. 243)*

28. In proactive interference, material learned later disrupts retrieval of information learned earlier.
   - ❑ *In retroactive interference, material learned later disrupts retrieval of information learned earlier. (p. 243)*

29. The decay theory suggests that when something new is learned, a neurochemical memory trace is formed.
   - ❑ *The decay theory suggests that when something new is learned, a neurochemical memory trace is formed. (p. 244)*

30. A person who suffers from retrograde amnesia will have problems retaining new information or events.
   - ❑ *A person who suffers from anterograde amnesia will have problems retaining new information or events. (p. 244)*

31. The method of loci refers to organizing memory around vivid imagery.
   - ❑ *The method of loci refers to organizing memory around vivid imagery. (p. 246)*

32. In the Cornell Method of taking notes, the notes are written and rewritten and the person reads the notes into a tape recorder.
   - ❑ *In the Cornell Method of taking notes, the notes are written into two columns. (p. 248)*

33. The PQ4R stands for Preview, Question, Read, Reflect, Recite, and Review.
   - ❑ *The PQ4R stands for Preview, Question, Read, Reflect, Recite, and Review. (p. 248)*

Practice Test

1. Which of the following is the **correct** definition of *memory?*
   a. the retention of information over time
   b. the retention of time through conditioning
   c. the conditioning of thoughts via observation
   d. the neural processing of subconscious material

a.	RIGHT
b.	no; this is not the correct definition of memory
c.	no; this is incorrect
d.	no; memory is not defined in this way

2. The encoding of memory refers to how information is
   a. retained.
   b. retrieved.
   c. placed into memory
   d. all of the above

a.	no; how information is retained refers to storage
b.	no; this sounds like retrieval
c.	YES; encoding refers to how information gets into memory
d.	no

3. Storage is the memory process **primarily** concerned with
   a. getting information into memory.
   b. retaining information over time.
   c. taking information out of storage.
   d. registering information with our senses.

a.	no; this option defines encoding
b.	YES; storage consists of retention of information over time
c.	no; this describe retrieval
d.	no; this option best relates to encoding

4. Which of the following is **not** a disadvantage of rehearsal?
   a. It doesn't help with retaining information for the long term.
   b. It doesn't connect meaning to the information.
   c. It doesn't help with remembering information for a brief time.
   d. It doesn't process information at a deeper level.

a.	no; rehearsal does help us retain information for the long term
b.	no; rehearsal does help connect meaning to the information
c.	YEA; this is not a disadvantage of rehearsal
d.	no; rehearsal does help process information at a deeper level

5. Thinking of examples of a concept is a good way to help yourself understand the concept. This approach is referred to as
   a. deep processing.
   b. storage.
   c. imagery.
   d. elaboration.

a.	no; although at deep processing the stimulus' meaning is processed
b.	no; storage refers to retaining information over time
c.	no; imagery is the use of mental images and may or may not involve examples
d.	RIGHT; thinking of examples increases the extensiveness of processing information

6. A teacher who wants to help students with long-term retention should present information in which manner?
   a. organized randomly
   b. without any specific order
   c. organized alphabetically
   d. organized logically or hierarchically

a.	no; this would also reduce long-term retention since it lacks organization	
b.	no; in fact this would decrease long-term retention	
c.	no; but only if there is a more logically organization	
d.	YES; when information is presented in an logically organized way, memory is helped	

7. The capacity of working memory can be expanded by grouping information into higher-order units. This technique is called
   a. rehearsal.
   b. eidetic imagery.
   c. chunking.
   d. the phonological loop.

a.	no; rehearsal is the conscious repetition of information
b.	no; this is a type of photographic memory
c.	CORRECT; chunking packs information into higher-order units
d.	no; the phonological loop is a subsystem of working memory

8 Which memory system can retain information in its original form for only an instant?
   a. sensory memory
   b. working memory
   c. long-term memory
   d. short-term memory

a.	THAT'S RIGHT; sensory memory holds information for only a short time
b.	no
c.	no
d.	no

9. According to the Atkinson-Shiffrin theory of memory, the **best** way to move information into long-term memory is to
   a. rehearse the information and keep it in short-term memory as long as possible.
   b. move the information directly from sensory memory into long-term memory.
   c. rehearse the information in sensory memory as long as possible.
   d. move complex information directly to long-term memory.

a.	YES; this is correct according to the Atkinson-Shiffrin theory
b.	no; the model includes short-term memory located between sensory and long-term
c.	no; information lasts for only a short time in sensory memory
d.	no; complex memory must first go through sensory and short-term memory

10. Which of the following statements about sensory memory is **incorrect?**
   a. Information does not stay in sensory memory for very long.
   b. Sensory memory processes more information than we may realize.
   c. Sensory memory retains information from our senses.
   d. Information in sensory memory is resistant to decay.

a.	no; this statement is correct
b.	no; this statement is correct
c.	no; this statement is correct
d.	YES; information in sensory decays very rapidly

11. Visual images that are stored in the sensory registers are called _____ memory.
   a. iconic
   b. echoic
   c. semantic
   d. nondeclarative

a.	CORRECT; the iconic refers to visual images
b.	no; echoic memory refers to auditory stimuli
c.	no; semantic memory is memory of the meanings of words
d.	no; nondeclarative memory refers to implicit memory

12. Auditory information that is stored in the sensory memory is referred to as
   a. iconic memory.
   b. echoic memory.
   c. nondeclarative memory.
   d. memory span.

a.	no; iconic memory refers to visual images
b.	YES; the word echoic includes the word echo
c.	no; this term refers to memory that cannot be verbalized or consciously recalled
d.	no; memory span describes the storage capacity of working or short-term memory

13. You are reading a book, and your friend Rachel asks you a question. By the time you say, "Sorry, what did you say?" you "hear" her question in your head. This is due to
   a. echoic memory.
   b. long-term sensory memory.
   c. working memory.
   d. iconic memory.

a.	YES; this demonstrates echoic memory or auditory information in sensory memory
b.	no; this is no long-term sensory memory
c.	no; working memory would not cause this experience
d.	no; iconic memory refers to visual images not auditory information

14. You have just looked up a phone number in a phone book. Which of the following strategies would be the **most effective** for remembering this phone number longer than 30 seconds?
   a. transferring the phone number to short-term memory
   b. processing the phone number in sensory memory
   c. thinking of as many phone numbers as possible
   d. rehearsing the phone number

a.	no; the information is already in short-term memory
b.	no; remember information in sensory memory decays very rapidly
c.	no; this would cause interference and you would forget the correct phone number
d.	THAT'S CORRECT; by rehearsal, the number will last longer in working memory

15. Which of the following can store information for up to 30 seconds?
   a. sensory memory
   b. working memory
   c. long-term memory
   d. iconic memory

16.   The storage capacity of working memory is _____ units of information
    a.   12
    b. 7 ± 2
    c. 2.8×10^{20}
    d.   .45

    a.   no; but that is close
    b.   THAT'S CORRECT
    c.   no; this is the estimated storage capacity of long-term memory
    d.   no; not even close

17.   Declarative memory is subdivided into
    a.   procedural and virtual memory.
    b.   episodic and semantic memory.
    c.   echoic and iconic memory.
    d.   automatic and deliberate memory.

    a.   no
    b.   RIGHT
    c.   no; these refer to the types of information found in sensory memory
    d.   no

18.   Early network theories of memory were **primarily** criticized for
    a.   underestimating the complexity of human memory.
    b.   being too abstract.
    c.   including too many hierarchical levels.
    d.   focusing exclusively on semantic memory.

    a.   THAT'S RIGHT; hierarchical networks are too simple
    b.   no; if anything, network theories are too concrete
    c.   no; that is not a primary criticism
    d.   no; this is not a primary criticism

19.   Which of the following theories are most consistent with reconstructive memory?
    a.   network theories
    b.   schema theories
    c.   script theories
    d.   none of the above

    a.   no; network theories are not consistent with reconstructive memory
    b.   YES; schemas are used when we reconstruct information
    c.   no; a script is a schema for an event
    d.   no

20. Experiments with sea slugs led to the speculation that memories are related to activity of
    a.   the hippocampus.
    b.   the amygdala.
    c.   brain chemicals.
    d.   the cell nucleus.

a.	no; the hippocampus is involved in human memory	
b.	no; the amygdala is involved in human memory	
c.	CORRECT; in particular, serotonin may play a role in memory	
d.	no	

21. Your brother gives you a list of items he wants you to pick up at the grocery store on her way home
    from work. You glanced over the list during your lunch hour but inadvertently left the list on your
    desk when you left work. When you get to the grocery store, which items on the list are you **most
    likely** to remember?
    a.   the items at the beginning of the list
    b.   the items at the end of the list
    c.   the items in the middle of the list
    d.   the items at the beginning and end of the list

a.	no; although this is half correct	
b.	no; although this is half correct	
c.	no; these items would not likely be remembered	
d.	YES; the primacy and the recency effect would be observed	

22. The typical serial position effect pattern shows which of the following?
    a.   stronger recency effect than primacy effect
    b.   stronger primacy than recency effect
    c.   equal strength for primacy and recency effect
    d.   weaker recency effect than primacy effect

a.	YES; this describes the typical serial position effect pattern	
b.	no; this does not describes the typical serial position effect	
c.	no; the typical pattern is stronger recency effect than primacy effect	
d.	no; this is just the opposite of the typical serial position effect	

23. Essay questions measure which type of memory?
    a.   recognition
    b.   recall
    c.   serial position
    d.   none of the above

a.	no; the student simply needs to recognize learned items	
b.	CORRECT; in recall, the study must retrieve learned information	
c.	no; serial position refers to the pattern of information remembered	
d.	no; multiple choice questions involve recognition	

24. An essay examination is to recall as a multiple-choice test is to
    a.   recognition.
    b.   reconstruction.
    c.   reorganization.
    d.   restructuring.

a.	YES; multiple-choice tests require the learned to recognize learned items	
b.	no; recognition is the type of retrieval used in multiple choice tests	
c.	no; reorganization is not involved in multiple-choice tests	
d.	no; this is not correct	

25. According to the _____, associations formed at the time of encoding tend to be effective retrieval cues.
    a. recall
    b. serial position effect
    c. PQ4R
    d. encoding specificity principle

a.	no; recall is a type retrieval in which previously learned information
b.	no; this describes how retrieval is affected by the position of information in a list
c.	no; PQ4R is a study method
d.	CORRECT; this describes the encoding specificity principle

26. When people are in a sad mood, they are more likely to remember negative experiences. This describes:
    a. retroactive interference.
    b. proactive interference.
    c. mood-congruent memory.
    d. decay theory.

a.	no; retroactive interference describes how new information disrupts old
b.	no; proactive interference describes how old information disrupts new
c.	RIGHT; mood-congruent memory is correct
d.	no; decay theory says that the neurochemical of memory tends to disintegrate

27. Adam took a Spanish course during his first semester at university; during his second semester, he took a French course. Retroactive interference would suggest that Adam
    a. should now consider taking German.
    b. is going to have a difficult time learning French.
    c. is not going to remember his Spanish as well.
    d. is going to have a difficult time with both Spanish and French.

a.	no; German?
b.	no; this would describe proactive interference of old disrupting new
c.	YES; retroactive interference occurs when new information disrupts old
d.	no; retroactive interference would predict problems remembering Spanish

28. Which theory suggests that forgetting is caused by a fading memory trace?
    a. reconstruction theory
    b. repression
    c. decay
    d. interference theory

a.	no; reconstruction describes how we remember information
b.	no; repression blocks memories from the conscious
c.	YES; decay theory says that the neurochemical memory trace disintegrates
d.	no; interference theory says memories are forgotten because of other information

29. In retrograde amnesia, there is memory loss
    a.   only for new information.
    b.   only for segments of new information.
    c.   for the complete past.
    d.   only for a segment of the past.

a.	no; this more accurately describes anterograde amnesia	
b.	no; this more accurately describes anterograde amnesia	
c.	no; only segments of the past are forgotten in retrograde amnesia	
d.	THAT'S RIGHT; this is the definition of retrograde amnesia	

30. Which of the following is **not** an effective study strategy?
    a.   rotely rehearse and memorize information
    b.   pay attention and minimize distraction
    c.   organize what you put into memory
    d.   use mnemonic strategies

a.	YES; instead you should try to understand the material	
b.	no; this is an effective strategy	
c.	no; this is an effective strategy	
d.	no; this is an effective strategy	

Chapter 8 - Thinking and Language

The Big Picture: Chapter Overview

In the late 1950s and 1960s, many psychologists began to realize that human behavior could not be fully understood without appreciating the importance of mental processes. Cognitive psychology was beginning to challenge behaviorism, which was the dominant force in psychology. The development of computers stimulated the growth of cognitive psychology. Although some cognitive psychologists draw an analogy between human cognition and the functioning of computers, important differences exist. The computer's role in cognitive psychology has given rise to a field called artificial intelligence.

Psychologists study thinking by examining concepts and their formation. Concepts help us to make sense of information in the world. When thinking about concepts, we use prototype matching. Another ability studied in cognitive psychology is problem solving. As we solve problems we find and frame the problem, develop good problem solving strategies by utilizing subgoaling, algorithms, and heuristics, evaluate solutions, and rethink and redefine problems and solutions. Fixation, functional fixedness, and mental set are obstacles in solving problems.

Critical thinking, another area of thinking studied by psychologists, is thinking reflectively, productively, and evaluating the evidence; critical thinking is similar to the concept of mindfulness. Reasoning is the mental activity of transforming information to reach conclusions. Inductive reasoning is reasoning from the specific to the general; analogies draw on inductive reasoning. Reasoning from the general to the specific is called deductive reasoning. Evaluating alternatives and making choices among them is called decision-making. Rules that we use in decision making are not established and this increases the biases and flaws that we are prone to make: confirmation bias, belief perseverance, overconfidence bias, hindsight bias, availability heuristic, and representativeness heuristic.

Language is a form of communication based on a system of symbols that can be spoken, written, or signaled. All languages have infinite generativity which allows individuals to generate an unending number of meaningful sentences from a finite number of words and rules. Languages also have organizational rules that include phonology, morphology, syntax, and semantics. Noam Chomsky argues for the role of biology in language; humans are biologically prewired to learn language at a certain time and in a certain way.

Among the strongest arguments for the influence of biology on language is that children all over the world acquire language milestones at about the same time developmentally and in about the same order. On the other hand, reinforcement and imitation may also play a role in language development, which suggests an interaction between biological and environmental influences.

Language development proceeds from babbling in infants to single words, two-word statements, then to telegraphic speech. Children also learn morphological rules such as word endings to indicate plural nouns. Psychologists believe in a critical period for language acquisition where there is learning readiness. The case of Genie illustrates the critical period for language acquisition. There is some controversy regarding the best way to educate children whose first language is not English. Bilingualism attempts to teach academic subjects to immigrant children while slowly and simultaneously adding English instruction. Ellen Bialystok has argued that bilingual education fosters metalinguistic awareness and hence intellectual development. Another controversy centers on the best way to teach children to read. The whole language approach stresses that reading instruction should parallel children's natural language learning. The basic-skills-and-phonetics approach emphasizes that reading instruction should stress phonetics and its basic rules for translating written symbols into sounds. An important issue in the study of language is teaching human language to animals. One issue involves whether animals can understand the meaning of symbols and if animals can learn syntax.

Whorf suggested that language determines the way we think. The linguistic relativity hypothesis states that language determines the structure of thinking and shapes our basic ideas. Some have argued that words reflect, not cause, the way we think. Moreover, language is always dependent on thought and each can direct the other.

Learning Objectives

When you have studied the material in this chapter, you should be able to:

1. explain the similarities and differences in the functioning of computers and human cognition. (p. 256)
2. discuss the concept of artificial intelligence and list several applications of AI. (pp. 253-256)
3. define thinking. (p. 256)
4. explain why concepts are important to cognitive process. (pp. 256-258)
5. give examples of problem finding and framing. (p. 259)
6. identify and describe techniques that improve problem-solving skills. (pp. 259-261)
7. define and give an example of an algorithm and an heuristic. (p. 260)
8. define and give examples of fixation, functional fixedness, and mental set. (p. 261)
9. identify and discuss the critical thinking skills that are necessary in everyday life. (pp. 262-263)
10. distinguish between inductive and deductive reasoning. (pp. 263-264)
11. give an example that illustrates each of the common flaws or biases that can result in faulty conclusions: conformation bias, belief perseverance, the overconfidence bias, hindsight bias, the availability heuristic, and the representative heuristic. (pp. 264-267)
12. define language. (p. 268)
13. discuss the common organizational rules that bound all languages. (p. 268)
14. describe the following components of language: phonology, morphology, syntax, and semantics. (pp. 268-269)
15. summarize evidence supporting a critical period for language development. (pp. 273-274)
16. describe the progression of language development in infants and young children. (pp. 272-273)
17. discuss the issues involved in bilingual education, including Ellen Bialystok's ideas about metalinguistic awareness. (pp. 274-275)
18. present information supporting and refuting each side of the reading program debate: whole language versus basic skills education. (p. 275)
19. identify the issues in the debate regarding the ability of animals to use language. (pp. 275-276)
20. discuss the significance of the linguistic relativity hypothesis in terms of culture. (p. 277-279)
21. From *Explorations in Psychology: In Pursuit of Language in Animals*, cite evidence that supports and refutes the contention that animals use or can use language to communicate. (p. 278)
22. From *Explorations in Psychology: How to Talk with Babies and Toddlers*, summarize and relate the information to the material on the progression of language development in children and the material on critical periods in language development. (p. 270)

Guided Review

The Cognitive Revolution in Psychology

An approach that seeks to explain behavior by investigating mental processes and structures that cannot be directly observed is called _____ psychology. According to the cognitive approach, observable behavior is often explained in _____ terms. Interest in cognitive psychology was stimulated with the development of the _____. Although analogies are often drawn between the functioning of computers and the human brain, they function quite differently in some respects. Each brain cell, for example, is alive and can be altered in its _____. Most computers receive information from humans who have coded the information and removed much of the _____ in the natural world. The human brain can also learn new _____, relationships, _____, and patterns. In recent years, interest has grown in a field called _____ _____, the science of creating machines capable of performing activities that require intelligence when performed by people. AI is useful in tasks that require _____, persistence, and vast _____.

cognitive - p. 254
unobservable - p. 254

computer - p. 254

functioning - p. 255

ambiguity - p. 255
rules/concepts - p. 255
artificial intelligence - p. 256

speed/memory - p. 256

Thinking

When we mentally manipulate information as when we form concepts, solve problems, reason, and make decisions, we are _____. A category used to group objects, events, and characteristics on the basis of common properties is called a _____. Concepts help to make memory more _____. An important process in the formation of concepts is to develop _____ about them. According to Rosch, real-life concepts often have " _____ _____." When we decide if an item is a member of a particular category through comparison with the most typical items of the category, we are using _____ _____.

Problem solving is defined as an attempt to find an appropriate way of reaching a _____ when it is not readily available. The steps of problem solving include finding and framing _____, developing good problem solving strategies, evaluating _____, and rethinking and redefining problems and solutions. Setting intermediate goals is called _____. Two general strategies that people engage in while trying to solve problems are heuristics and _____. Heuristics are rules of thumb that can suggest a solution but do not _____ a solution. A procedure that guarantees a solution is called an _____. One trap that may be experienced in solving a problem is _____, which is using a prior strategy without considering a new perspective. _____ fixedness refers to when we fail to solve a problem because we view it in terms of its usual functions. Psychologists use the term _____ _____ when individuals try to solve a problem in a particular way that has worked in the past.

_____ _____ is defined as thinking reflectively, productively, and evaluating the evidence. In other words, _____ _____ is a very important aspect of everyday reasoning that

thinking - p. 256

concept/efficient - p. 265

hypotheses (definitions) - p. 258
fuzzy boundaries - p. 258

prototype matching - p. 258

goal - p. 259

problems - p. 259
solutions - p. 259
subgoaling - p. 259

algorithms - p. 260
guarantee - p. 260
algorithm - p. 260
fixation - p. 261
Functional - p. 261

mental set - p. 261

Critical thinking - p. 262
critical thinking - p. 263

involves grasping the deeper meaning of problems, of keeping an open mind, and deciding for oneself. According to Brooks and Brooks, schools should place greater emphasis on getting students to _____ their thinking. A mindful person creates new ideas, is _____ to new information, and is aware of more than one _____.

_____ is the mental activity of transforming information to reach conclusions. The process of deriving abstract principles, concepts, or hypotheses from specific observations is called _____ reasoning. Reasoning from the general to the specific is called _____ reasoning. _____ draw on inductive reasoning. If a student is evaluating alternative and making choices among them, she is engaged in _____ _____. When we make decisions, we are prone to _____ and _____. If you seek out and use information that supports your ideas rather than refutes them, you have committed the _____ _____. When we have a hard time letting go of a belief, we have experienced belief _____. In making decisions, we often tend to be more confident than correct; this is called _____ bias. Psychologists study the tendency that people have of falsely reporting they accurately predicting an event, but only after the event has occurred. These psychologists study _____ bias. We evaluate the probability of an event based on the ease with which prior occurrences come to mind and this is called the _____ heuristic. The strategy which suggests that we make estimates based on matching a prototype, is called the _____ heuristic.

- expand - p. 263
- open - p. 263
- perspective - p. 263
- Reasoning - p. 263

- inductive - p. 263
- deductive/Analogies - p. 263

- decision making - p. 264
- biases/flaws (errors) - p. 264

- confirmation bias - p. 264
- perseverance - p. 265

- overconfidence - p. 265

- hindsight - p. 266

- availability - p. 266
- representativeness - p. 266

Language

All human languages have some common characteristics. Language is a form of _____ and consists of a system of _____. It allows individuals to produce an endless number of sentences from a finite set of rules, a quality called _____ _____ The study of the sound systems of language is called _____. The term that refers to word formation is _____. The way in which words are combined is called _____. The actual meaning of words and sentences is called _____.

- communication - p. 268
- symbols - p. 268
- infinite generativity - p. 268
- phonology - p. 268
- morphology - p. 268
- syntax - p. 268
- semantics - p. 268

Although many theorists stress the biological basis of language, others suggest that language is shaped more by environment and _____ factors. Noam Chomsky believes that language is strongly related to _____ factors. Chomsky argues that human are _____ to acquire language. B. F. Skinner argued that language is acquired through _____ and Bandura thought that language is acquired through _____.

- biological - p. 269
- biological - p. 269
- prewired - p. 269
- reinforcement - p. 269
- imitation - p. 269

Language researcher Roger Brown has concluded that a child's ability to learn grammar is not based on _____. Children from middle-income families and professional parents have a _____ vocabulary than children from disadvantaged families. The research on language acquisition illustrates that _____ and _____ factors play roles.

Early language development in infants consists of _____

- reinforcement - p. 269

- greater (larger) - p. 271
- biological - p. 271
- environmental - p. 271
- babbling - p. 272

105

which even deaf babies do suggesting _____ readiness. When children reach 18 to 24 months, they utter _____ _____ statements that are described by the term _____ speech. Berko found that preschool and first grade children can apply _____ _____ to indicate the plural of "wug."

A period in which there is a learning readiness, beyond which learning is different or impossible, is called a _____ _____ . After conducting research on atypical populations, Lenneberg concluded that language development during the preschool years is the result of _____ . The stunted language development of "wild child" Genie and other similarly deprived children supports the _____ _____ hypothesis.

Bilingualism is an important issue in Canada. Wallace Lambert has shown that bilingual children perform _____ than unilingual children on measures of intelligence. Ellen Bialystok has proposed that this is true because bilingual children have a better-developed _____ _____ . Adolescents and adults can learn a second language, but will be more difficult for them than for

_____.

There are two approaches to teach children to read. The _____ _____ approach stress reading instruction should be parallel to children's natural language learning. In this approach, reading is _____ with listening, writing, subjects, and real-world activities. The _____-_____-_____-_____ approach stress that reading instruction should emphasize phonetics and the rules for translating written symbols into _____ . Research indicates that a _____ approach is the best strategy.

The debate about chimpanzees' ability to use language focuses on whether they can understand the meaning of _____ and whether they can learn the mechanics and rules of language, called _____ . While researchers agree that animals can communicate with each other and that some can _____ language-like symbols, their language abilities do not show the same degree of generativity and _____ as human language.

According to the _____ _____ hypothesis, language determines the structure of our thought and shapes our basic ideas. This hypothesis was developed by _____. Although the hypothesis is controversial, many researchers would agree that language can influence thought but probably does not _____ it. Language can be thought of as a _____ for representing ideas. _____ is believed to be the foundation for language.

Explorations in Psychology

To respond to the questions and exercises presented in this section, please write your thoughts, perspectives, and reactions on a separate piece of paper.

Explorations in Psychology: How to Talk with Babies and Toddlers

- Why is it important to be an active conversational partner with a baby or toddler?
- Is there any piece of advice presented that would be appropriate to apply when speaking with people of any age?

Explorations in Psychology: In Pursuit of Language in Animals

- Some pet owners believe that their pets really do understand language. What would you say to them after reading this material?
- Is language in animals the same as language in humans?
- Why should we be concerned about teaching animals language? What possible benefits do you see in pursuing such a task?

In Your Own Words

To respond to the questions and exercises presented in this section, please write your thoughts, perspectives, and reactions on a separate piece of paper.

- ✓ Using your own words, describe the difference in approach of behaviorism and cognitive psychology.
- ✓ Brainstorm and develop a list of encounters you have had with computers that have artificial intelligence.
- ✓ Give an example of inductive reasoning and deductive reasoning as you meet a person for the first time.
- ✓ Paraphrase the textbook's definitions of hindsight bias and availability heuristic.
- ✓ Think of a problem that you are currently experiencing. Using the steps of problem solving described in this chapter, develop a solution.
- ✓ Are you bilingual? Have you experienced bilingual education? Would you agree with Ellen Bialystok that bilingualism improves metalinguistic awareness?
- ✓ Carefully read the section on Whorf's linguistic relativity hypothesis. Imagine that you have a hobby (e.g., stamps, gardening, wood working). How would your expertise influence your thinking or perception of the hobby compared to someone who knows nothing or very little of the hobby?

Correcting the Incorrect

Carefully read each statement. Determine if the statement is correct or incorrect. If the statement is incorrect, make the necessary changes to correct it. Then look directly under the statement for the correct statement and page reference in the textbook.

1.   Cognitive psychology challenged behaviorism.
   - *Cognitive psychology challenged behaviorism.* *(p. 254)*
2.   The growth of cognitive psychology was stimulated by Noam Chomsky's theories.
   - *The growth of cognitive psychology was stimulated by the development of the computer. (p. 254).*
3.   Cognitive psychologists use animals as an analogy to explain the relation between cognition and the brain.
   - *Cognitive psychologists use the computer as an analogy to explain the relation between cognition and the brain. (p. 255)*
4.   Mentally manipulating information is referred to as decision making.
   - *Mentally manipulating information is referred to as thinking. (p. 256)*
5.   Concepts are solutions we use to solve problems.
   - *Concepts are mental categories that we use to group objects, events, and characteristics. (p. 256).*

6.   In real-life, concepts are well-defined.
   - ❏ *In real-life, concepts are not well-defined. (p. 258)*
7.   The least typical item of a category is used as the prototype.
   - ❏ *The most typical item of a category is used as the prototype. (p. 258)*
8.   The first step in problem solving is to develop good problem solving strategies.
   - ❏ *The first step in problem solving is to find and frame problems. (p. 259).*
9.   If you are using an algorithm, you are using a strategy that is guaranteed to solve a problem.
   - ❏ *If you are using an algorithm, you are using a strategy that is guaranteed to solve a problem. (p. 260)*
10.   Functional rigidity is a term used to describe when an individual fails to solve a problem by viewing it in terms of its usual functions.
    - ❏ *Functional fixedness is a term used to describe when an individual fails to solve a problem by viewing it in terms of its usual functions. (p. 261)*
11.   The candle, nine-dot, and six-matchstick problems illustrate fixation in problem solving.
    - ❏ *The candle, nine-dot, and six-matchstick problems illustrate fixation in problem solving. (p. 260)*
12.   Schools probably spend the right amount of time on teaching critical thinking.
    - ❏ *Schools probably do not spend the right amount of time on teaching critical thinking. (p. 263)*
13.   A mindless person creates new ideas, is open to new information, and is aware of more than one perspective.
    - ❏ *A mindful person creates new ideas, is open to new information, and is aware of more than one perspective. (p. 263)*
14.   Inductive reasoning involves reasoning from general to specific; deductive reasoning is reasoning from specific to general.
    - ❏ *Inductive reasoning involves reasoning from specific to general; deductive reasoning is reasoning from general to specific. (p. 263-264)*
15.   Sherlock Holmes was a master at inductive reasoning
    - ❏ *Sherlock Holmes was a master at deductive reasoning. (p. 264)*
16.   If you seek out information that supports your own ideas rather than refutes them, you have experienced the confirmation bias.
    - ❏ *If you seek out information that supports your own ideas rather than refutes them, you have experienced the confirmation bias. (p. 264)*
17.   People tend to falsely report that they accurately predicted an event; this is called the availability heuristic.
    - ❏ *People tend to falsely report that they accurately predicted an event; this is called the hindsight bias. (p. 266)*
18.   The tendency to hold on to a belief even in the face of contradictory evidence is belief perseverance.
    - ❏ *The tendency to hold on to a belief even in the face of contradictory evidence is belief perseverance. (p. 265)*
19.   The representativeness heuristic says that we can produce an endless number of meaningful sentences using a finite set of words and rules.
    - ❏ *Infinite generativity says that we can produce an endless number of meaningful sentences using a finite set of words and rules. (p. 268)*
20.   Language is based on a system of symbols.
    - ❏ *Language is based on a system of symbols. (p. 268)*
21.   Syntax refers to the way words are combined to form acceptable phrases and sentences.
    - ❏ *Syntax refers to the way words are combined to form acceptable phrases and sentences. (p. 268)*
22.   Morphology refers to a language's sound system and phonology the meaning of words.
    - ❏ *Phonology refers to a language's sound system and semantics the meaning of words. (p. 268)*
23.   B. F. Skinner suggested that we are biologically prewired to learn language.
    - ❏ *Noam Chomsky suggested that we are biologically prewired to learn language. (p. 269)*
24.   Children in welfare families hear only about 600 words an hour compared to children in professional families hearing about 2,100 words per hour.
    - ❏ *Children in welfare families hear only about 600 words an hour compared to children in professional families hearing about 2,100 words per hour. (p. 271)*
25.   Telegraphic speech is also known as babbling.

❑ *Telegraphic speech is also known as the use of short and precise words. (p. 272).*

26. To say there is a critical period in language acquisition means that there is learning readiness during a particular period.

❑ *To say there is a critical period in language acquisition means that there is learning readiness during a particular period. (p. 273)*

27. A child is learning to read using a method that parallels natural language learning; this is called the whole language approach.

❑ *A child is learning to read using a method that parallels natural language learning; this is called the whole language approach. (p. 275)*

28. Chimps cannot understand symbols.

❑ *Chimps can understand symbols. (p. 276)*

29. The idea that language determines the structure of thinking and shapes our basic ideas is called infinite generativity.

❑ *The idea that language determines the structure of thinking and shapes our basic ideas is called the linguistic relativity hypothesis. (p. 277)*

30. Memory is just stored in terms of words.

❑ *Memory is stored in terms of words, sounds, and images. (p. 278)*

31. Thought can direct language, but language does not direct thought.

❑ *Thought can direct language and language can direct thought. (p. 279)*

Practice Test

1. When comparing the computer to the human brain, which statement is **incorrect?**
    a. Computers perform complex numerical calculations faster than the human brain.
    b. Computers apply rules more consistently than the human brain.
    c. Computers can develop more sophisticated learning goals than the human brain.
    d. Computers can represent complex mathematical patterns better than the human brain.

a.	no; this statement is accurate
b.	no; this statement is accurate
c.	CORRECT; the human brain can develop more sophisticated learning goals
d.	no; this statement is accurate

2. Which of the following was the most important in stimulating the growth of cognitive psychology?
    a. the development of MRI scan
    b. the development of the computer
    c. a study done by B. F. Skinner supporting cognitive psychology
    d. the case of Genie

a.	no; the development of MRI scan is less important
b.	THAT'S RIGHT; computers provide information about how thinking might work
c.	no; in fact Skinner would never support cognitive psychology
d.	no; the case of Genie is more important in linguistics

3. Artificial intelligence systems have been used successfully in all of the following areas **except** which one?
    a. resolving interpersonal conflicts
    b. playing chess
    c. diagnosing medical illness
    d. evaluating loan applicants

a.	YES; AI systems cannot resolving conflicts between people	
b.	no; AI systems have played chess	
c.	no; AI systems are able to diagnose medical illness	
d.	no; AI systems evaluate loan applicants	

4. The ability to form concepts helps us with all of the following cognitive activities **except** which one?
   a. generalizing experiences
   b. relating experience and objects
   c. feeling tired after a workout
   d. remembering associations

a.	no; concepts allow us to make generalizations	
b.	no; concepts allow us to relate experiences and objects	
c.	RIGHT; concepts do not make us feel tired after a workout	
d.	no; concepts allow us to remember associations	

5. The use of concepts allows us to:
   a. avoid the hindsight bias.
   b. extend the critical learning period for language.
   c. make memory less efficient.
   d. make generalizations.

a.	no; the hindsight bias occurs independently of our use of concepts	
b.	no; the critical learning period is not related to our use of concepts	
c.	no; in fact, concepts make memory more efficient	
d.	YEP; generalizations are possible because of concepts	

6. You are watching a professional basketball game where most of the players are over 6' 6" tall. You are surprised to see a player under 6' tall. You are surprised because this player does not match your idea of a professional basketball player. Which of the following best describes your experience?
   a. prototype matching
   b. infinitive generativity
   c. syntax
   d. linguistic relativity hypothesis

a.	CORRECT; we use prototypes to decide if something belongs to a category	
b.	no; this refers to one of the characteristics of language	
c.	no; syntax is the way we combine words to form phrases and sentences	
d.	no; this refers to the idea that language influences thought	

7. Your text describes the experiences of Fred Smith who asked, "Why can't there be reliable overnight mail service?" His question represents which problem-solving step?
   a. rethinking and redefining the problem
   b. evaluating the solutions
   c. employing good problem-solving strategies
   d. finding and framing the problem

a.	no; identifying the problem must occur first	
b.	no; identifying the problem must occur first	
c.	no; identifying the problem must occur first	
d.	THAT'S RIGHT; the question is always the problem to be recognized	

8. A good strategy for subgoaling is to
   a.   work without a specific plan.
   b.   work backward in establishing subgoals.
   c.   set no more than three subgoals.
   d.   work randomly in establishing subgoals.

a.	no; a plan is needed
b.	RIGHT; this is a good strategy in establishing subgoals
c.	no; maybe, but this can limit our thinking
d.	no; subgoals must be ordered and logical, not random

9. In order to complete your algebra homework, you would be using which problem-solving strategy?
   a.   heuristics
   b.   trial-and-error
   c.   algorithms
   d.   subgoaling

a.	no; heuristics do not guarantee a solution to a problem
b.	no; this can be time consuming and ineffective
c.	YEA; an algorithm is a strategy that always produces a solution, and this is desired
d.	no; an algorithm is the better strategy

10. A(n) algorithm is:
    a.   a rule of thumb that does not a guarantee a solution
    b.   a rule of thumb that guarantees a problem
    c.   a strategy that guarantees a solution
    d.   a strategy for framing problems

a.	no; this describes heuristics
b.	no; the problem has already been identified; you don't need to identify again
c.	YES; this is the definition of algorithms
d.	no; asking questions is effective for framing problems

11. "A paper clip is a paper clip and nothing more." This person is most likely experiencing:
    a.   inductive reasoning.
    b.   mindfulness.
    c.   functional fixedness.
    d.   hindsight bias.

a.	no; inductive reasoning is reasoning from specific to general
b.	no; mindfulness is similar to critical thinking, which this person appears to lack
c.	AYE; functional fixedness is failing to see other uses of an object
d.	no; hindsight bias is

12. A person who had just used a penny to tighten a screw has
    a.   solved an anagram.
    b.   overcome functional fixedness.
    c.   learned that heuristics can be ill-defined.
    d.   demonstrated the contiguity principle.

a.	no; this is not an anagram
b.	CORRECT; the penny is being used in an unusual function
c.	no; heuristics are rules of thumb
d.	no

13. According to Brooks and Brooks, schools should focus more on teaching what kind of thinking skills?
    a.   operational thinking skills
    b.   heuristic thinking skills
    c.   critical thinking skills
    d.   all of the above

a.	no
b.	no
c.	THAT'S CORRECT; schools focus now on lower skills not critical skills
d.	no

14. According to Ellen Langer, a mindful person is characterized by all of the following **except** which one?
    a.   continues to create new ideas
    b.   engages in automatic behavior
    c.   is open to new information
    d.   is aware of more than one perspective

a.	no; this is part of mindfulness
b.	GOOD; a mindful person thinks about what he or she is doing
c.	no; this is part of mindfulness
d.	no; this is part of mindfulness

15. Inductive reasoning may be related to
    a.   confirmation bias.
    b.   analogies.
    c.   overconfidence bias.
    d.   belief perseverance.

a.	no; in this bias we seek out information that confirms our beliefs
b.	GOOD; analogies draw on inductive reasoning
c.	no; in this bias we show too much confidence in our decisions
d.	no; this is the tendency to hold on to a belief when there is contradictory evidence

16. A specific conclusion derived from general information involves
    a.   representative heuristic.
    b.   simulation heuristics.
    c.   inductive reasoning.
    d.   deductive reasoning.

a.	no; in this heuristics we use prototypes to make decisions
b.	no
c.	no; inductive reasoning is going from specific to general
d.	YES; this is the definition of deductive reasoning

17. Dwayne just got a promotion to a new department, but he has been told that his new supervisor is a cranky, disagreeable, critical person. According to the confirmation bias, what will Dwayne **most likely** do on his first day in the new supervisor's department?
    a.   He will forget about the things he has been told about his new supervisor.
    b.   He will look for positive behaviors on part of his supervisor.
    c.   He will tell the new supervisor what he was told.
    d.   He will look for negative behaviors on part of the supervisor.

a.	no; the confirmation bias would not predict this
b.	no; on the contrary, the bias would say he would seek out negative behaviors
c.	no; this is not the confirmation bias
d.	RIGHT; the bias predicts that people seek out information that fits their ideas

18. "I knew it all along" is an example of
   a. the availability heuristic
   b. the simulation heuristic
   c. the representativeness heuristic
   d. hindsight bias

a.	no; this heuristic focuses on recalling the frequency of past occurrences
b.	no
c.	no; this bias says that we use prototypes to make decisions
d.	YES; the hindsight bias says that people falsely report an event after it has occurred

19. The heuristic that involves judging the probability of an event by how well it matches a prototype is the
   a. availability heuristic
   b. similarity heuristic
   c. representativeness heuristic
   e. subgoaling strategy

a.	no; this heuristic focuses on recalling the frequency of past occurrences
b.	no
c.	GOOD; this defines the representativeness heuristic
d.	no; this is a problem solving strategy

20. A system of symbols that can be spoken, written, or signed is considered a
   a. transfer set.
   b. language.
   c. method.
   d. signal.

a.	no
b.	THAT'S RIGHT; this is how language is defined
c.	no
d.	no

21. All human languages have the capacity to create an endless number of meaningful sentences using a finite set of words and rules. This is called _____.
   a. linguistic relativity hypothesis
   b. heuristics
   c. semantics
   d. infinite generativity

a.	no; this hypothesis describes the relationship between language and thought
b.	no; heuristics are rules of thumb that do not guarantee solutions to problems
c.	no; semantics refer to the meaning of words and sentences
d.	RIGHT; using finite sets of words and rules, we can create infinite sentences

22. How many phonemes are found in the word "tree"?
    a. 1
    b. 2
    c. 3
    d. 4

a.	no	
b.	no	
c.	CORRECT; there are three sounds in "tree," t - r - e	
d.	no	

23. Language is made up of basic sounds called
    a. morphemes
    b. syntax
    c. semantics
    d. phonemes

a.	no; all words are made up of one or more morphemes	
b.	no; syntax refers to how words are combined to form phrases and sentences	
c.	no; semantics refers to the meaning of words and sentences	
d.	YES; a phoneme is a basic sound	

24. The meaning of words and sentences is called
    a. morphology
    b. semantics
    c. syntax
    d. infinitive generativity

a.	no; morphology refers to word formation	
b.	RIGHT; semantics refers to the meaning of words and sentences	
c.	no; syntax refers to how words are combined to form phrases and sentences	
d.	no; using finite sets of words and rules, we can create infinite sentences	

25. Skinner is to _____ as Chomsky is to _____.
    a. imitation; reinforcement
    b. reinforcement; biology
    c. biology; reinforcement
    d. reinforcement; imitation

a.	no; it was Bandura who emphasized imitation	
b.	CORRECT; Skinner emphasized reinforcement in language acquisition, Chomsky emphasized prewired biological predispositions	
c.	no; close, but it is actually the other way	
d.	no; Chomsky focused on biological predispositions	

26. How do children convey meaning in their telegraphic speech?
    a. with the words only
    b. with rapid expression
    c. with eye contact and volume
    d. with gestures, tone, and context

a.	no; the child's conveys meaning in other ways beside the words	
b.	no	
c.	no; maybe, but this is not entire story	
d.	THAT'S RIGHT; children convey meaning in other ways besides actually words	

27. A _____ period is when there is learning readiness for language acquisition.
   a.   critical
   b.   sensitive
   c.   primary
   d.   secondary

a.	THAT'S CORRECT; critical period is when there is learning readiness
b.	no
c.	no
d.	no

28. A 15-month-old child pounds the tray of her high chair with a cup and firmly says, "My milk." As a student of psychology, you recognize this use of language as
   a.   generative speech.
   b.   telegraphic speech.
   c.   babbling
   d.   the heuristic property of language.

a.	no
b.	YES; short sentences are characteristic of telegraphic speech
c.	no; babbling is repeating sounds and syllables
d.	no

29. According to advocates of bilingual education,
   a.   teaching immigrants in their native language leave them behind in the workplace.
   b.   teaching immigrants using their native language increases their self-esteem.
   c.   the whole language approach is flawed.
   d.   the whole language approach is the best strategy to teach immigrants English.

a.	no; in fact, this is a criticism of bilingual education
b.	CORRECT; also, they claim that bilingual education values others' culture
c.	no; the whole language approach is an approach to teaching children to read
d.	no; the whole language approach is an approach to teaching children to read

30. Which statement **best** describes reading experts' consensus on the most effective method of reading instruction?
   a.   The whole language approach works best for most children.
   b.   Reading instruction should focus exclusively on the basic-skills-and-phonetics approach.
   c.   The best approach is to combine the whole language and the basic-skills-and-phonetics approach.
   d.   The basic-skills-and-phonetics approach works better with younger readers.

a.	no; this does not best describe the experts' consensus
b.	no; this does not best describe the experts' consensus
c.	YES; a combination of the two approaches is best
d.	no; this does not best describe the experts' consensus

31. Which of the following is true regarding chimpanzees' ability to use language?
   a.   Evidence suggests that chimps can understand symbols.
   b.   Researchers agree that chimps can learn syntax.
   c.   Researchers agree that chimps can use language to create fairly complex sentences.
   d.   all of the above

a.	no; but the answer is partially correct
b.	no; but the answer is partially correct
c.	no; but the answer is partially correct
d.	RIGHT; all have been found

32. According to the linguistic relativity hypothesis,
   a. language determines our thoughts.
   b. thinking determines our language.
   c. language influences but does not determine thought.
   d. language can create an endless number of sentences

a.	YES; this is correct
b.	no; actually this is the opposite of what they hypothesis argues
c.	no; but this is what the research on the linguistic relativity hypothesis has found
d.	no; this sounds more like infinitive generativity

Chapter 9 - Intelligence

The Big Picture: Chapter Overview

Most experts would say that intelligence is an abstract concept that can only be measured indirectly, and includes verbal ability, problem-solving skills, and an ability to adapt to and learn from everyday experiences. Sir Francis Galton made the first attempt at wide-scale intelligence testing. Galton, the father of mental tests, used simple sensory, perceptual, and motor responses to measure intelligence. The term "mental test" was developed by James Cattell; he used the same approach as Galton in measuring intelligence.

An intelligence test must be reliable, valid, and standardized. Reliability refers to the consistency of scores on a test. Three measures of reliability are test-retest, alternate forms, and split-half reliability. Validity is the extent to which a test measures what it is intended to measure and includes content validity and criterion validity. Two types of criterion validity are concurrent validity and predictive validity. Standardization refers to tests that are developed with uniform procedures for administration and scoring. Norms are established standards of performance on the test and are created by giving the test to a large group of individuals who are representative of the population.

Alfred Binet developed the first intelligence test and the concept of mental age. In 1905 William Stern devised the term IQ, which is defined as a child's mental age divided by chronological age and multiplied by 100. The scores on the Binet test approximate a normal distribution with the majority of scores falling in the middle of the possible range of scores. Binet believed that the core of intelligence consists of memory, imagery, judgment, and other complex memory processes. Two widely used intelligence tests are the Stanford-Binet test and the Wechsler scales. The Wechsler scales allow an examiner to obtain separate verbal and nonverbal scores. There are also intelligence tests that can be administered to groups of individuals such as the CTCS and the SAT, which has been criticized for including items that favor males. Psychologists distinguish between aptitude tests such as the CTBS, which are designed to predict an individual's ability to learn a skill, and achievement tests such as the CAT, which are designed to measure what has been learned

Psychologists have long debated whether intelligence is composed of one general ability or a number of specific abilities. Spearman's two-factor theory and Thurstone's multiple-factor theory argued that a number of factors are involved. Spearman also thought that intelligence was a general ability. A recent classification of intelligence, proposed by Gardner, includes seven components. Sternberg's triarchic theory emphasizes three essential components: componential intelligence, experiential intelligence, and contextual intelligence. Both Gardner's and Sternberg's ideas have implications for how we define intelligence and educate students.

Arthur Jensen has sparked debate with his thesis that intelligence is primarily inherited and therefore the differences in average intelligence between groups, races, nationalities, and social classes were due to genetics. Douglas Wahlsten has argued that it is impossible to demonstrate that human intelligence is primarily inherited. Many have questioned the ability of intelligence tests to accurately measure a person's intelligence and that they are culturally biased. Today's experts view intelligence as being determined by both genetics and the environment. Intelligence can be modified by providing an intellectually stimulating environment, such as is the case in Head Start. In response, psychologists have attempted to develop culture-fair tests since many early intelligence tests were culturally biased. Using intelligence tests as the sole indicator of intelligence is an example of their misuse and may lead to stereotypes and expectations. The tests should be used in conjunction with other information about an individual and can still be valuable tools.

Mental retardation is a condition of limited mental ability (usually an IQ of below 70) and difficulty in adaptive behavior. There are several classifications of mental retardation: mild, moderate, severe, and profound. The two main causes of mental retardation are organic, which involves genetic disorder or brain damage, and cultural-familial, involving no evidence of organic brain damage. A gifted individual has a well-above-average IQ and/or a superior talent in a certain area. There are three criteria described gifted children: precocity, learning in qualitatively different ways than ordinary children, and a passion to master. Creativity is the ability to think about something in a novel and unusual way and to come up with unique solutions to problems. Convergent thinking refers to producing one correct answer; divergent thinking produces many answers to the same question and is more characteristics of creativity. Creative thinkers share several characteristics such as flexibility, inner motivation, risk taking, and objectively evaluating their creative work. Individual can become more creative by first developing curiosity and interest.

Learning Objectives

When you have studied the material in this chapter, you should be able to:

1. define intelligence. (p. 286)
2. discuss the contributions of Galton, Cattell, and Stern to early conceptions of intelligence. (pp. 286-288)
3. list the three criteria required of any instrument for measuring intelligence. (p. 288)
4. explain the concept of reliability and identify three methods of measuring reliability. (pp. 288-289)
5. explain the concept of validity and identify two methods of measuring validity. (p. 289)
6. explain the importance of standardization and norms in the measurement process. (p. 290)
7. describe how mental age is used to generate an intelligence quotient. (p. 291)
8. discuss the importance of both verbal and non-verbal components in intelligence testing. (p. 292)
9. identify the strengths and weaknesses of individual and group intelligence tests. (pp. 292-295)
10. summarize Spearman's and Thurstone's early views of multiple intelligences. (p. 295)
11. list the seven components of Gardner's multiple intelligences. (pp. 295-296)
12. identify and discuss the three components of intelligence in Sternberg's triarchic theory. (pp. 298-299)
13. summarize the ideas of Jensen, Herrnstein, and Murray, and Wahlsten in the heredity-environment controversy. (pp. 299-303)
14. analyze arguments that refute heredity and support environment as a critical factor in intelligence. (p. 303)
15. explain how intelligence tests have been biased towards white, middle-class, urban people. (p. 304)
16. describe the Raven Progressive Matrices Test and the SOMPA and discuss why these tests are considerably more culture-fair. (pp. 305-306)
17. explain the appropriate use of intelligence tests and their potential for misuse. (pp. 306-307)
18. define mental retardation and differentiate between organic and cultural-familial retardation. (p. 308)
19. define giftedness and identify the characteristics associated with gifted people. (p. 309)
20. contrast convergent and divergent thinking and relate these thinking styles to creativity. (p. 310)
21. list the steps in the creative process. (p. 311)
22. From *Explorations in Psychology: Project Spectrum*, relate the material on multiple intelligences to Gardner's Project Spectrum. (p. 297)
23. From *Explorations in Psychology: The Repository for Germinal Choice*, analyze arguments that support and arguments that disfavor breeding for intelligence. (p. 302)

Guided Review

The Nature of Intelligence and Its Early History

The only way we can study a person's intelligence is _____.
There is general agreement that intelligence consists of _____
_____, problem-solving skills, and the ability to _____ to and
_____ from life's everyday experiences. The consistent and stable
ways we are different from each other are _____ _____. The
early German psychologists, such as Wundt, ignored "higher mental
processes" and focused on _____ and perception. In 1884 in
London, the first attempt at wide-scale intelligence testing was made
by Sir Frances _____. The term "mental test" was developed by
James _____.

indirectly - p. 286
verbal ability - p. 286
adapt - p. 286
learn – p. 286
individual differences - p. 286

sensation - p. 286

Galton - p. 286-287
Cattell - p. 287

Intelligence Tests

_____ is how consistently an individual performs on a
test. When reliability is measured by giving an individual the same test
on two different occasions, this is called _____-_____
reliability. A second form involves giving _____ forms of the
same test on two different occasions. Another form of reliability, in
which test items are divided into halves and compared for
consistency, is called _____-_____ reliability. When split-half
reliability is high, the test is said to be _____ _____. The
extent to which a test measures what it is intended to measure is
called _____. A form of validity that gives a broad picture of
what is supposed to be measured is called _____ validity. A type
of validity that predicts other measures or criteria of the attribute is
called _____ validity. The relation of a test's scores to a criterion
that is presently available is called _____ validity. The type of
validity that assesses the relation of a test's scores to an individual's
performance at a point in the future is called _____ validity. Tests
developed with uniform procedures for giving and scoring them are
_____. The test constructor also develop established standards
of performance, called _____.

Reliability - p. 288

test-retest - p. 288
alternative - p. 288

split-half - p. 288
internally consistent - p. 289

validity - p. 289
content - p. 289

criterion - p. 289
concurrent - p. 289

predictive - p. 289

standardized - p. 290
norms - p. 290

In France in 1904, the French Ministry of Education
commissioned Alfred Binet to work with the school system. His
work led to the development of the concept of _____ age. In
1912, William Stern devised the term _____ _____. It
consists of a child's _____ age divided by a child's _____ age
and multiplied by 100. It has been found that intelligence as measured
by the Binet test approximates a _____ distribution, which means
that the scores in the distribution are symmetrical, with a majority of
cases falling in the middle ranges. The current Stanford-Binet test can
be given to individuals from the age of 2 through _____. In
addition to the Stanford-Binet, another widely used series of
individual intelligence tests are the _____ scales. These tests
allow an examiner to obtain separate _____ and nonverbal scores.

mental - p. 291
intelligence quotient - p. 291
mental/chronological - p. 291

normal - p. 291

adulthood - p. 291

Wechsler - p. 292
verbal - p. 292

Group intelligence tests are more _____ and
_____ than individual intelligence tests, but they offer a
disadvantage: an examiner cannot establish _____ with, or
determine anxiety levels of, the subjects being tested. Two group

convenient - p.293
economical - p.293
rapport - p. 294

119

tests that many students take are the _____ _____ _____

_____ _____ and the _____ _____ _____ .

In recent years, a controversy has developed over whether _____ _____ can raise SAT scores. Another controversy is the discovery that some items on the SAT favor _____ . Psychologists distinguish between tests designed to predict an individual's ability to learn a skill, called _____ tests, and those designed to measure what has already been learned, called _____ tests.

Do We Have a Single Intelligence or Multiple Intelligences?

Some theorists have characterized intelligence as composed of one general ability, whereas others have focused on a number of _____ abilities. Charles Spearman's two-factor theory argued that we have a general ability, which he called _____ , and a number of specific intelligences, which he called _____ . Thurstone's theory, called the _____-_____ theory of intelligence, proposed the existence of seven _____ mental abilities. A more recent attempt to classify intelligence, proposed by Gardner, also suggests that intelligence is comprised of _____ components. Gardner's theory of multiple intelligences has been applied to _____ .

According to Sternberg's triarchic theory, intelligence consists of three factors. The first, composed of analytical thinking and abstract reasoning, is called _____ intelligence. The second type, _____ intelligence, consists of insightful and creative thinking. Sternberg calls the third type, which is "street smarts" or practical knowledge, _____ intelligence. Students with high _____ ability tend to be favored in conventional classes.

Issues and Controversies in Intelligence

Arthur Jensen has sparked debate with his thesis that intelligence is primarily _____ . Jensen believes that heredity accounts for about _____ percent of intelligence. Other experts in the field of intelligence suggest that genetics do not determine intelligence to the extent Jensen thought. Douglas Wahlsten argues that it is _____ to isolate the effects of heredity on human intelligence. Researchers increasingly manipulate the early environment of children's lives when they are at risk for _____ intelligence. The emphasis is on _____ rather than remediation.

Many of the early intelligence tests were culturally _____ . In response to these problems, psychologists have developed _____ _____ tests. Two types of culture-fair tests have been devised. One type includes items that are _____ to individuals from all socioeconomic and ethnic backgrounds; the other type has all the _____ items removed. A single IQ score may lead to _____ and _____ about an individual. The use of intelligence tests as the sole indicator of intelligence is an example of the _____ of intelligence tests.

The Extremes of Intelligence and Creativity

Limited mental ability, an IQ score below 70, and difficulty in adapting to everyday life are characteristic of _____ _____. Most individuals with mental retardation fall into the _____ category. The causes of mental retardation include those associated with genetic disorders or brain damage, called _____ retardation, and those with no evidence of organic retardation, referred to as _____-_____ retardation. Having above-average IQ and/or a superior talent in one area is referred to as _____. Despite a commonly held belief, there is no relationship between giftedness and _____ _____.

With regard to creativity, most researchers believe that it is not the same thing as _____. One distinction is between the type of thinking that produces one correct answer, called _____ thinking, and the type that produces many answers and is associated with creativity, called _____ thinking. Creativity is defined as the ability to think in a _____ and unusual way and to come up with _____ solutions to problems. The steps in the creative process include _____, incubation, insight, evaluation, and _____. A group that is encouraged to come up with as many ideas as possible is engaging in _____.

mental retardation - p. 308
mild - p. 308

organic - p. 308

cultural-familiar - p. 308
giftedness - p. 309

mental disorder - p. 309

intelligence - p. 310
convergent - p. 310

divergent - p. 310
novel - p. 310
unique - p. 310
preparation/elaboration - p. 311

brainstorming - p. 312

Explorations in Psychology

To respond to the questions and exercises presented in this section, please write your thoughts, perspectives, and reactions on a separate piece of paper.

Explorations in Psychology and Life: Project Spectrum

- Do you think most school districts would embrace the concept of Project Spectrum? Defend your answer.
- As you look back to your education, what type of intelligence, from Gardner's seven, was valued and what type was minimized?
- If you were a student in a Spectrum class, what would you discover to be your strengths and weakness as they are related to Gardner's theory of intelligence?

Explorations in Psychology and Life: The Repository for Germinal Choice

- Do you have any moral objections to the purpose of the Repository for Germinal Choice? If so, what are they? If not, why not?
- If you were a parent of a young woman wanting to become a mother and considering the use of a contribution from the Repository for Germinal Choice, what would be your reaction?
- How do you react to the statement that the Repository for Germinal Choice encourages breeding for intelligence? Should we be breeding for other characteristics such as height, personality, or other physical characteristics?

In Your Own Words

To respond to the questions and exercises presented in this section, please write your thoughts, perspectives, and reactions on a separate piece of paper.

✓ Develop a metaphor to explain reliability and validity.

✓ Have you ever taken a standardized intelligence, aptitude, or achievement test? What was it? How do you know it was standardized? Did you receive a report of your scores compared to others?

✓ What does Douglas Wahlsten mean when he says that the heritability of human intelligence is impossible to estimate?

✓ Look at Gardner's seven frames of mind. Give an example of each that illustrates intelligence.

✓ Give an example of creativity that you have observed in the last 2 hours. Does the example fit the definition of creativity offered in the textbook?

✓ Are you intelligent? How does your answer reflect your definition of intelligence? To what degree is your definition similar to the definition presented in the textbook?.

✓ Imagine you are a developmental psychologist. You are an expert in how enriched environments help children to increase their intelligence and creativity. Recently you have been called to Ottawa, to give testimony to a Parliamentary Committee on what parents can do to help their young children improve intelligence and creativity. What do you say? What can parents do?

✓ Describe a time in your life when you were creative. What were you doing? Did you develop some novel solution to a problem? Did you create some work? How do you know that you were creative?

Correcting the Incorrect

Carefully read each statement. Determine if the statement is correct or incorrect. If the statement is incorrect, make the necessary changes to correct it. Then look directly under the statement for the correct statement and page reference in the textbook.

1.   A person's intelligence can be directly measured.
   ❑ *A person's intelligence can only be indirectly measured. (p. 286)*
2.   Intelligence is defined by doing well on IQ tests.
   ❑ *Intelligence is defined verbal ability, problem-solving skills, and the ability to adapt and learn. (p. 286).*
3.   In the late 1800s, David Wechsler used simple sensory, perceptual, and motor responses to measure intelligence.
   ❑ *In the late 1800s, Francis Galton used simple sensory, perceptual, and motor responses to measure intelligence. (p. 286-287)*
4.   Reliability refers to the extent that a test yields a consistent, reproducible, measure of performance.
   ❑ *Reliability refers to the extent that a test yields a consistent, reproducible, measure of performance. (p. 288)*
5.   Giving alternate forms of the same test on two different occasions measures split-half reliability.
   ❑ *Giving alternate forms of the same test on two different occasions measures alternative forms reliability. (p. 288)*
6.   Criterion validity is a form of concurrent validity.
   ❑ *Concurrent validity is a form of criterion validity. (p. 289)*
7.   If the CTBS can predict a person's academic achievement in university, it then has good content validity.
   ❑ *If the CTBS can predict a person's academic achievement in university, it then has good predictive validity. (p. 289)*
8.   The standards of performance of a test are known as norms.
   ❑ *The standards of performance of a test are known as norms. (p. 290)*
9.   If you take a test that involves uniform procedures for administration and scoring, then it has been normed.
   ❑ *If you take a test that involves uniform procedures for administration and scoring, then it has been standardized. (p. 290)*
10. Binet developed the concept of mental age (MA).

     ❑ *Binet developed the concept of mental age (MA). (p. 291)*

11.   Average mental age scores correspond to chronological age (CA).
     ❑ *Average mental age scores correspond to chronological age (CA). (p. 291)*

12.   In a normal distribution, there are a few scores in the middle and many toward the extremes.
     ❑ *In a normal distribution, there are a few scores toward the extremes and many in the middle. (p. 291).*

13.   IQ scores around 100 are considered average.
     ❑ *IQ scores around 100 are considered average. (p. 291)*

14.   Intelligence measured by the Binet test approximates a normal distribution.
     ❑ *Intelligence measured by the Binet test approximates a normal distribution. (p. 291)*

15.   The Wechsler scales yields three scores: verbal, nonverbal, and critical thinking.
     ❑ *The Wechsler scales yields two scores: verbal and nonverbal. (p. 292)*

16.   Achievement tests can predict if a person can learn a skill.
     ❑ *Aptitude tests can predict if a person can learn a skill. (p. 294)*

17.   Spearman believed that intelligence is made up of two factors.
     ❑ *Spearman believed that intelligence is made up of two factors. (p. 295)*

18.   Howard Gardner developed a theory of intelligence that describes seven components.
     ❑ *Howard Gardner developed a theory of intelligence that describes seven components. (p. 295)*

19.   One component of Sternberg's triarchic theory of intelligence is musical skill.
     ❑ *One component of Gardner's seven frames of mind is musical skill. (p. 296)*

20.   According to Sternberg, "smart" students usually are those who have high creativity.
     ❑ *According to Sternberg, "smart" students usually are those who have high analytic ability. (p. 298).*

21.   Jensen argued that environment accounts for about 80% of intelligence.
     ❑ *Jensen argued that genetics accounts for about 80% of intelligence. (p. 301)*

22.   Intelligence is mainly determined by genetic influences.
     ❑ *Intelligence is determined by both genetic and environmental influences. (p. 301-302)*

23.   The distribution of scores on standardized intelligence tests for African Americans and white Americans do not overlap.
     ❑ *The distribution of scores on standardized intelligence tests for African Americans and white Americans do overlap. (p. 304)*

24.   All cultures define intelligence the same way.
     ❑ *All cultures do not define intelligence the same way. (p. 304)*

25.   A type of culture-fair test involves removing all verbal questions.
     ❑ *A type of culture-fair test involves removing all verbal questions. (p. 305)*

26.   Scores on intelligence tests alone are valid enough to place a child in a special education class.
     ❑ *Scores on intelligence tests alone are not valid enough to place a child in a special education class. (p. 306)*

27.   The sole determinant of mental retardation is below average intelligence.
     ❑ *The determinants of mental retardation is below average intelligence, difficulty in adapting to everyday life and under 18 years of age. (p. 308)*

28.   Most individuals with mental retardation can be classified as having moderate mental retardation.
     ❑ *Most individuals with mental retardation can be classified as having mild mental retardation. (p. 308)*

29.   Down syndrome is a form of cultural-familial retardation.
     ❑ *Down syndrome is a form of organic retardation. (p. 308)*

30.   A person who is gifted has an IQ of 100 or higher.
     ❑ *A person who is gifted has an IQ of 120 or higher. (p. 309)*

31.   Convergent thinking is an important type of thinking in creativity.
     ❑ *Divergent thinking is an important type of thinking in creativity. (p. 310)*

32.   Creativity is the ability to think about something in novel and unusual ways.
     ❑ *Creativity is the ability to think about something in novel and unusual ways. (p. 310)*

Practice Test

1. Which of the following represents the **least comprehensive** definition of intelligence?
   a. being original
   b. having problem solving skills and the ability to adapt to and learn from everyday experiences
   c. becoming immersed in one's domain
   d. having verbal ability

a.	no; this includes multiple intelligences
b.	no; this is rather comprehensive definition
c.	no; this includes several intelligences
d.	YES; this is the least comprehensive definition of intelligence

2. Which of the following is a component of the definition of "intelligence"?
   a. verbal ability
   b. problem-solving skills
   c. adapting to everyday experiences
   d. all of the above

a.	no; but partially correct
b.	no; but partially correct
c.	no; but partially correct
d.	CORRECT

3. Both Galton and Cattell were pioneers in the study of intelligence. What was their **primary** contribution to the field?
   a. They developed the first standardized intelligence test.
   b. They established a standard definition of intelligence.
   c. They started the tradition of studying individual differences in intelligence.
   d. They operationalized intelligence in terms of sensory and motor processes.

a.	no; they used different measures that we not standardized
b.	no; this was not their primary contribution
c.	YES; both believed that individual differences had to be measured
d.	no; but they both believed these processes were at the heart of intelligence

4. Which of the following theories of intelligence emphasizes the importance of "g"?
   a. Spearman's two-factor theory
   b. Thurstone's multiple-factor theory
   c. Sternberg's triarchic theory
   d. Wechsler's applied theory

a.	YES; Spearman's two-factor theory included g (general intelligence) and s (specific intelligences)
b.	no; Thurstone's theory included seven primary mental abilities
c.	no; Sternberg's theory includes componential, experiential, and contextual
d.	no

5. Intelligence consists of seven factors according to the theory proposed by
   a. Thurstone
   b. Galton
   c. Spearman
   d. Sternberg

a.	CORRECT; Thurstone proposed seven primary mental factors	
b.	no	
c.	no; Spearman proposed a general intelligence (g) and specific intelligences (s)	
d.	no; Sternberg proposed a triarchic theory of intelligence	

6. If a person was given an intelligence test, and later given the same test again, the scores on the two test administrations should be close to identical if the test is
   a. reliable.
   b. standardized.
   c. normalized.
   d. valid.

a.	GOOD; reliability refers to the extent to which scores are consistent
b.	no; standardization refers to developing uniform procedures for giving and scoring
c.	no; norms are established standards of performance for a test
d.	no; validity refers to extent to which test measures what it is suppose to measure

7. The consistency of test scores is measured by
   a. content validity.
   b. criterion validity.
   c. reliability.
   d. standardization.

a.	no; this refers to test's ability to test a broad range of the content of what measures
b.	no; this refers to relationship of score on this test or other test scores
c.	CORRECT; reliability refers to the extent to which scores are consistent
d.	no; standardization refers to developing uniform procedures for giving and scoring

8. The internal consistency of a test can be measured by
   a. test-retest reliability.
   b. split-half reliability.
   c. alternate forms.
   d. content validity.

a.	this is a reliability examining consistency in scores from two test versions
b.	RIGHT; this divides the test into two parts; scores on each part are compared
c.	no; this a form of reliability that uses two alternate versions of the same test
d.	no; this refers to test's ability to test a broad range of the content of what measures

9. When a test measures what it is intended to measure, it is called
   a. validity.
   b. reliability.
   c. standardization.
   d. test-retest reliability

a.	GOOD; reliability refers to the extent to which scores are consistent
b.	no reliability refers to the extent to which scores are consistent
c.	no; standardization refers to developing uniform procedures for giving and scoring
d.	no; this is a reliability examining consistency in scores from two test versions

10. You have an A in advanced French. If a French achievement test has good concurrent validity, your score on this test should be
   a. high.
   b. average.
   c. low.
   d. unpredictable.

a.	THAT'S RIGHT; concurrent validity refers to validity between score and something available now like course grade
b.	no
c.	no
d.	no

11. An employer wished to develop a test to identify employees who will be successful at selling his company's products. The employer is seeking a test with good
   a. criterion validity.
   b. content validity.
   c. concurrent validity.
   d. predictive validity.

a.	no; but close, this refers to relationship of score on this test or other test scores
b.	no; this refers to test's ability to test a broad range of the content of what measures
c.	no; concurrent validity refers to validity between score and something available now
d.	YEA; an employer wants to be able to predict who will be successful

12. You want to establish norms for a newly developed test. What would be your **most appropriate** strategy?
   a. give the test many times to a small group
   b. make sure the test measures what it is supposed to measure
   c. administer the test to a large representative group
   d. write up a series of standardized instructions

a.	no; the small group would not be representative of the entire population
b.	no; validity is important, but is more a characteristics of a test that a way to norm it
c.	YES, THAT'S RIGHT; this is done to determine what are the "normal" responses
d.	no; standardization is important, but will not identify the norms

13. In terms of intelligence testing, chronological age (CA) means
   a. years in school.
   b. actual age of the child in years.
   c. number of years until school is finished.
   d. predicted mental age of the child.

a.	no
b.	RIGHT
c.	no
d.	no

14. According to the IQ test score calculation developed by Stern, a child with a mental age of 8 and a chronological age of 10 would have an IQ of
   a. 80.
   b. 125.
   c. 100.
   d. 95.

a.	THAT'S GOOD; MA/CA x 100; 8/10 x 100 = 80
b.	no; MA/CA x 100
c.	no; MA/CA x 100
d.	no; MA/CA x 100

15. If IQ scores form a normal distribution, it means that
   a. the scores are symmetrical.
   b. most scores fall at the extremes.
   c. most scores fall in the middle range.
   d. all scores are below average.

a.	no
b.	no; there are few scores at the extremes
c.	RIGHT; a normal distribution is shaped like a bell with few scores on the ends
d.	no; that would not be a normal distribution

16. Which child would probably perform better on the Wechsler scales than the Stanford-Binet?
   a. ten-year-old Jose who has only spoken English for the past two years
   b. ten-year-old Austin who always has high grades in language arts
   c. twelve-year-old Elizabeth who likes to read and write
   d. fifteen-year-old Tasha who scored very high on the PSAT

a.	RIGHT; the Stanford-Binet reports just one IQ score; the Wechsler scale report both verbal and nonverbal IQ scores
b.	no; Austin would do equally well on both tests
c.	no; Elizabeth would do equally well on both tests
d.	no; Tasha would do equally well on both tests

17. Which of the following statements about group intelligence tests is **incorrect**?
   a. Group intelligence tests do not allow the examiner to establish rapport with the examinees.
   b. When testing many individuals, group intelligence tests are more convenient and economical.
   c. The Army Alpha Test was the first group intelligence test.
   d. Schools may use group intelligence tests to make special education placement decisions.

a.	no; this is correct
b.	no; this is also correct
c.	no; this is correct
d.	YEP; group intelligence testing does not allow decisions to be made about individuals

18. Which of the following issues has been raised regarding the SAT?
   a. whether there is a correlation between SAT scores and scores on other achievement tests
   b. whether certain items are gender-biased
   c. security issues regarding the test
   d. the effects of computerizing the SAT

a.	no
b.	PERFECT; the issues is whether there are some questions that favor one gender or the other
c.	no
d.	no

19. Which of the following statements is **true** about Gardner's concept of multiple intelligences?
   a.   Gardner's seven intelligences are merely revisions of Thurstone's 7 primary mental abilities.
   b.   Most experts reject Gardner's concept of multiple intelligences.
   c.   The problem with Gardner's multiple intelligences is that they are difficult to apply.
   d.   Gardner views each of his seven intelligences as involving unique cognitive skills.

a.	no; Gardner's seven frames of mind are very different from Thurstone's 7
b.	no; more research needs to be completed
c.	no; Gardner's multiple intelligences are being applied in education
d.	CORRECT

20. Both the ability to analyze the world spatially and musical intelligence are important components in the theory of intelligence proposed by
   a.   Thurstone.
   b.   Galton.
   c.   Sternberg.
   d.   Gardner.

a.	no
b.	no
c.	no; Sternberg talks about componential, contextual, and experiential intelligence
d.	YES; these are among Gardner's seven frames of mind

21. According to Sternberg, a person who is street smart and gets along well with other people **most likely** has high
   a.   experiential intelligence.
   b.   contextual intelligence.
   c.   componential intelligence.
   d.   visuo-spatial intelligence.

a.	no; this refers to solve familiar problems in more automatic ways
b.	RIGHT; this refers to getting along in school and in the world
c.	no; this is related to store and retrieve information and to solve problems
d.	no

22. Which element in Sternberg's theory of intelligence is commonly measured by intelligence tests?
   a.   componential
   b.   contextual or practical intelligence
   c.   experiential
   d.   all of the above

a.	YES; this is related to store and retrieve information and to solve problems
b.	no; this refers to getting along in school and in the world
c.	no; this refers to solve familiar problems in more automatic ways
d.	no

23. When compared to the correlation of intelligence scores for identical twins raised apart, the correlation of intelligence scores for identical twins raised together is usually
   a.   lower.
   b.   no different.
   c.   higher.
   d.   not comparable.

a.	no	
b.	no	
c.	THAT'S CORRECT; this suggests there is some genetic contribution to intelligence	
d.	no	

24. According to Jensen, which of the following factors is most important in the determination of intelligence?

   a. culture
   b. genetics
   c. family environment
   d. quality of education

a.	no; this is an environmental factor which Jensen downplayed
b.	RIGHT; Jensen stated that intelligence is primarily inherited
c.	no; this is an environmental factor which Jensen downplayed
d.	no; this is an environmental factor which Jensen downplayed

25. According to Jensen, the influence of heredity on intelligence is about _____ percent.

   a. 20
   b. 50
   c. 80
   d. 90

a.	no
b.	no
c.	THAT'S TRUE; Jensen based his research on comparisons of twins
d.	no

26. The finding that African American schoolchildren score, on average, 10 to 15 points lower on standardized intelligence tests than White American schoolchildren indicates

   a. poor standardization of intelligence tests.
   b. cultural bias of intelligence tests.
   c. poor reliability of intelligence tests.
   d. inconsistency of intelligence tests.

a.	no; intelligence tests are very well standardized
b.	THAT'S CORRECT; intelligence tests tend to favor certain backgrounds and classes
c.	no; intelligence tests have good reliability
d.	no; intelligence tests have good reliability or consistency

27. What do the Raven Progressive Matrices Test and the SOMPA have in common?

   a. Both are entirely nonverbal.
   b. Both represent efforts to develop culture-fair intelligence tests.
   c. Both are designed for children from low-income families.
   d. Both have strict time limits.

a.	no; there is a verbal component on the SOMPA
b.	CORRECT
c.	no; both tests can measure intelligence in children from different backgrounds
d.	no

28. Down syndrome is associated with
   a.   cultural-familiar retardation.
   b.   organic retardation.
   c.   giftedness in certain, specific areas.
   d.   all of the above.

a.	no; Down syndrome is not due to cultural or familiar factors
b.	YES; Down syndrome is a genetic condition
c.	no; people with Down syndrome are not gifted
d.	no

29. Mental retardation is **likely** to be diagnosed in which of the following individuals?
   a.   James: 14 years of age; IQ of 120; no apparent cognitive deficits.
   b.   Barbara: 16 years of age; IQ of 100; has a reading disability.
   c.   Andrew: 18 years of age; IQ of 80; has difficulty when several instructions are given at once.
   d.   Julia: 8 years old; IQ below 70; has difficulty adapting to changes in everyday situations.

a.	no; James' IQ is above average
b.	no; Barbara's IQ is average
c.	no; Andrew's IQ does not meet the cut off of an IQ of 70 or below
d.	RIGHT; Julia's case fits the definition of mental retardation

30. If your psychology teacher held up a piece of string, a candle, a match, and a spoon and asked you to find as many ways as possible to involve all of these objects in a cake recipe, she would be asking you to use
   a.   convergent thinking.
   b.   associative convergence.
   c.   divergent thinking.
   d.   construction intuition.

a.	no; convergent thinking refers to producing one correct answer
b.	no
c.	RIGHTO!; divergent thinking produces many answers and is related to creativity
d.	no

31. The kind of thinking associated with creativity is called
   a.   divergent thinking.
   b.   convergent thinking.
   c.   critical thinking.
   d.   none of the above.

a.	RIGHT AGAIN; divergent thinking produces many answers and is related to creativity
b.	no; convergent thinking refers to producing one correct answer
c.	no
d.	no

Chapter 10 - Human Development

The Big Picture: Chapter Overview

Development is defined as a pattern of movement or change that begins at conception and continues throughout the life cycle. Development involves biological processes (e.g., individual's physical nature), cognitive processes (e.g., thought, intelligence, language), and socioemotional processes (e.g., relationships with others, emotions, personality). Development can be organized into periods with approximate age ranges. There are a number of developmental issues. The nature-nurture issue involves the extent to which behavior is influenced by nature (heredity) and nurture (environment). The continuity view states that development involves gradual change, whereas the discontinuity view suggests there are distinct developmental stages. The early-later experience issue centers on whether children are malleable throughout development and that later experiences are just as important as early experience.

Conception occurs when a sperm cell unites with an ovum. The fertilized egg is called a zygote. The first 2 weeks after conception are referred to as the germinal period; the period from 3 to 8 weeks is the embryonic period. The fetal period begins 2 months after conception and lasts about the next 7 months. Teratogens are agents that cause birth defects. Thalidomide, the HIV virus, and alcohol are examples of teratogens. Smoking during pregnancy can increase the risk for fetal and neonatal death and may be associated with later language and cognitive skills in the child. A full-term infant is born 38 to 42 weeks following conception, while a preterm infant is born prior to 38 weeks after conception.

Infants come into the world with a number of reflexes, including the Moro reflex. As the child shows advances in motor skills, changes in its brain are occurring. In childhood, the growth rate slows down and motor development becomes more smooth and coordinated. Piaget's theory of cognitive development focuses on how children actively construct their cognitive world and the stages that they go through. Children use schemas; a schema is a concept or framework that organizes and interprets information. In the process of assimilation, the individual adjusts to new information by incorporating it into existing knowledge. In accommodation, the individual adjusts to new information. Piaget believed humans pass through four cognitive stages where each represents a different way of understanding the world: sensorimotor, preoperational, concrete operational, and formal operational. Erik Erikson proposed an influential theory of psychosocial development. In each of the stages in his theory, the individual is confronted with a crisis or challenge that must be resolved. The more successfully the individual resolves the crisis, the more competent they are likely to become.

Developmental psychologists have been interested in studying the process of attachment, which is the close emotional bond between the infant and its caregiver. Lorenz described attachment by using the process of imprinting. Some infants have more positive attachment experience than others. Ainsworth has described how attachment differs in the degree to which the caregiver is sensitive to the infant's signals. Children can also differ in temperament, which is an individual's behavioral style and characteristic way of responding. There are three basic types of temperament in children: easy child, difficult child, and slow-to-warm-up child. Parenting styles describe how parents interact with their children. According to Baumrind, there are four basic styles: authoritarian, authoritative, neglectful, and indulgent. Reciprocal socialization refers to the idea that children socialize parents just as parents socialize children. Mothers and fathers both have role in their children's development.

G. Stanley Hall described adolescence as a time of storm-and-stress, a turbulent time charged with conflict and mood swings. In actuality, adolescents do not make up a homogeneous group with the majority of adolescents successfully reaching adult maturity. A significant physical event that occurs in adolescence is puberty. The hormones testosterone and estradiol reach high concentrations during puberty in boys and girls, respectively. According to Piaget, children between the ages of 11 and 15 develop the ability to think abstractly and logically and engage in hypothetical-deductive reasoning. Piaget called this stage formal operational thought. Adolescent egocentrism describes the belief of an adolescent that others are as preoccupied with the adolescent as she is herself, that one is unique, and that one is indestructible. Another component of cognitive development is moral development. Kohlberg's theory suggests that moral development involves internalization, a change from behavior that is externally controlled to behavior that is controlled by internal, self-generated standards and principles. He also believed that moral development progresses through three levels: preconventional, conventional, and postconventional. Gilligan has suggested that Kohlberg's theory under-represents the care perspective in moral development and overrepresents the justice perspective. In adolescence, the individuals are developing their sense of identity according to Erikson's stage of identity versus identity confusion. The search for identity can lead to adolescents wanting to gain independence from their parents, but at the same time fearing making the wrong decisions. Some adolescents are at risk of not becoming productive adults. Successful programs for at-risk youths include providing individual attention and broad community-wide interventions.

The peak of our physical skills and health comes in early adulthood, although research suggests that the more active an individual is in late adulthood, the happier and healthier he or she is. Our culture values a youthful appearance; middle adulthood may be difficult to handle. The majority of women do not experience psychological or physical problems from menopause. Life-span refers to the upper boundary of a specie's life, which is believed to be 120 years for humans. Life expectancy is the number of years that will probably be lived by the average person born in a particular year; since 1900 life expectancy has increased 30 years. In explaining aging, the cellular clock theory suggests that cells can only divide a maximum number of about 100 times. The free-radical theory states that people age because of free radicals inside their body damaging DNA and other cellular structures. Alzheimer's disease is characterized by progressive, irreversible brain disorders that involve gradual deterioration of memory, reasoning, language, and physical functioning.

Cognitive skills are strong in early adulthood. Memory may decline in middle adulthood, but strategies such as imagery and organization can reduce the decline. Although older adults show decline in the speed of processing information, when general knowledge and wisdom are considered, older adults often outperform younger adults. Social development is concerned with such issues as careers, work, and lifestyle choices. During midlife, many individuals reach the highest satisfaction in their careers. Lifestyle and marriage is influenced by many individuals' desire for personal fulfillment. While the theories of Erikson and Levinson propose that adult development passes through a series of stages, other theories emphasize life events, cohort effects, and social clocks. Late adulthood can be lived passively or actively. The activity theory states that the more active and involved older people are, the more satisfied they are and the more likely they will stay healthy. Kübler-Ross has suggested that we go through five stages in facing death: denial and isolation, anger, bargaining, depression, and acceptance.

Learning Objectives

When you have studied the material in this chapter, you should be able to:

1. define development and processes involved in development. (pp. 320-321)
2. list the eight developmental periods. (pp. 321)
3. defend arguments on both sides of the nature-nurture controversy. (p. 323)
4. distinguish between continuity and discontinuity as related to development. (pp. 323-324)
5. distinguish between early and later experience views of development. (p. 324)
6. describe the process of prenatal development, including conception, the germinal period, the embryonic period, and the fetal period. (pp. 324-326)
7. discuss the impact of teratogens on development. (p. 326)
8. describe the course of physical developmental in from birth through infancy and childhood. (pp. 326-331)
9. list and describe each of Piaget's cognitive stages. (pp. 331-335)
10. differentiate between assimilation and accommodation. (p. 331)
11. explain the relevance of object permanence, egocentrism, and conservation to cognition. (pp. 332-334)
12. analyze arguments supporting and refuting Piaget's cognitive stages. (pp. 335-336)
13. list and describe Erickson's eight psychosocial stages and the tasks associated with each stage. (pp. 336-338)

14. define attachment and explain the relationship between early attachment patterns and adult relationships. (pp. 339-340)
15. define temperament. (p. 341)
16. identify and describe Baumrind's parenting styles. (pp. 341-342)
17. define reciprocal socialization and give an example of this process. (p. 342)
18. summarize Hall's "storm-and-stress" theory of adolescence and research refuting his hypothesis. (pp. 345-346)
19. discuss cognitive development in adolescence, including the concepts of formal operations, idealism, hypothetical-deductive reasoning, and adolescent egocentrism. (pp. 346-347)
20. distinguish between Kolhberg's and Gilligan's theories of moral development. (pp. 347-349)
21. outline the physical, cognitive, and social developments of adolescence and adulthood. (pp. 350-358)
22. distinguish between Erickson's and Levinson's theories of adult personality development. (p. 358)
23. explain two theories of aging: the Hayflick cellular clock theory and the free-radical theory. (pp. 353-354)
24. identify the physical, cognitive, and socioemotional challenges of late adulthood. (pp. 355-360)
25. describe the challenges that accompany death and dying. (pp. 361-362)
26. from *Explorations in Psychology and Life: Child Care in North America*, identify the issues involved in the availability of child care for working parents and the relationship between attachment in high- versus low-quality child care settings. (p. 343)

Guided Review

What is Development?

Psychologists use the term development to mean a pattern of movement or change that begins at _____ and continues through the _____ _____ . Development is the product of several processes: biological, cognitive, and _____ . _____ processes involve changes in an individual's physical nature. Changes in an individual's thought, intelligence, and language involve _____ processes. _____ processes include changes in an individual's relationships with other people, changes in emotion, and changes in personality. A commonly used approach to classifying developmental periods includes the prenatal period, infancy, early _____ , middle and _____ childhood, adolescence, early _____ , middle adulthood, and late _____ .

The debate about whether development is primarily influenced by maturation or by experience is referred to as the _____ - _____ controversy. Nature refers to the contribution of _____ ; the role of the environment refers to the term _____ . The _____ of development view suggest that development involves distinct stages. The fact that a caterpillar changes into a butterfly illustrates the _____ of development.

conception - p. 320	
life span - p. 320	
socioeconomic/Biological - p. 320	
cognitive - p. 320	
Socioeconomic - p. 320	
childhood - p. 321	
late/adulthood - p. 321	
adulthood - p. 321	
nature-nurture - p. 322	
heredity - p. 323	
nurture/continuity - p. 323/ p. 324	
discontinuity - p. 323-324	

Child Development

The union of single sperm cell and an ovum is called _____ , or fertilization. The fertilized egg, called a _____ , receives _____ of its chromosomes from each parent. The first 2 weeks after conception is referred to as the _____ period; the period from 3 to 8 weeks is the _____ period. This embryonic period is marked by increasing cell _____ and the appearance of _____ . The _____ period begins 2 months after conception and lasts for about 7 months. Scientists label any agent that causes birth defects a _____ . The substance that caused specific birth defects like leg malformation was the drug _____ . Mothers who are heavy drinkers, for example, risk giving birth to children with _____ _____ _____ . Infants born prior to 38 weeks after conception are called _____ infants. Preterm infants who are very small are more likely than their larger counterparts to have _____ problems.

A child is born with several "wired" _____ , some of which disappear after 1 month as higher brain functions mature. At the age of 3, the human brain is _____ percent of its adult weight. Although physical development slows during the childhood years, _____ development becomes smoother and more coordinated. Education experts recognize the importance of spontaneous _____ .

With regard to cognitive development, Jean Piaget stressed that children _____ construct their own cognitive world. A _____ is a concept or framework that is already present in a person's mind and is used to organize and interpret information. Piaget believed that we adapt in two ways: when we incorporate new

conception/zygote - p. 325	
half - p. 325	
germinal - p. 325	
embryonic - p. 325	
differentiation - p. 325	
organs/fetal - p. 325	
teratogen - p. 326	
thalidomide - p. 326	
fetal alcohol syndrome - p. 326	
preterm - p. 327	
developmental - p. 327	
reflexes - p. 328	
75 - p. 330	
motor - p. 330	
play - p. 330	
actively - p. 331	
schema - p. 331	

information into our existing knowledge, it is called _____ .
When we have to adjust to new information, it is called _____ .
Piaget believed we pass through four stages in understanding the
world. According to Piaget, the thinking in one stage is _____
different than thinking in another stage. The first stage of
development, which lasts from birth to age 2, is called the _____
stage. In his stage, infants realize that objects continue to exist even
when they are not in sight; Piaget called this _____ _____ .
According to Piaget, preschool children have trouble understanding
the concept of reversibility; they cannot perform _____ .
Children between the ages of 2 and 7 are in a stage Piaget referred to
as _____ thought. Children in this stage have not yet grasped the
concept of _____ , which is the recognition that a quantity stays
the same even though its shape has changed. Children in this stage
are also unable to distinguish between their perspective and someone
else's perspective, a quality Piaget called _____ . The thinking in
this stage is more _____ than the previous stage. Piaget also
called preoperational thought _____ . Between the ages of 7 and
11, children are in a stage Piaget called _____ operational thought.
In this stage, mental reversibility is possible and intuitive thought is
replaced by _____ reasoning. Another important skill that
characterizes concrete operational thought is the ability to _____
or divide things and to consider their interrelations. The final stage is
called _____ _____ when the thinking is more _____ ,
idealistic, and logical. People in this stage can develop hypotheses
about ways to solve problems and this is called _____-_____
_____ . Piaget's theory has been criticized by psychologists because
he ignored _____ differences in thinking. _____ , a Russian
psychologist, recognized that development must be understood in
_____ context.

   Erik Erikson proposed an influential theory of _____
development. Each of the eight stages in his theory confronts
individuals with a _____ that must be resolved. The first year of
life represents the stage of _____ versus. _____ . Erikson
believes that the focus of the second year of life is on _____
versus _____ and _____ . During the preschool years,
children face the conflict of _____ versus guilt. Developing a
sense of _____ increases initiative. During the elementary school
years, children are challenged by industry versus _____ .
According to Erikson, the adolescent stage of development is
characterized by identity versus _____ _____ . During this
stage, according to Erikson, adolescents must determine who they are.
The state of development that characterizes early adulthood is
_____ versus isolation. In middle adulthood, the stage is called
generativity versus. _____ , with the crisis associated with late
adulthood of integrity versus _____ .

   In developmental psychology, _____ refers to a close
emotional bond between an infant and its caregiver. Harlow and
Zimmerman's research with infant monkeys illustrated the importance
of _____ _____ . Lorenz's research with goslings
demonstrated the process of _____ . Bowlby and Ainsworth

have suggested that, in humans, attachment to the _____ during the first year provides an important foundation. _____ attached infants use caregivers as a secure base from which to explore the environment; these infants are likely to have mothers who are more _____, accepting, and expressive of affective. An _____ attached infant avoids or is ambivalent toward caregivers. Kagan has argued that _____ and temperament characteristics are important factors; other critics have pointed out that there is a diversity of _____ agents and contexts in an infant's world. A child's behavioral style and characteristic way of responding is called _____, of which there are three types: easy child, _____ child, and slow-to-warm-up child. Baumrind has proposed a classification scheme for parenting styles. She refers to a restrictive, punitive style as _____ parenting. Children are encouraged to be independent but still have limits and controls on their actions in _____ parenting. A parenting style characterized by lack of parental involvement is _____ parenting. A style of parenting in which parents are highly involved with their children but place few demands on them is called _____ parenting. The process by which children and parents socialize each other is called _____ socialization. In our society, motherhood has been given _____ prestige. There is _____ evidence that when mothers work full-time, harm will come to the their children's development.

	caregiver - p. 340
	Securely - p. 340
	sensitive/insecurely - p. 340
	genetic - p. 340
	socializing - p. 340
	temperament/difficult - p. 341
	authoritarian - p. 341
	authoritative - p. 341
	neglectful - p. 342
	indulgent - p. 342
	reciprocal - p. 342
	low - p. 343
	no - p. 343

Adolescence

The transition from childhood to adulthood is called _____. G. Stanley Hall viewed adolescence as a turbulent time charged with conflict; his perspective is known as the _____-_____-_____ view. Although adolescents are commonly portrayed as being rebellious and self-centered, most adolescents are _____ human beings who are not experiencing deep emotional turmoil.

The lower age of menarche is associated with higher standards of _____. The rapid maturation that occurs mainly during early adolescence is called _____. During adolescence there is a dramatic increase in the hormone _____ in boys and in the hormone _____ in girls. The hormonal and body changes associated with adolescence is about _____ years earlier in _____ than in _____. In Piaget's theory, children between the ages of 11 and 15 are able to think abstractly; they are able to engage in _____ operational thought. Adolescents are also able to think logically and engage in _____-_____ reasoning. The belief that others are as _____ with the adolescent as he or she is with himself or herself, the belief that one is _____, and the belief that one is _____ are all components of adolescent egocentrism.

Lawrence Kohlberg has identified three levels of _____ development. The first, which shows no internalization of moral values, is the _____ level. At the second level, called the _____ level, internalization is intermediate. At the highest level, called _____ level, morality is completely internalized. One criticism of Kohlberg's theory is that moral reasons are often a shelter

	adolescence - p. 345
	storm-and-stress - p. 345
	competent - p. 345
	living - p. 346
	puberty - p. 346
	testosterone - p. 346
	estradiol - p. 346
	two - p. 346
	females/males - p. 346
	formal - p. 346
	hypothetical-deductive - p. 346
	preoccupied - p. 347
	indestructible - p. 347
	unique - p. 347
	moral - p. 347
	preconventional - p. 347
	conventional - p. 347
	postconventional - p. 348

for _____ behavior. Carol Gilligan has criticized Kohlberg's approach because it doesn't adequately reflect _____ with others; her view is the _____ perspective, in contrast with Kohlberg's _____ perspective. Erikson argued that adolescents experience a gap between the security of childhood and the autonomy of adulthood and is called psychological _____. Conflicts between adolescents and their parents involve the adolescent's desire to become _____ from their parents. Four areas of concern that make up a large portion of at-risk youths are _____, substance use, _____, and adolescent pregnancy. Successful programs designed to help at-risk youths emphasize the _____ between the youth and the _____.

Adult Development and Aging

Most people reach their peak physical performance during _____ _____. This is also the time when most people are their _____. As individuals enter middle adulthood, the three greatest health concerns are _____ _____, cancer, and _____. During midlife, women experience _____ when their menstrual periods cease completely because the production of _____ declines. _____ is the maximum number of years an individual can live and is 120 years. A person's _____ _____ refers to how long she will probably live if born in a particular year. The world's population of individuals _____ years of age has _____ from 1950 to 1990. Cells can only divide a maximum number of times according to the _____ _____ theory. Cells may die because of their _____ getting shorter and shorter. According to the free-radical theory, people age because inside their cells _____ _____ molecules are produced that damage DNA and other structures. A degenerative, irreversible brain disorder that impairs memory and social behavior is called _____ disease, which involves the neurotransmitter _____.

Memory decline in middle age is more likely when _____ _____ are involved; _____ _____ are not as affected by age. Among older adults, _____ of processing information is slower than in younger adults. _____ may increase with age because of life experiences.

Most new jobs will be in _____, health, and _____ services through the year 2005. Companies that employ university graduates say that the most important skills are _____ skills, interpersonal skills, and _____ skills.. Contrary to popular opinion, only about _____ percent of North Americans change careers in mid-life. In the last 50 years, the desire for a stable marriage has received competition from the desire for personal _____. The idealistic expectations of marriage help to explain the nation's high _____ rate. Many myths continue to exist about marriage and being _____.

Levinson's view of adulthood, based on interviews with middle-aged men, also emphasizes a _____ approach. Critics of Erikson's and Levinson's theories have pointed out that they are not based on _____ research, and they tend to describe the stages as _____. Life _____ rather than stages may be responsible for changes in our adult lives. Some developmental psychologists believe that changes in our society influence how different _____ move through the life cycle. Others believe that the timetable according to which individuals are expected to accomplish life's tasks, called the _____ _____ , depends on the social environment. According to _____ theory, older people who are more active and involved are more satisfied with life. An excellent way to maintain health in late adulthood is with _____ .

cohorts - p. 359

social clock - p. 359
activity - p. 359

success - p. 360

Death and Dying

In most cultures, death is not seen as the _____. According to Elisabeth Kübler-Ross we go through the following five stages in facing death: _____ and isolation, anger, _____, depression, and _____. Those who are left behind after the death of a loved one often experience psychological disorders like _____. The poorest group of individuals in North America are _____ _____.

end - p. 361

denial/bargaining - p. 361
acceptance - p. 361

depression - p. 361
widowed women - p. 362

Explorations in Psychology

To respond to the questions and exercises presented in this section, please write your thoughts, perspectives, and reactions on a separate piece of paper.

Explorations in Psychology and Life: The Power of Touch and Massage in Development

- This section describes the effects of touch and massage on preterm babies. Do you suppose that touch has the same type of positive effects on adults? Describe the basis of your view.
- Speculate on what touch and massage given to babies might be doing to create the effects Dr. Field has reported.
- What implications do Dr. Field's studies have on parents, child-care providers, teachers, and others who work with children?

Explorations in Psychology and Life: Child Care in North America

- Describe the findings of the Canadian Transition to Child Care and the National Institute of Child Health and Human Development studies.
- Do you think that mothers return to work too early after the birth of their baby?
- If you are a parent looking for quality child care, what do you look for?
- Given the information presented in the section, what would you say to a young mother who is apprehensive about returning to work 5 months after the birth of her son?

In Your Own Words

To respond to the questions and exercises presented in this section, please write your thoughts, perspectives, and reactions on a separate piece of paper.

✓ Describe some biological, cognitive, and socioemotional changes that you have experienced in the past year.
✓ As you think about the formal operations stage, what was the last decision you made where you used hypothetical-deductive reasoning?
✓ How might a middle-age person help the next generation as they experience generativity?

✓ Have you ever met parents who represents Baumrind's four parental styles? Describe them.
✓ When you were in eighth grade what types of arguments did you have with your parents or other adults? Did the arguments revolve around your search for independence?
✓ What type of outlook on life do you suppose people born during the 1930s may have compared to people born during 1950s and 1970s?
✓ Knowing what you do now about the changes that take place throughout the life-span, what is the best age to be?
✓ In what ways would you be different if you were born into a different family?
✓ How will you know if you've had a successful life?

Correcting the Incorrect

Carefully read each statement. Determine if the statement is correct or incorrect. If the statement is incorrect, make the necessary changes to correct it. Then look directly under the statement for the correct statement and page reference in the textbook.

1. Development refers to the changes that take place from conception through adolescence.
   ❑ *Development refers to the changes that take place from conception through the life span. (p. 320)*
2. Biological processes include the development of the brain, height and weight, and motor skills.
   ❑ *Biological processes include the development of the brain, height and weight, and motor skills. (p. 320)*
3. An infant's smile in response to his mother's smile illustrates cognitive processes.
   ❑ *A infant's smile in response to his mother's smile illustrates socioemotional processes. (p. 320)*
4. According to Neugarten, our society has become more age-relevant.
   ❑ *According to Neugarten, our society has become more age-irrelevant. (p. 323)*
5. The nature and nurture theory refers to the contributions of heredity and environment on behavior.
   ❑ *The nature and nurture theory refers to the contributions of heredity and environment on behavior. (p. 323)*
6. The example of the caterpillar turning into a butterfly illustrates continuity of development.
   ❑ *The example of the caterpillar turning into a butterfly illustrates discontinuity of development (p. 324)*
7. The stages of prenatal development are the germinal period, the embryonic period, and the fetal period.
   ❑ *The stages of prenatal development are the germinal period, the embryonic period, and the fetal period. (p. 325)*
8. A teratogen refers to the tip of the chromosome.
   ❑ *A teratogen refers to any agent that causes a birth defect. (p. 326).*
9. Object permanence is a concept or framework that already exists that organizes and interprets information.
   ❑ *A schema is a concept or framework that already exists that organizes and interprets information. (p. 332)*
10. A preterm infant is born prior to 40 weeks after conception.
    ❑ *A preterm infant is born prior to 38 weeks after conception. (p. 327)*
11. In assimilation, the individual adjusts to new information.
    ❑ *In accommodation, the individual adjusts to new information. (p. 331)*
12. Object permanence takes place in the preoperational stage.
    ❑ *Object permanence takes place in the sensorimotor stage. (p. 332)*
13. Infants are more cognitively competent than Piaget thought.
    ❑ *Infants are more cognitively competent than Piaget thought. (p. 336)*
14. The thinking of a child during the concrete operational stage is logical.
    ❑ *The thinking of a child during the concrete operational stage is logical. (p. 334)*
15. A person who can engage in hypothetical-deductive reasoning is most likely to be in the concrete operational stage.
    ❑ *A person who can engage in hypothetical-deductive reasoning is most likely to be in the formal operational stage. (p. 335)*
16. Vygotsky ignored the role of culture in development.
    ❑ *Vygotsky stressed the role of culture in development. (p.336)*

17. Erikson developed eight stages of psychosocial development.
   - ❑ *Erikson developed eight stages of psychosocial development. (p. 337)*
18. Individuals during their 20s and 30s are in the identity versus identity-confusion stage according to Erikson.
   - ❑ *Individuals during their 20s and 30s are in the intimacy versus isolation stage according to Erikson. (p. 338)*
19. A parent who is restrictive and has a punitive style that demands obedience on the part of the child has an authoritative parenting style.
   - ❑ *A parent who is restrictive and has a punitive style that demands obedience on the part of the child has an authoritarian parenting style. (p. 341)*
20. The fact that children influence their parents as parents influence their children describes reciprocal socialization.
   - ❑ *The fact that children influence their parents as parents influence their children describes reciprocal socialization. (p. 342)*
21. G. Stanley Hall believed that adolescence was a time of serene-and-solemness.
   - ❑ *G. Stanley Hall believed that adolescence was a time of storm-and-stress. (p. 345).*
22. Estradiol is a hormone found in girls responsible for development of breasts, uterus, and skeleton.
   - ❑ *Estradiol is a hormone found in girls responsible for development of breasts, uterus, and skeleton. (p. 346)*
23. An adolescent yells to her mother, "You just don't understand me!" This illustrates the preconventional stage of moral development.
   - ❑ *An adolescent yells to her mother, "You just don't understand me!" This illustrates adolescent egocentrism (p. 347)*
24. As the control of behavior shifts from the external to the internal, internalization occurs.
   - ❑ *As the control of behavior shifts from the external to the internal, internalization occurs. (p. 347)*
25. During the conventional stage of moral thinking, the individual shows no internalization of moral values.
   - ❑ *During the conventional stage of moral thinking, the individual shows an intermediate level of internalization of moral values. (p. 347)*
26. Moral development is completely internalized at the postconventional level of moral thinking.
   - ❑ *Moral development is completely internalized at the postconventional level of moral thinking (p. 348)*
27. Carol Gilligan argues that people see their connectedness with others as important in moral thinking.
   - ❑ *Carol Gilligan argues that people see their connectedness with others as important in moral thinking. (p. 349)*
28. The elementary years are an important time for identity changes.
   - ❑ *The adolescent years are an important time for identity changes. (p. 350)*
29. Most women who experience menopause report psychological problems or physical problems.
   - ❑ *Most women who experience menopause do not report psychological problems or physical problems. (p. 352)*
30. The life expectancy of a person born in Canada in 2000 is about 120 years.
   - ❑ *The life expectancy of a person born in Canada in 2000 is about 78.6 years. (p. 353)*
31. Cells can divide only about 25 times according to the cellular clock theory.
   - ❑ *Cells can divide only about 100 times according to the cellular clock theory. (p. 353)*
32. Parkinson's disease is characterized by gradual deterioration of memory, reasoning, language, and eventually, physical functioning.
   - ❑ *Alzheimer's disease is characterized by gradual deterioration of memory, reasoning, language, and eventually, physical functioning. (p. 354)*
33. Memory tends to decline if automatic processing is involved.
   - ❑ *Memory tends to if controlled processing is involved. (p. 355)*
34. Erikson and Levinson both emphasize the importance of life events in different cohorts.
   - ❑ *Erikson and Levinson both emphasize the importance of stages. (p. 358)*
35. People who don't follow the social clock find their lives less stressful than those who do.
   - ❑ *People who don't follow the social clock find their lives more stressful than those who do. (p. 359)*
36. The generativity theory of aging states that the more active and involved older people are, the more satisfied they are and the healthier they are likely to stay.

❑ *The activity theory of aging states that the more active and involved older people are, the more satisfied they are and the healthier they are likely to stay. (p. 359)*

37. Only cultures in the West have rituals for death.
   ❑ *Most cultures in the West have rituals for death. (p. 361)*

38. Kübler-Ross describes six stages in facing death
   ❑ *Kübler-Ross describes six stages in facing death. (p. 361)*

Practice Test

1. Psychologists define development as
   a. behavioral changes.
   b. patterns of movement or change.
   c. cognitive maturity.
   d. physical growth.

a.	no; development involves more than just behavior changes
b.	THAT'S RIGHT; development refers to pattern of movement or change
c.	no; development involves more than just cognitive maturity
d.	no; development involves more than just physical growth

2. Which of the following is part of the term "development"?
   a. a pattern of movement or change
   b. continues throughout the life cycle
   c. begins at conception
   d. all of the above

a.	no; but you're partially correct
b.	no; but you're partially correct
c.	no; but you're partially correct
d.	YES; development involves all of the above

3. Which of the following processes are involved in development?
   a. biological processes
   b. cognitive processes
   c. socioemotional processes
   d. all of the above

a.	no; but biological processes are involved in development
b.	no; but cognitive processes are involved in development
c.	no; but socioemotional processes are involved in development
d.	THAT'S RIGHT; it involves biological, cognitive, and socioemotional processes

4. Developmental psychologists divide the life span into
   a. 10 periods of development.
   b. 8 periods of development.
   c. 5 periods of development.
   d. 3 periods of development.

a.	no
b.	CORRECT; the most widely used classification of development involves 8 periods
c.	no
d.	no

5.   The debate over whether development is primarily a matter of heredity or experience is also known as the
     a.   mechanics versus pragmatics controversy.
     b.   storm and stress view.
     c.   continuity/discontinuity problem.
     d.   nature/nurture issue.

a.	no	
b.	no	
c.	no; this refers to how the change occurs, suddenly or slowly	
d.	YES; nature refers to heredity and nurture refers to experience	

6.   To his parents, it seems that Alyssa is able to think abstractly "all of a sudden." Which developmental approach are they demonstrating?
     a.   continuity of development
     b.   discontinuity of development
     c.   the authoritative approach
     d.   the interaction approach

a.	no; continuity of development refers to gradual, cumulative change	
b.	YES; discontinuity of development refers to development in distinct stages	
c.	no; this is a parenting style	
d.	no	

7.   Although development frequently seems to take place all of a sudden, it actually involves gradual change according to the
     a.   continuity of development approach.
     b.   discontinuity of development approach.
     c.   qualitative development approach.
     d.   none of the above

a.	YEP; continuity of development refers to gradual, cumulative change	
b.	no; discontinuity of development refers to development in distinct stages	
c.	no; qualitative changes describes discontinuity of development	
d.	no	

8.   Suppose you are studying a theory of development that divides the life span into five distinct stages. Given this information, you know that this theory is most likely a(n)
     a.   socioemotional theory.
     b.   experiential theory.
     c.   discontinuous theory.
     d.   continuous theory.

a.	no; socioemotional theory refers to changes in emotion and personality	
b.	no	
c.	YEAH; discontinuity of development refers to development in distinct stages	
d.	no; continuity of development refers to gradual, cumulative change	

9.   Maria is in her fifth week of pregnancy. Which prenatal stage is present?
     a.   embryonic period
     b.   germinal stage
     c.   conception
     d.   fetal period

a.	YES; the fifth week is in the embryonic period (three to eight weeks)	
b.	no; the germinal stage is the first two week	
c.	no; conception refers to the union of sperm and ovum	
d.	no; the fetal period is 2 months to 9 months	

10. A young woman, who is a heavy drinker, confides in you that she thinks she might be pregnant. What advice would you give her?
   a. See a doctor immediately and cease drinking.
   b. Don't worry; it's probably a false alarm.
   c. Wait another month and then see a doctor if you still think you might be pregnant.
   d. There is no need to do anything until you are at least five months pregnant.

a.	CORRECT; her unborn child is at-risk for fetal alcohol syndrome	
b.	no; why think it is a false alarm?	
c.	no; damage from alcohol might occur	
d.	no; damage from alcohol can occur in early pregnancy	

11. Which of the following characterize physical and motor development in late childhood?
   a. The growth rate accelerates in late childhood.
   b. The child's brain is closer to full growth than the rest of its body.
   c. Child development experts believe that children do not yet have the expertise to plan and select their own activities.
   d. Spontaneous play should be kept to a minimum at this stage of development

a.	no; the rate actually slows down in late childhood	
b.	YES: the brain has attained 90% of adult weight	
c.	no; this is not correct	
d.	no; play is very important in childhood	

12. Little Miranda screams with delight as she sees a horse. She yells to her dad, "See doggie." According to Piaget, what process has occurred?
   a. assimilation
   b. accommodation
   c. object permanence
   d. reversibility

a.	YES; new information (horse) is adjusted to fit existing knowledge (doggie)	
b.	no; the horse is perceived as a doggie	
c.	no; object permanence is an understanding that objects exist even if they aren't seen	
d.	no; this refers to the ability to think in reverse	

13. A preoperational thinker cannot yet do which of the following?
   a. think symbolically
   b. understand words
   c. reverse mental representations
   d. participate in "pretend" play

a.	these children can think symbolically; they can use language and can draw	
b.	no; these children understand words	
c.	RIGHT; a preoperational thinker (ages 2-7 years) cannot yet reverse their thinking	
d.	no; these children can do "pretend" play	

14. Children are able to grasp the principle of conservation in which stage of development?
    a. sensorimotor thought
    b. preoperational thought
    c. concrete operational thought
    d. none of the above

a.	these children are not capable of conservation	
b.	no; these children are not yet capable of conservation	
c.	CORRECT; children (ages 7-11 years) grasp conservation	
d.	no	

15. Piaget's enduring contributions to the field of developmental psychology include all of the following except which one?
    a. his view of children as active, constructive thinkers
    b. his extensive analysis of individual differences in cognitive development
    c. his focus on qualitative change in cognitive development
    d. his identification of an orderly sequence of cognitive development

a.	this is an enduring contribution	
b.	THAT'S CORRECT; Piaget focused on differences between groups of children	
c.	no; this is an enduring contribution	
d.	no; this is an enduring contribution	

16. According to Erikson, the first psychosocial stage of development is called
    a. autonomy versus shame and doubt.
    b. industry versus inferiority.
    c. initiative versus guilt.
    d. trust versus mistrust.

a.	no; this is the second stage	
b.	no; this is the fourth stage	
c.	no; this is the third stage	
d.	RIGHT; trust is built when the child's needs are met	

17. Four-year-old Allison sees all of the adults pitch in to clear the dinner table. Not wanting to be left out, she picks up a glass and carries it to the kitchen. Unfortunately, the glass slips out of her hand and breaks, just as she is trying to put it on the kitchen counter. According to Erikson's theory of psychosocial development, what would be the most appropriate response by Allison's mother?
    a. The mother should scold Allison severely.
    b. The mother should tell Allison that she is stupid and clumsy.
    c. The mother should ask Allison if she is OK and thank her for trying to help.
    d. The mother should make Allison clean up the mess.

a.	no; this could lead to guilt over her willingness to help	
b.	no; this could lead to guilt over her willingness to help	
c.	RIGHT; she is in initiative versus guilt; she shows initiative in helping with the glass	
d.	no; maybe, but is not according to Erikson's theory of psychosocial development	

18. According to Erikson, the final developmental stage is called
    a. generativity versus stagnation.
    b. intimacy versus isolation.
    c. integrity versus despair.
    d. ageism versus activity theory.

a.	no; this stage occurs in the 40s and 50s
b.	this stage occurs in early adulthood
c.	YES; this is the last stage where the person looks back on their lives
d.	these are theories of aging and are not among Erikson's stages

19. According to Erikson, adolescents who experience identity confusion
   a. withdraw and isolate themselves from peers and family.
   b. eventually develop thoughts that are concrete and irrational.
   c. develop a sense of inferiority
   d. develop postconventional level of moral thinking

a.	THAT'S CORRECT
b.	no; just the opposite occurs; thoughts become more abstract and logical
c.	no; inferiority is part of an earlier stage (6 years to puberty)
d.	this is the highest level of moral thinking

19. According to Erikson, the two stages of early and middle adulthood consist of intimacy versus isolation and
   a. integrity versus despair.
   b. identity versus identity confusion.
   c. generativity versus despair.
   d. generativity versus stagnation.

a.	no; this occurs in late adulthood
b.	this stage takes place in adolescence
c.	no
d.	YES; this stage occurs in the 40s and 50s

21. Natalie is an infant who usually displays a sunny disposition, follows a regular sleep/wake schedule, and adjusts quickly to new routines and experiences. Natalie would most likely be classified as a(n)
   a. easy child.
   b. difficult child.
   c. slow-to-warm-up child.
   d. withdrawn child.

a.	RIGHT; Natalie has an easy child temperament
b.	a difficult child reacts negatively, cries frequently and has an irregular routines
c.	this type involves low activity and shows low adaptability
d.	this is not a temperament type

22. Authoritarian parents often have children who are
   a. overly self-confident.
   b. good communicators.
   c. socially incompetent.
   d. cognitively deficient.

a.	no
b.	no
c.	CORRECT
d.	no

23. A parenting style that encourages children to be independent but still places limits on their behavior is called
    a. authoritative.
    b. authoritarian.
    c. neglecting.
    d. indulgent.

a.	RIGHT; this style is characterized by limits and control and verbal give-and-take
b.	no; this style involves a restrictive, punitive style
c.	no; a neglecting style refers to a parent who is uninvolved in the child's life
d.	no; indulgent style involves involvement but few demands

24. A parenting style in which parents are highly involved with their children but place few demands on them is called
    a. authoritative.
    b. authoritarian.
    c. neglecting.
    d. indulgent.

a.	no; this style is characterized by limits and control and verbal give-and-take
b.	no; this style involves a restrictive, punitive style
c.	no; a neglecting style refers to a parent who is uninvolved in the child's life
d.	YES; indulgent style involves involvement but few demands

25. G. Stanley Hall described adolescence as a time of "storm and stress." Modern developmental psychologists
    a. agree that he was correct.
    b. find there is no more conflict with parents at this time than at any other stage in life.
    c. believe that adolescents are competent human beings and, for the most part, maintain a positive self-image.
    d. have shown that the turmoil is caused by hormonal disturbances.

a.	no
b.	no
c.	no; this is the belief of most modern developmental psychologists
d.	no

26. The author of your text suggests that adolescence should be regarded as all of the following except which one?
    a. a time of evaluation
    b. a time of acute crisis
    c. a time of decision making
    d. a time of commitment

a.	no; adolescence is a time of evaluation
b.	CORRECT; for most adolescents, it is not a time of acute crisis
c.	no; adolescence is a time of decision making
d.	no; adolescence is a time of commitment

27. Adolescent egocentrism involves all of the following except which one?
    a. the perception of self as unique
    b. the perception of self as indestructible
    c. the inability to see an issue from another's point of view
    d. the belief that others are aware of and watching one's every action

a.	no; this is part of adolescent egocentrism	
b.	no; this is part of adolescent egocentrism	
c.	CORRECT; this is not the same as egocentrism in childhood	
d.	no; this is part of adolescent egocentrism	

28. Which of the following characterizes adolescent cognitive development?
   a. formal operational thought
   b. hypothetical-deductive reasoning
   c. adolescent egocentrism
   d. all of the above

a.	no; formal operational thought characterizes cognitive development
b.	no; this type of reasoning characterizes cognitive development
c.	no; egocentrism characterizes cognitive development
d.	RIGHT; all are characteristics of adolescent cognitive development

29. Individuals are able to engage in hypothetical-deductive reasoning after they achieve _____ thought.
   a. sensorimotor
   b. preoperational
   c. concrete operational
   d. formal operational

a.	no; this stage refers to nonsymbolic stage
b.	no; the child in this stage is capable of symbolic thinking
c.	no; the child in this stage engages in logical thinking about concrete events
d.	YES; in formal operational though, people are able to engage in this reasoning

30. According to Kohlberg, at what level is moral development completely internalized and not based on others' standards?
   a. preconventional
   b. conventional
   c. postconventional
   d. justice

a.	in this stage there is no internalization of moral values
b.	this is the intermediate level of internalization
c.	RIGHT; this is the highest level of moral thinking
d.	no; this is the type of orientation that Kohlberg takes

31. Kohlberg's theory of moral development has been criticized because
   a. it does not reflect the care perspective.
   b. it does not reflect the justice perspective.
   c. it is unconcerned with culture.
   d. Kohlberg excluded males in his study.

a.	RIGHT; a care perspective considers people's connectedness
b.	no; Kohlberg's theory does take a justice perspective
c.	no; this is a criticism of Piaget's theory
d.	no; most of his research was with males

32.   Karen who is 52 years old is going through menopause. This means that her
      a.   children are leaving the home.
      b.   menstrual periods are ceasing.
      c.   ovaries are producing too much estrogen.
      d.   cells are approaching the Hayflick limit.

a.	no
b.	RIGHT
c.	no; in fact her ovaries are producing less estrogen
d.	no; the Hayflick limit refers to the cellular clock theory of aging

33.   Of the following statements, which one is **incorrect?**
      a.   Life span and life expectancy are really the same thing.
      b.   The life span of humans is about 120 years.
      c.   The life-expectancy of humans has increased in the last 100 years.
      d.   The fastest growing segment of the population is the 85 years and older group.

a.	RIGHT; life span refers to the maximum number of years an individual can live; life-expectancy is the number of years an average person born in a particular year will live
b.	no; this is correct
c.	no; this is correct
d.	no; this is correct

34.   Which of the following best represents the research findings on the memory skills of middle-aged adults?
      a.   memory for controlled processes declines more than memory for automatic processes
      b.   long-term memory skills tend to be enhanced
      c.   no discernible declines have been found
      d.   keeping irrelevant information separate in one's mind becomes easier with age

a.	CORRECT;
b.	no; long-term memory skills are not enhanced in middle age
c.	no
d.	no; keeping irrelevant information separate in one's mind becomes harder with age

35.   Which theory suggests that the more active and involved older people are, the more satisfied they are, and the more likely they will stay healthy?
      a.   integration theory
      b.   activity theory
      c.   "second childhood" theory
      d.   socialization theory

a.	no
b.	AYE; the activity theory focuses on activity and involvement
c.	no
d.	no

36. People tend to become more concerned about their health status in
      a.   early adulthood.
      b.   adolescence.
      c.   middle adulthood.
      d.   late adulthood.

a.	no	
b.	no	
c.	THIS IS CORRECT	
d.	no; the concern starts earlier, in middle adulthood	

37. The _____ theory of aging is related to the Hayflick limit on cell division.
   a. cellular clock
   b. free-radical
   c. activity
   d. cohort

a.	RIGHT; cells can divide a maximum number of times	
b.	no; free radicals refer to unstable oxygen molecules	
c.	no; this refers to the importance of remaining active and involved	
d.	no; a cohort refers to a group of people born during the same time or time period	

38. Of the following, which one is not among the five stages in facing death according to Kübler-Ross?
   a. denial
   b. anger
   c. bargaining
   d. fear

a.	no; this is one of the stages	
b.	no; this is one of the stages	
c.	no; this is one of the stages	
d.	AYE; fear is not among the five stages	

Chapter 11 - Motivation and Emotion

The Big Picture: Chapter Overview

Motivation refers to the question of "why" we behave, think, and feel the way we do. Motivated behavior is energized, directed, and sustained. Biological influences in motivation include instincts, needs, and drives. At one time, it was believed that much of human behavior was controlled by instincts, which are biological patterns of behavior assumed to be universal in a species, although this is no longer the case. Drive reduction theory suggests that drives and needs motivate behavior; a drive is an aroused state that occurs because of a physiological need. The goal of drive reduction is homeostasis or the body's tendency to maintain equilibrium. Many of our behaviors are carried out to increase rather than decrease drive. Another perspective, ethology, is the study of the biological basis of behavior in natural habitats. In addition, there are physiological and cognitive processes that are important in motivation. In the study of motivation, external stimuli are called incentives. Behavior is energized by both positive and negative incentives. Sociocultural influences play an important role in motivation. Maslow's theory views motivation as a hierarchy of motives with self-actualization as the highest and most elusive of needs. The contemporary view of motivation emphasizes the interactive biological, cognitive, and sociocultural factors.

Cannon found that stomach contractions are related to hunger; a full stomach stimulates the hormone CCK to signal the brain to stop eating. Blood sugar level, insulin, and glucose play a role in regulating hunger. The brain is involved in hunger as it monitors the stomach and blood sugar levels. Brain lesions of the ventromedial hypothalamus cause animals to become obese, while lesions of the lateral hypothalamus causes animals to stop eating. External cues such as seeing someone else eat can influence hunger, especially in obese individuals who may be more sensitive to external cues. Obesity is a serious and pervasive problem with about one-third of North Americans being overweight. Heredity may give individuals a tendency to be overweight. Weight is also influenced by set point (i.e., the weight maintained when no effort is made to gain or lose weight) and basal metabolism rate. Environmental influences on weight include the taste of food. Some psychologists have studied dieting by examining restrained eaters, who are people who chronically restrict their food intake to control their weight. Many people on diets initially lose weight, but then gain it back. Exercise is an effective way to lose weight by increasing metabolism. There may be a harmful side of dieting. Anorexia nervosa and bulimia represent eating disorders that involve thinness through starvation and a bingeing-purging cycle, respectively. Chronic dieting may actually cause bingeing.

In humans, sexuality is influenced by hormones (e.g., estrogens, androgens) and brain processes. Cognitive factors such as thoughts, imagery, and interpretation are important in sexuality as well. Pheromones are odorous hormones released in animals that are powerful attractants; aphrodisiacs are substances that supposedly arouse sexual desires and increase sexual capacity. The wide variation in what is considered normal sexuality is influenced by cultural factors. Sexual scripts influence sexual motivation and are stereotyped patterns of expectancies for how people should behave sexually; examples of scripts include the traditional religious script and the romantic script. According to Masters and Johnson, the human sexual response pattern consists of four stages: excitement, plateau, orgasm, and resolution. Psychosexual dysfunctions influence these stages either as impairments of desire or as achievement of the response pattern. Sexual behavior and attitudes among heterosexuals have become more permissive in the twentieth century. Today, many experts in the field of human sexuality view sexual orientation as a continuum ranging from exclusively heterosexual to exclusively homosexual. An individual's sexual orientation is determined by a combination of genetic, hormonal, cognitive, and environmental factors.

The need for achievement is the desire to accomplish something to reach a standard of excellence and to expend effort to excel. McClelland has extensively studied achievement using ambiguous pictures shown to subjects. The internal desire to achieve is called intrinsic motivation, whereas motivation influenced by external rewards and punishment is called extrinsic motivation. Intrinsic motivation seems to be more likely to produce competent behavior and mastery. Attribution theory says that individuals are motivated to discover the underlying causes of behavior as they make sense of behavior. Goal-setting, planning, and self-monitoring are studied as important factors in achievement motivation. People in North America are often more achievement-oriented than people in other countries suggesting that there are cultural, ethnic, and socioeconomic effects. For studies involving ethnic minorities, socioeconomic status is a better predictor of achievement than ethnicity. To increase achievement, goals should be set that are specific, proximal, and challenging.

An emotion is made up of affect, physiological arousal, and behavioral expression. The autonomic nervous system is divided into the sympathetic nervous system that is responsible for quick responses to stressors and the parasympathetic nervous system that calms the body. Polygraphs, used to determine if someone is lying, monitor changes in the body thought to be influenced by emotional states. The Yerkes-Dodson law suggests that performance is best under moderate rather than low or high levels of arousal.

The James-Lange theory of emotion holds that we perceive a stimulus, our body responds, and we interpret the body's reaction as emotion. The Cannon-Bard theory suggests that we experience an emotion and bodily changes simultaneously. The amygdala appears to be an important part of the brain involved in neural circuitry of emotion. Endorphins, dopamine, and norepinephrine may also be involved in emotions. The two-factor theory of emotion developed by Schachter and Singer suggests that cognitive factors affect emotion; in this theory, emotion is determined by physiological arousal and cognitive labeling as we look at the external word to explain the arousal and then label the emotion.

Examining the behavioral expression of emotion, Ekman has found six basic emotions: happiness, anger, sadness, surprise, disgust, and fear. Facial expressions may also influence emotions according to the facial feedback hypothesis. While there are strong universal, biological ties to the facial expression of emotion, there are cultural factors that influence it. Display rules are sociocultural standards that determine when, where, and how emotions should be expressed. The master stereotype of gender and emotion is that females are emotional and males are not. Researchers have not found differences between males and females with regard to experiencing emotions. In reality the relationship between emotion and gender is more complex. Emotions often involve social contexts and relationships; gender differences are more likely to occur in contexts that emphasize social roles and relationships. According to Plutchik, emotions have four distinctions: they are positive or negative, they are primary or mixed, many are polar opposites, and they vary in intensity. Psychologists have researched such powerful emotions as happiness and anger. For instance, psychologists have found that catharsis is not a good way to deal with anger.

Learning Objectives

When you have studied the material in this chapter, you should be able to:

1. define motivation. (p. 368)
2. distinguish between instincts, drives, and needs. (pp. 368-370)
3. explain drive reduction theory and its relationship to homeostasis. (p. 369)
4. identify important contributions from the biological, cognitive, and sociocultural perspectives regarding motivation. (pp. 368-371)
5. explain the role of stomach cues and blood sugar in the regulation of hunger. (pp. 373-374)
6. explain the role of the lateral hypothalamus and the ventromedial hypothalamus in the regulation of hunger. (pp. 374-375)
7. discuss the roles of external and environmental factors in hunger. (pp. 375-378)
8. compare and contrast anorexia nervosa and bulimia nervosa. (p. 378)
9. differentiate between androgens and estrogens and their respective roles in male and female sexual motivation. (p. 380)
10. describe the roles that cognitive, sensory, and perceptual processes play in sexual desire. (pp. 380-381)
11. define sexual script. (p. 382)
12. identify the four phases of the sexual response cycle and physiological processes associated with each stage. (pp. 382-383)
13. discuss the causes and treatments of common sexual dysfunctions. (pp. 383-384)

14. summarize research investigating factors that may influence sexual orientation. (p. 384-387)
15. define the need for achievement. (p. 388)
16. discuss the relationship between intrinsic motivation and the need for achievement. (pp. 388-389)
17. explain why definitions of achievement motivation are culturally dependent. (pp. 390-392)
18. define emotion and name three aspects of emotion. (p. 393-394)
19. explain the Yerkes-Dodson Law and its relationship to performance. (p. 394)
20. compare and contrast the James-Lange, Cannon-Bard, and two-factor theories of emotion. (pp. 396-398)
21. describe the experiments of Schachter and Singer that support cognitive labeling in emotional experience. (pp. 397-398)
22. explain the facial feedback hypothesis. (p. 399)
23. give examples of display rules. (pp. 400-401)
24. list the four dimensions in Plutchik's classification of emotion. (p. 402)
25. summarize the results of research on happiness and anger. (pp. 402-405)
26. list and discuss Carol Tavris's suggestions for managing anger. (p. 405)
27. from *Explorations in Psychology: Evaluating Lie Detectors*, relate the information on lie detectors to the Yerkes-Dodson Law. Discuss the Guilty Knowledge Test. (p. 395)
28. summarize the information from *Explorations in Psychology: Comparing Math Achievement in Asian and North American Cultures*, and analyze the reasons why Asian children outperform North American children in math achievement. (p. 391)

Guided Review

Some Ideas Behind The "Whys" Of Behavior

The question of why individuals behave, think, and feel the way they do is studied by the field of _____ . Behaviors that have an innate, biological determinant are called _____ . Psychologists have historically believed that much human behavior was controlled by _____ . A _____ is an aroused state that occurs because of a physiological need. A _____ is a deprivation that energizes a drive. One theory of motivation suggests that, as a drive becomes stronger, we are motivated to reduce it; this is the _____ reduction theory. Whereas drives pertain to a _____ state, needs involve a _____ state. The body's tendency to maintain a balanced equilibrium is called _____ . One weakness of this theory is that it doesn't explain well why many people behave in ways that _____ rather _____ a drive.

Lorenz suggested that _____ may provide insight into the motivation of human behavior. External stimuli that motivate behavior are called _____ . Behavior is energized by both _____ and _____ incentives. Abraham Maslow's theory uses a _____ of motivation. The highest level of motivation, according to Maslow, is _____ . The contemporary view of motivation stresses biological, _____ , and behavior/social/cultural processes. Psychologists continue to debate the role of conscious versus _____ thought in motivation.

motivation - p. 368
instincts - p. 368

instincts - p. 368/drive - p. 369
need - p. 369

drive - p. 369
psychological - p. 369
physiological - p. 369
homeostasis - p. 369

increase/reduce - p. 369
ethology - p. 370

incentives - p. 371
internal/external - p. 371
hierarchy - p. 371
self-actualization - p. 372
cognitive - p. 372

unconscious - p. 372

Hunger

Peripheral factors involved in hunger include contractions of the _____ and blood _____ levels. The stomach produces the hormone _____ , which signals the brain to stop eating. Insulin causes excess sugars in the blood to be stored in cells as _____ and _____ . Two important areas of the hypothalamus involved in eating are the _____ hypothalamus and the _____ hypothalamus. The _____ hypothalamus is involved in reducing hunger, whereas the _____ hypothalamus stimulates eating. Stanley Schachter believes that an important difference between obese and normal individuals is their response to _____ cues. It is believed that people of normal weight pay more attention to _____ cues than do those who are overweight. The weight that is maintained without effort to lose or gain is called the _____ _____ . During adolescence and adulthood, the basal _____ rate declines, leading to gradual weight increases over many years. Exercise burns calories, but also lowers a person's _____ _____ and increases _____ rate following exercising. The eating disorder characterized by the pursuit of thinness through starvation is called _____ _____ . A person who is consistently following a binge-and-purge eating pattern may suffer from _____ .

stomach/glucose (sugar) - p. 374
CCK - p. 374

fats/carbohydrates - p. 374
lateral/ventromedial - p.374/375
ventromedial - p. 375
lateral - p. 375

external - p. 375

internal - p. 375
set point - p. 376
metabolism - p. 377

set point - p. 378
metabolism - p. 378

anorexia nervosa - p. 378

bulimia - p. 378

Sexuality

Sex hormones are controlled by the master gland in the brain, the _____ . The main class of female hormones is the _____ . The main class of male hormones is the _____ . The pituitary gland monitors hormone levels, but it is regulated by the _____ . In higher animals, the _____ lobes of the neocortex help to moderate and direct sexual arousal. Men are more likely to _____ become sexual aroused compared to women. Women are more likely to become sexual aroused by _____ . Odorous substances released by animals that are powerful attractants are called _____ . _____ are substances that increase sexual desire and sexual capacity. There are _____ differences in sexuality that influence what is considered normal sexual behavior; examples of this are the island of Ines Beag and Mangaian culture. Sexual motivation is influenced by stereotyped expectancies of how people should behave sexually and these are called _____ and include the traditional _____ script and the _____ script. As identified by Masters and Johnson, the human sexual response pattern consists of _____ phases. Erotic responsiveness begins in the _____ phase; a continuing and heightening of sexual arousal occurs in the _____ phase; the third phase is _____ ; following orgasm, the individual enters the _____ phase. Disorders that involve impairments in the sexual response cycle are called psychosexual _____ . Although efforts at treating psychosexual dysfunctions have not been very successful, new treatments that focus directly on each _____ have led to greater success rates. The drug _____ has helped men with impotence. Kinsey conducted research on sexual behavior, but his samples were not _____ . According to more recent Canadian and American surveys of North American sexual behavior, North Americans' sexual lives are more _____ than previously believed. Many experts in the field of sexuality view sexual orientation as a _____ , ranging from exclusive heterosexuality to exclusive _____ . Some people are sexually attracted to people of both sexes and are _____ . Researchers have explored the possible biological basis of homosexuality by examining genetic, _____ , and anatomical variables. An individual's sexual orientation is most likely determined by a combination of _____ , hormonal, _____ , and environmental factors.

pituitary/estrogens - p. 380
androgens - p. 380
hypothalamus - p. 380
temporal - p. 380
quickly - p. 381

touch - p. 381
pheromones - p. 381
Aphrodisiacs - p. 381
cultural - p. 382

scripts - p. 382
religious/romantic - p. 382

4/excitement - p. 382

plateau/orgasm - p. 382-383
resolution - p. 383

dysfunctions - p. 383

dysfunction/Viagra - p. 383

representative - p. 384

conservative - p. 384

continuum - p. 385
homosexuality - p. 385
bisexual - p. 385

hormonal - p. 385

genetic/cognitive - p. 386

Achievement Motivation

Our motivation to accomplish something and to reach a standard of excellence is called the need for _____ . People with high achievement motivation take _____ risks and persist with efforts when tasks become _____ . The internal desire to be competent is called _____ motivation; motivation influenced by external rewards and punishments is called _____ motivation. Self-determination that is _____ produces a sense of personal control. We are motivated to understand the causes that underlie

achievement - p. 388
moderate - p. 388
difficult - p. 388
intrinsic - p. 389
extrinsic - p. 389
intrinsic - p. 389

behavior; this is the focus of _____ theory. An internal cause for achievement that is under an individual's control and amenable to change is _____. The best type of goal to set is one that is specific, proximal, and _____. If a person is ego-involved, he will focus on how smart he will look and his ability to outperform others. Individuals who set _____ goals focus on their ability and mastery of the task. In _____ goals, the individual will exert as little effort as possible on a task. People in North America are often more _____ than people in other countries. For studies involving ethnic minorities, _____ _____ is a better predictor of achievement than ethnicity.

attribution - p. 389

effort - p. 389
challenging - p. 389

task-involved - p. 390
work-avoidant - p. 390

achievement-motivated - p. 390
socioeconomic status - p. 392

Emotion

A feeling, or affect, that involves a mixture of physiological arousal, conscious experience, and overt behavior is called _____. The _____ nervous system regulates and monitors the body's internal organs and processes such as breathing and digestion. When the body needs to prepare for a response to a stressor, the _____ nervous system is activated. This quick response is sometimes referred to as the _____ response. It is the responsibility of the _____ nervous system to calm the body to promote relaxation and healing. A machine that tries to determine if a subject is lying by monitoring physiological changes in the body is called a _____. The principle that performance is best under moderate rather than low or high levels of arousal is the _____-_____ _____. When doing a simple task, optimal arousal is _____, whereas the optimal arousal for a difficult task is _____.

emotion - p. 393
autonomic - p. 393

sympathetic - p. 392

fight-or-flight - p. 393
parasympathetic - p. 394

polygraph - p. 394

Yerkes-Dodson law - p. 394
low - p. 394
high - p. 394

One theory of emotion holds that an individual perceives a stimulus in the environment, then the body responds, and the person interprets the body's reaction as emotion. This is the _____-_____ theory. According to the _____-_____ theory, one experiences an emotion and bodily changes _____. A part of the limbic system called the _____, is involved in emotion. Endorphins and dopamine may play roles in _____ emotions, while _____ is linked to the regulation of arousal. Cognitive theorists believe that both _____ _____ and _____ _____ are involved in emotion, as in the two-factor theory. Schachter and Singer believe that after emotional events produce physiological arousal, we look to the _____ world and then _____ the emotion. While some psychologists believe that cognitive activity is a _____ for emotion, others believe that thoughts are the _____ of emotions.

James-Lange - p. 396
Cannon-Bard - p. 396
simultaneously - p. 396
amygdala - p. 396
positive - p. 397
norepinephrine - p. 397
physiological arousal - p. 397
cognitive labeling - p. 397

external - p. 397
label - p. 397
precondition - p. 398
result - p. 398

Although much of the interest in emotion has focused on physiological and cognitive factors, emotion also takes place in a _____ context. Ekman's research has shown that the facial expressions of basic emotions are _____ across cultures and include _____, anger, _____, surprise, fear, and disgust. According to the _____ _____ _____, facial expressions may influence emotions. The _____ _____ for emotion are not universal and determine when, where, and how emotions are expressed. The _____ stereotype suggests that females are more emotional than males. Researchers have found that females and

behavioral - p. 398
universal - p. 400
happiness/sadness - p. 400
facial feedback hypothesis -p. 399/ display rules - p. 400

master - p. 401

males generally are _____ in the way they experience emotion. Female-male differences in emotion are more likely to occur in contexts that highlight _____ _____ and relationships.

      According to Plutchik, emotions have four dimensions: (1) they are positive or _____ , (2) they are _____ or mixed, (3) many are opposites, and (4) they vary in _____ . Plutchik believes that some emotions, such as happiness and disgust, are _____ emotions that can be mixed to form all the other emotions. Research on lottery winners has indicated that having more money _____ _____ lead to greater happiness. According to Diener, happiness is a reflection of the frequency of _____ emotions and the infrequency of _____ emotions. The release of anger by directly or vicariously engaging in anger or aggression is called _____ . The catharsis hypothesis states that behaving angrily or watching others do so reduces subsequent anger. Although _____ theory promotes catharsis, social cognitive theory argues against this view. Research has not supported the power of catharsis to _____ anger. Some recommended ways of controlling anger include: (1) waiting, (2) _____ with anger in other ways, (3) forming a _____ - _____ group, (4) taking action to help others, and (5) breaking out of your usual _____ .

alike - p. 401	
social roles - p. 402	
negative/primary - p. 402	
intensity - p. 402	
primary - p. 412	
does not - p. 404	
positive - p. 404	
negative - p. 404	
catharsis - p. 405	
psychoanalytic - p. 405	
reduce - p. 405	
coping - p. 405	
self-help - p. 405	
perspective - p. 405	

Explorations in Psychology

To respond to the questions and exercises presented in this section, please write your thoughts, perspectives, and reactions on a separate piece of paper.

Explorations in Psychology and Life: North America's Sexual Landscape and Its Myths

- What are several myths about sexuality that you held as you were entering sexual maturity and adulthood? How did you discover that they were not accurate?
- What advantages may exist as society confronts and rebukes myths of sexuality?
- Is there a downside to the changing sexual landscape?

Explorations in Psychology and Life: Comparing Math Achievement in Asian and North American Cultures

- As you look back to your mathematics education from elementary through high school, what strengths and weaknesses do you see? What approaches did your teachers take? Did the approach influence your motivation to learn more about mathematics?
- Are there any long-term negative effects of North American children doing poorly in math achievement compared to other countries?
- What recommendations would you make to education majors planning to teach mathematics that would assist them in improving mathematics education?

Explorations in Psychology and Life: Evaluating Lie Detectors

- Imagine this: Your supervisor at the local store where you work has wrongly accused you of stealing some money from the cash register. Based on what you've learned in this section, should you offer to take a lie detector test to clear your good name? Why?
- Do lie detector tests actually detect lying?
- What is the Guilty Knowledge Test and why is it a better way of applying the lie detector?

In Your Own Words

To respond to the questions and exercises presented in this section, please write your thoughts, perspectives, and reactions on a separate piece of paper.

✓ What instincts do we generally believe people possess?

✓ Put on paper the sequence of events as we establish homeostasis according to the drive reduction theory.

✓ List some incentives that motivate you. Are these incentives generally positive or negative?

✓ Looking at Maslow's hierarchy of motives, at what level would you estimate yourself to be? What steps could you take to help you move to the next level?

✓ In the last 24 hours, what external cues to eat have you encountered?

✓ Describe 10 activities you have engaged in the past week that meet your need for achievement. Which ones are internally or intrinsically motivated?

✓ What situations in your life have activated the sympathetic nervous system?

✓ What makes you happy? Are these things consistent with the textbook's discussion of happiness?

✓ If you were the ruler of a country, what steps would you take to help your citizens meet the needs on Maslow's hierarchy of motives? Assume you have an unlimited budget!

✓ Look at the cartoon on page 383. What is the message it sends about sexuality for men and for women?

✓ Why are you taking university courses? Relate your response to the material on achievement motivation. What internal and external factors are motivating you?

Correcting the Incorrect

Carefully read each statement. Determine if the statement is correct or incorrect. If the statement is incorrect, make the necessary changes to correct it. Then look directly under the statement for the correct statement and page reference in the textbook.

1. Motivated behavior is energized, directed, and instinctual.
   - ❏ *Motivated behavior is energized, directed, and sustained. (p. 368)*
2. Ekman argued that all human behavior involves instincts.
   - ❏ *McDougall argued that all human behavior involves instincts. (p. 368)*
3. A need is an aroused state.
   - ❏ *A drive is an aroused state. (p. 369)*
4. As a drive becomes stronger, we are motivated to reduce it.
   - ❏ *As a drive becomes stronger, we are motivated to reduce it. (p. 369)*
5. Drive pertains to a psychological state, while a need refers to an emotional state.
   - ❏ *Drive pertains to a psychological state, while a need refers to a psychological state. (p. 369)*
6. Most behaviors that we engage in attempt to reduce arousal.
   - ❏ *Many behaviors that we engage in attempt to reduce arousal. (p. 369)*
7. Incentives can only be positive stimuli or events.
   - ❏ *Incentives can be positive or negative stimuli or events. (p. 371)*
8. Self-actualization is found at the peak of Maslow's hierarchy of motives.
   - ❏ *Self-actualization is found at the peak of Maslow's hierarchy of motives. (p. 372)*
9. The stomach signals only when to start eating..
   - ❏ *The stomach signals when to start eating and when to stop eating. (p. 374)*
10. When the lateral hypothalamus of a rat is stimulated, the rat stops eating.
    - ❏ *When the lateral hypothalamus of a rat is stimulated, the rat begins eating. (p. 375)*
11. People of normal weight are more attuned to internal cues of hunger.
    - ❏ *People of normal weight are more attuned to internal cues of hunger. (p. 375)*
12. The set point is fixed and cannot be modified.
    - ❏ *The set point is not fixed and can be modified. (p. 376)*
13. Few people with anorexia nervosa grow up in families with high achievement demands.
    - ❏ *Many people with anorexia nervosa grow up in families with high achievement demands. (p. 378)*
14. Estrogens include testosterone and are produced by the testes.

❑ *Androgens include testosterone and are produced by the testes.* *(p. 380)*

15. Hormones are more important in human females than human males with regard to sexual behavior.
❑ *Hormones are less important in human females than human males with regard to sexual behavior.* *(p. 380)*

16. Pheromones are substances that arouse a person's sexual desire and capacity for sexual activity.
❑ *Aphrodisiacs are substances that arouse a person's sexual desire and capacity for sexual activity.* *(p. 381)*

17. In the romantic script for sexual behavior, sex is synonymous with lust.
❑ *In the romantic script for sexual behavior, sex is synonymous with love.* *(p. 382)*

18. The four phases of the human sexual response pattern are excitement, plateau, orgasm, and resolution.
❑ *The four phases of the human sexual response pattern are excitement, plateau, orgasm, and resolution.* *(p. 382)*

19. Homosexuality is best viewed as an either/or proposition.
❑ *Homosexuality is best viewed as a continuum.* *(p. 385)*

20. The need for achievement refers to the desire to accomplish something, to reach a standard of excellence, and to expend effort to excel.
❑ *The need for achievement refers to the desire to accomplish something, to reach a standard of excellence, and to expend effort to excel.* *(p. 388)*

21. Providing extrinsic motivation is generally preferable to intrinsic motivation.
❑ *Providing intrinsic motivation is generally preferable to extrinsic motivation.* *(p. 389)*

22. Effort is an example of an internal cause for achievement.
❑ *Effort is an example of an internal cause for achievement.* *(p. 389)*

23. Ego-involved goals lead to a focus on mastery.
❑ *Task-involved goals lead to a focus on mastery.* *(p. 390)*

24. Emotion has three parts: affect, behavioral, and physiological.
❑ *Emotion has three parts: affect, behavioral, and conscious experience.* *(p. 393)*

25. If you think someone is following you back to the dorm on a dark night, your parasympathetic nervous system is probably very active in preparing you for the fight-or-flight response.
❑ *If you think someone is following you back to the dorm on a dark night, your sympathetic nervous system is probably very active in preparing you for the fight-or-flight response.* *(p. 393)*

26. The Yerkes-Dodson law states that performance is best under conditions of moderate rather than low or high arousal.
❑ *The Yerkes-Dodson law states that performance is best under conditions of moderate rather than low or high arousal.* *(p. 394)*

27. In the James-Lange theory of emotion, emotion occurs after physiological reaction.
❑ *In the James-Lange theory of emotion, emotion occurs after physiological reaction.* *(p. 396)*

28. In the Cannon-Bard theory of emotion, physiological reaction occurs after emotion.
❑ *In the Cannon-Bard theory of emotion, physiological reaction and emotion occur simultaneously.* *(p. 396)*

29. The two-factor theory states that physiological arousal and cognitive labeling determine emotion.
❑ *The two-factor theory states that physiological arousal and cognitive labeling determine emotion.* *(p. 397)*

30. The facial feedback hypothesis predicts that smiling could lead to feeling happiness.
❑ *The facial feedback hypothesis predicts that smiling could lead to feeling happiness.* *(p. 399)*

31. Display rules are sociocultural standards of when, where, and how emotions are expressed.
❑ *Display rules are sociocultural standards of when, where, and how emotions are expressed.* *(p. 400)*

32. Plutchik suggested that emotions have six dimensions.
❑ *Plutchik suggested that emotions have four dimensions.* *(p. 402)*

33. According to the wheel model of emotion, some emotions are primary and can be mixed with others to form all other emotions.
❑ *According to the wheel model of emotion, some emotions are primary and can be mixed with others to form all other emotions.* *(p. 402)*

34. Lottery winners tend to be much happier than normal.
❑ *Lottery winners are not much happier than normal.* *(p. 404)*

35. Happiness can be understood by examining the frequency of positive emotions and frequency of negative emotions.

❏ *Happiness can be understood by examining the frequency of positive emotions and infrequency of negative emotions. (p. 404)*

36.　Faith is a factor in happiness.
　　❏ *Faith is a factor in happiness. (p. 402)*
37.　An effective way to deal with anger is catharsis.
　　❏ *An ineffective way to deal with anger is catharsis. (p. 405)*

Practice Test

1.　"The question of why individuals behave, think, and feel the way they do" defines
　　a.　motivation.
　　b.　instinct.
　　c.　emotion.
　　d.　drive.

a.	YES; this is the definition of motivation; it energizes, directs, and sustains behavior
b.	no; an instinct is an innate, biological pattern of behavior
c.	an emotion is a feeling that has physiological and behavioral components
d.	no; drive is an aroused state that occurs because of a need

2.　Psychologists who focus upon why people and organisms do what they do are studying
　　a.　association.
　　b.　cognition.
　　c.　emotion.
　　d.　motivation.

a.	no
b.	no
c.	no; an emotion is a feeling that has physiological and behavioral components
d.	CORRECT; motivation is the question the "why" behind behavior

3.　Which aspect of motivation was supported by Darwin and Freud?
　　a.　drives
　　b.　instincts
　　c.　needs
　　d.　incentives

a.	no
b.	RIGHT; Darwin and Freud believe that instincts motivate behavior
c.	no
d.	no

4.　A need is to a physiological state as a drive is to a(n)
　　a.　innate state.
　　b.　psychological state.
　　c.　physical state.
　　d.　biological state.

a.	no
b.	THAT'S GOOD; a drive involves a psychological state
c.	no
d.	no

5. Which of the following is an example of homeostasis?
   a. An organism in pain cries out loudly.
   b. A cold organism shivers to reduce heat loss.
   c. A fearful organism huddles in the corner and cries.
   d. Two friends who have been separated for months greet each other with hugs.

a.	no; there is no indication that crying loudly leads to a return to a steady state
b.	YES; homeostasis refers to the body's equilibrium or steady state
c.	there is no reference that this behavior returns the organism to equilibrium
d.	this does not involve a return to the body's equilibrium

6. Ethological theory is related to which of the following dimensions of motivation?
   a. biological
   b. cognitive
   c. sociocultural
   d. psychodynamic

a.	THIS IS CORRECT; this refers to the biological basis of behavior in natural habits
b.	cognitive dimensions are not emphasized in ethology
c.	no; sociocultural dimensions are not emphasized in ethology
d.	no; psychodynamic dimensions are not emphasized in ethology

7. If you had to write a research paper on Maslow's hierarchy of motives, which of the following titles would you choose to capture the essence of Maslow's theory?
   a. Keep those reinforcements coming.
   b. The power of the unconscious.
   c. Easy come, easy go.
   d. Be all that you can be.

a.	no; this would be more appropriate for incentives
b.	the unconscious is emphasized in psychodynamic perspective
c.	no
d.	THAT'S RIGHT; we are motivated to become self-actualized

8. The highest and most elusive of needs, according to Maslow, is
   a. self-esteem.
   b. self-actualization.
   c. love and belongingness.
   d. safety.

a.	no; this is second from the top of the hierarchy
b.	YES; this refers to developing one's full potential and sits on top of the hierarchy
c.	no, this is third from the top of the hierarchy
d.	no; this is fourth from the top of the hierarchy

9. Which of the following is a peripheral factor involved in hunger?
   a. stomach contractions
   b. blood sugar
   c. sugar receptors in the liver
   d. all of the above

a.	no; but you're partially correct
b.	no; but you're partially correct
c.	no; but you're partially correct
d.	YES; all of these are peripheral factors involved in hunger

10. Which intervention would cause a rat to become obese?
    a.   destroy the ventromedial hypothalamus
    b.   stimulate the ventromedial hypothalamus
    c.   enhance the ventromedial hypothalamus
    d.   stimulate the mid-sagital hippocampus

a.	CORRECT; this area is involved in reducing hunger and restricting eating
b.	no; to stimulate the area leads to a reduction in hunger and restriction of eating
c.	no; the ventromedial hypothalamus is either destroyed or stimulated, not enhanced
d.	no

11. According to current views, which of the following is not an important factor in obesity?
    a.   social influences
    b.   neurotransmitter balance
    c.   cognitive processing
    d.   biological predisposition

a.	no; social influence plays a very information role in obesity
b.	YEP, THAT'S RIGHT; these is the least important factor in obesity
c.	cognitive processing does play an important role in obesity
d.	no; biological predisposition is important

12. According to statistics, which of the following is at highest risk for anorexia nervosa?
    a.   21-year-old White university student who works 30 hours a week to pay for school
    b.   18-year-old African American female whose parents are both teachers
    c.   16-year-old Hispanic female who works at a fast food place after school
    d.   15-year-old White female whose parents are both lawyers

a.	no; this person does not have the highest risk
b.	no; this person does not have the highest risk
c.	no; this person does not have the highest risk
d.	CORRECT; this person has the most risk factors (age, race, family background)

13. When it comes to sex, as we move from animals to humans,
    a.   the role of hormones becomes less clear.
    b.   hormonal control over sexual behavior disappears.
    c.   cognitive factors become less important.
    d.   sexuality becomes less variable.

a.	THAT'S RIGHT; sexual behavior in humans is individualized and variable
b.	no; hormones do play some role in sexuality; what the role is remains unclear
c.	no; cognitive factors play a greater part in human sexuality than in animals
d.	no; in fact there is great variability in human sexuality

14. People's ability to control their sexual behavior relates most strongly to
    a.   sensory factors.
    b.   perceptual factors.
    c.   social factors.
    d.   cognitive factors.

a.	no; sensory factors play a lesser role in our ability to control sexual behavior
b.	no; perceptual factors play a role in sexual behavior, but probably not in its control
c.	no; while important, social factors are not most strongly related to control
d.	RIGHT; our ability to think about sexuality can control our sexual behavior

15. A man is more likely than a woman to link sexual intercourse with
    a. love.
    b. conquest.
    c. commitment.
    d. attachment.

a.	no; females are more likely to link intercourse with love	
b.	YES; the script for men suggests that men emphasize sexual conquest	
c.	no	
d.	no	

16. As males get older, they can expect which of the following?
    a. a longer refractory period
    b. more intense orgasms
    c. a shorter plateau phase
    d. no orgasms

a.	YES; men enter a refractory period in which they cannot have another orgasm	
b.	no	
c.	no	
d.	no; as males get older they continue to have orgasms	

17. Which of the following is true regarding the refractory period?
    a. Only males experience a refractory period.
    b. Only females experience a refractory period.
    c. Males and females both experience a refractory period.
    d. The refractory period occurs immediately following the excitement phase.

a.	THAT'S RIGHT; men a period of time when they cannot have another orgasm	
b.	no; females may experience several orgasms without delay	
c.	no; males only experience a refractory period	
d.	no; the refractory period follows orgasm	

18. The treatment of sexual dysfunctions has been largely
    a. successful using traditional forms of psychotherapy.
    b. successful using treatments that focus directly on the dysfunction.
    c. unsuccessful regardless of the treatment.
    d. successful when they are treated as personality disorders.

a.	no; these treatments have not been successful	
b.	YES; treatment that focuses directly on the dysfunction are very effective	
c.	no; there are successful treatments that focus directly on the dysfunction	
d.	these treatments are ineffective	

19. _____ is a drug that is designed to treat impotence.
    a. Viagra
    b. Prozac
    c. Rogaine
    d. none of the above

a.	RIGHT; Viagra has a success rate of about 60-80%	
b.	no; Prozac is an antidepressant	
c.	no; Rogaine is a baldness remedy	
d.	no	

20. If male homosexuals are given androgens, their sexual
   a. desire decreases.
   b. orientation changes.
   c. orientation does not change.
   d. desire increases.

a.	no
b.	no
c.	YES; this suggests that the role of hormones in homosexuality is unclear
d.	no

21. A child who cleans up his room every day so he can receive his two-dollar allowance on Saturday is
   a. self-actualizing.
   b. extrinsically motivated.
   c. intrinsically motivated.
   d. probably a Type B personality.

a.	no; self-actualization refers to fulfilling one's potential
b.	THIS IS CORRECT; extrinsic motivation involves external rewards for doing a task
c.	no; intrinsic motivation involves internal rewards for a task
d.	no; Type B personality actually describes someone who is laid back and calm

22. The desire to do a job well for its own sake is called
   a. extrinsic motivation.
   b. intrinsic motivation.
   c. the Yerkes-Dodson law.
   d. ethological motivation.

a.	no; extrinsic motivation refers to an external reward for doing a job well
b.	YES; this illustrates intrinsic motivation since the desire is internal
c.	no; this refers to the relationship between performance and arousal
d.	no

23. When first-graders work hard on a project in order to collect praise and gold stars from their teacher, what kind of motivation are they demonstrating?
   a. achievement motivation
   b. competence motivation
   c. extrinsic motivation
   d. intrinsic motivation

a.	while children may what to accomplish something, this is not the best option
b.	no
c.	YES; the children are receiving praise and gold stars, both of which are external
d.	no; the rewards are external

24. When both ethnicity and socioeconomic status are taken into account, the best predictor of achievement is
   a. race.
   b. socioeconomic status.
   c. ethnicity.
   d. none of the above

a.	no
b.	THAT'S RIGHT; all middle SES individuals have higher aspirations
c.	no
d.	no

25. Emotion is defined as
   a. a feeling that involves physiological arousal, conscious experience, and behavioral expression.
   b. a feeling that involves physiological arousal.
   c. physiological arousal
   d. behavior that involves facial expressions

a.	RIGHT; these characteristics define emotion
b.	no; emotion includes other components
c.	no; but you're partially correct
d.	no; there's more to emotion that this option

26. According to the Yerkes-Dodson law, your performance on an exam will be best if you are
   a. extremely aroused.
   b. minimally aroused.
   c. moderately aroused.
   d. extremely happy.

a.	too much arousal will impair your performance
b.	no; too little arousal will impair your performance
c.	THAT'S RIGHT; moderate arousal tends to maximize performance
d.	no; the Yerkes-Dodson law describes arousal and performance, not happiness

27. According to the James-Lange theory, an environmental stimulus
   a. is perceived as emotional by the hypothalamus.
   b. triggers emotional arousal, which is labeled by the brain.
   c. is emotional because of cultural and social expectations.
   d. causes arousal if it appears threatening.

a.	the Cannon-Bard theory of emotion includes the hypothalamus
b.	RIGHT; emotional arousal is interpreted or labeled by the brain to create emotion
c.	no; this theory doesn't directly include cultural and social expectations
d.	no; the brain first interprets arousal before anything is perceived as threatening

28. According to Schachter and Singer, the specific emotion we experience depends on the
   a. rate of firing of fibers leading from the hypothalamus to the neocortex.
   b. amount of serotonin released in the peripheral nervous system
   c. specific pattern of heart rate, blood pressure, and skin resistance.
   d. environmental circumstances to which we attribute our arousal.

a.	no; this is not relevant in this theory
b.	no; Schachter and Singer do not consider serotonin
c.	no; the pattern of arousal is less important than the external cues for it
d.	THIS IS RIGHT; we look for reasons or external cues to explain our arousal

29. The Cannon-Bard theory predicts that after witnessing a shocking event, a person will
    a. first experience shock and then be motivated to turn away.
    b. be motivated to turn away and then will experience shock.
    c. experience cathartic shock as a release of anxiety.
    d. experience physical and emotional reactions simultaneously.

a.	no
b.	no; this option sounds more like James-Lange theory
c.	no
d.	RIGHT; this theory says that physiological arousal and the emotion are experienced at the same time

30. Researchers have found universality in each of the following except
    a. facial expressions of happiness.
    b. facial expressions of fear.
    c. facial expressions of surprise.
    d. facial expression of contentment.

a.	happiness is expressed in a universal way
b.	fear is expressed in a universal way
c.	surprise is expressed in a universal way
d.	RIGHT; contentment is not expressed in a universal way

31. Bill was raised to believe that males should not cry in public except at an immediate relative's funeral. Bill adheres to these
    a. flow responses.
    b. display rules.
    c. stereotypes.
    d. set points.

a.	no
b.	AYE; display rules are sociocultural standards that determine when, where, and how emotions should be expressed
c.	no
d.	no

32. Plutchik suggests that our emotions can be classified according to four dimensions. Which of the following is not one of the four?
    a. Emotions are primary or mixed.
    b. Emotions are strong or weak.
    c. Emotions are bright or dull.
    d. Emotions are positive or negative.

a.	emotions can be primary or mixed
b.	no; emotions can be strong or weak
c.	RIGHT; Plutchik does not classify emotions in this way
d.	no; emotions can be positive or negative

33. According to Plutchik, mixing primary emotions leads to
    a. psychological difficulties.
    b. polar opposites.
    c. other emotions.
    d. negative emotions.

34. Anthony expected to get a nice raise after having had the most sales in his department for the past year. When Anthony found out the amount of his raise, he considered it "unfair." Anthony was most likely
    a. sad.
    b. happy.
    c. satisfied.
    d. angry.

a.	no; sadness is not likely
b.	no; Anthony is not likely to be happy
c.	no
d.	GOOD; angry is most likely the result of when we believe we have been treated unfairly or when expectations are violated

35. What is the main problem with using polygraph results as an indication of whether or not a person is lying?
    a. Different emotions can cause the same physiological changes.
    b. Most people can camouflage their response patterns.
    c. Examiners are usually biased against the person being tested.
    d. The accuracy rate of polygraphs is very low.

a.	YES; guilt, anxiety, and worry can create the same physiological response
b.	only some people can camouflage their response patterns
c.	there's no evidence that examiners are biased
d.	this may be true, but there is a problem underlying the accuracy rate

Chapter 12 - Personality

The Big Picture: Chapter Overview

     Personality refers to our enduring, distinctive thoughts, emotions, and behaviors, which characterize the way we adapt to our world. Some theorists believe that biological and genetic factors are responsible for our personality, whereas others hold that life experiences are more important. Some theorists stress the importance of how we think about ourselves; other theorists focus on how we behave toward each other. The psychoanalytic view sees personality as primarily unconscious, occurring in stages, and being linked to early experiences. Freud believed that much more of our mind is unconscious than conscious, and that the unconscious was the key to understanding personality. According to Freud, personality has three structures: the id, the ego, and the superego. The id houses biological instincts, is completely unconscious, and operates according to the pleasure principle. The ego operates according to the reality principle and the superego is the moral branch of the personality. The conflicting demands of the personality structures produce anxiety. In response to the anxiety, the ego uses defense mechanisms as protective methods to resolve conflicts and reduce the anxiety. Defense mechanisms include repression, which is the most powerful and pervasive defense mechanism. When used in moderation or on a temporary basis, defense mechanisms are not unhealthy; defense mechanism are also unconscious and we are not aware of their use.

     Freud argued that we go through five psychosexual stages and at each stage we experience pleasure in one part of the body more than in others; these body parts are known as erogenous zones. Freud maintained that adult problems stem primarily from early childhood experiences. The five psychosexual stages we go through are oral, anal, phallic, latency, and genital stages. We can become fixated at any stage if our needs are under- or overgratified. The main objections to Freud's theory are his overemphasis on sexuality and on the events of the first 5 years of life. Other objections are that sociocultural factors are more important than Freud believed and that the ego and conscious thought are more important. One Freud revisionist, Karen Horney, rejected the notion that "Anatomy is destiny." She emphasized the need for security as a prime motivator. Jung, a contemporary of Freud's, emphasized the collective unconscious and archetypes or ideas and images; another contemporary, Adler, believed that we can consciously monitor and direct our lives. The concepts of striving for superiority, inferiority complex, superiority complex, and compensation are important in Adler's individual psychology. Concepts in the psychoanalytic perspective that seem to be validated are the importance of early experiences in shaping personality, understanding personality developmentally, and how we mentally transform environmental experiences. The main concepts of psychoanalysis have been difficult to test since they involve inference and interpretation.

     Behaviorists believe that personality is observable behavior learned through experience with the environment. Social cognitive theorists emphasize person/cognitive factors in personality. Behaviorism asserts that the external environment determines an individual's behavior and that if the environment changes, so too does behavior. Social cognitive theory focuses on behavior, environment, and person/cognitive factors and how these three factors interact in determining personality. Bandura's emphasis on observational learning and Mischel's research on delay of gratification illustrate the cognitive aspects of social cognitive theory. One criticism of the behavioral perspective is of the view that cognitive factors play no role in behavior, with too much emphasis placed on environmental factors. The behavioral and social cognitive points of view have been criticized for being too concerned with change and for ignoring the biological determinants of personality.

     The humanistic perspective stresses the importance of people's capacity for personal growth, freedom to choose their destinies, and for their positive qualities. Rogers' approach suggests that each of us is a victim of conditional positive regard. As a result, our real self is not valued as positively as it should be. Rogers advocated unconditional positive regard to enhance our self-concept. A more positive self-concept can be achieved by showing unconditional positive regard, empathy, and genuineness. When our real self and ideal self are different, we fail to become fully functioning people. According to Maslow, people strive for self-actualization. Maslow believed that human needs can be arranged in a hierarchy of motives, with self-actualization as the motivation to develop one's full potential as a human being. An important component of personality is self-esteem, which is the evaluative and affection dimension of self-concept. Self-esteem can be improved through achievement and coping. While the humanistic perspective reminds us of the importance of the whole person, its concepts are difficult to test scientifically.

Trait theories suggest that personality is best understood by studying the organization of traits within the person. Traits are broad dispositions that lead to characteristic responses. Allport and Eysenck are trait theorists. Allport grouped traits into cardinal traits, central traits, and secondary traits depending upon how influential they were within the individual. Eysenck found three dimensions that explain personality: introversion-extraversion, stable-unstable, psychoticism. Recent analysis has revealed the existence of the Big Five factors of personality: emotional stability, extroversion, openness, agreeableness, and conscientiousness. These Big Five factors may be able to predict physical and mental health. The trait perspective argues that personality is consistent across situations and time. However, according to situationism, personality often varies considerably from one context to another. A view of personality called interactionism suggests that both person and situation variables are necessary to understand personality.

Some assessments of personality from palmistry include Barnum statements. Psychologists have conducted empirical research into many areas of personality. Psychologists use a number of tests and measures to assess personality. Projective tests present the individual with an ambiguous stimulus and then ask for a description or story. Two projective tests are the Rorschach Inkblot Test and the Thematic Apperception Test. Self-report tests are used to assess personality by asking individuals whether items describe their personality. Tests which select items that predict a particular criterion are called empirically keyed tests, are not based on face validity, and attempt to control social desirability. A widely used self-report test is the Minnesota Multiphasic Personality Inventory (MMPI). The MMPI-2 has four validity scales and 10 clinical scales. The Big Five factors can also be assessed using self-report tests. Behavioral assessment is an approach that observes an individual's behavior directly. Cognitive assessment is used to determine what thoughts underlie behavior.

Three important issues pertaining to personality theories are (1) whether personality is innate or learned, (2) whether personality is conscious or unconscious, and (3) whether personality is due to internal or external determinants.

Learning Objectives

When you have studied the material in this chapter, you should be able to:

1. define personality. (p. 412)
2. summarize the psychoanalytic perspective of Freud. (pp. 413-414)
3. describe the following Freudian personality structures: id, ego, and superego. (p.415)
4. list and identify Freudian defense mechanisms. (pp. 415-417)
5. describe each of Freud's psychosexual stages of development. (pp. 417-419)
6. discuss the Freudian concept of the Oedipus complex. (p. 418)
7. summarize criticisms of Freud's theories. (p. 419)
8. discuss modifications of Freud's theories by each of the following theorists: Horney, Jung, and Adler. (pp. 419-421)
9. critically evaluate the psychoanalytic perspective. (p. 421-422)
10. describe the behavioral and social cognitive theory approaches to personality. (pp. 423-424)
11. define Bandura's concepts of reciprocal determinism, self-efficacy, and observational learning. (p. 424)
12. describe the humanistic perspectives of personality and distinguish between the perspectives of Carl Rogers and Abraham Maslow. (pp. 425-428)
13. distinguish between the following humanistic concepts: self and ideal self, self-actualization, and self-esteem. (pp. 427-429)
14. describe trait theories. (pp. 429-430)
15. distinguish between the trait theories of Gordon Allport and Hans Eysenck. (pp. 430-431)
16. list and describe the "Big Five" personality traits. (p. 431-432)

17. explain situationism and trait-situation interactionism. (pp. 442-443)
18. describe the philosophy behind projective tests such as the Rorschach and TAT. (pp. 435-436)
19. distinguish between projective tests and self-report tests such as the MMPI, NEO-PI-R, HPI, and the Jackson Personality Inventory. (pp. 435-438)
20. evaluate the pros and cons of self-report tests. (p. 439)
21. describe the characteristics of behavioral and cognitive assessment. (p. 439)
22. relate the different personality approaches to the following issues: innate versus learned, conscious versus, unconscious, and internal versus external determinants. (pp. 439-442)
23. from *Explorations in Psychology: Freud, da Vinci and Dali*, describe the relationship between these artists and Freudian theory. (p. 414)
24. from *Explorations in Psychology: Freud's Oedipus Complex: Cultural and Gender Biases*, summarize information demonstrating gender and cultural bias in Freud's Oedipus theory. (p. 418)
25. from *Explorations in Psychology: Being skeptical about Graphology*, evaluate arguments as to the legitimacy of determining personality characteristics based on handwriting. (p. 437)

Guided Review

What is Personality?

The enduring, distinctive thoughts, emotions, and behaviors that characterize the way an individual adapts to the world is what psychologists call _____ . In trying to understand the "why" of our behavior, some personality theorists believe that biological and _____ factors are responsible, whereas other theorists hold that _____ _____ are more important.

personality - p. 412

genetic - p. 412
life experiences - p. 422

Personality Perspectives

Personality from the _____ perspective is seen as primarily unconscious and as occurring in stages; this perspective also views _____ experiences as important. Freud was a medical doctor who developed his ideas for his theory from his work with _____ patients. Freud believed that much more of our mind is _____ than conscious. Even trivial behaviors may have a special unconscious meaning; sometimes they emerge in our behavior without our awareness, a situation known as a _____ _____ . Freud also believed that _____ are unconscious representations of the conflicts and tension in our everyday lives. According to Freud, personality has _____ structures. One, which is a reservoir of psychic energy and instincts and continually presses to satisfy our basic needs, is called the _____ . The id works according to the _____ _____ . As a child experiences the demands and constraints of reality, a second personality structure called the _____ is formed. The ego tries to bring pleasure to the individual within the boundaries of society, a concept called the _____ _____ . The third personality structure, the moral branch, is called the _____ . The superego corresponds to our _____ . The demands for reality, the wishes of the id, and the constraints of the superego produce _____ . One way to resolve these conflicts is by means of _____ mechanisms. The most powerful and pervasive defense mechanism is _____ . This works by pushing id impulses out of awareness into our _____ mind. When the real motive for an individual's behavior is replaced by a "cover" motive, this is called _____ . The shifting of unacceptable feelings from one object to a more acceptable object is called _____ . A type of displacement that occurs when a socially useful course of action replaces a distasteful one is _____ . When we attribute our own shortcomings and problems to others, this is referred to as _____ .

When we express an unacceptable impulse by transforming it into its opposite, this is _____ _____ . Reverting back to behaviors characteristic of a previous level of development is called _____ . Defense mechanisms are unconscious and not necessarily unhealthy when used in _____ . Freud believed that individuals experience pleasure in different parts of the body at different stages of development; he called these body parts _____ _____ . If an individual's needs at any level of development are under- or overgratified, the result is a _____ . During the first 18

psychoanalytic - p. 413

early - p. 413

psychiatric - p. 413
unconscious – p. 413

Freudian slip - p. 413
dreams - p. 412

3 - p. 415

id - p. 415
pleasure principle - p. 415

ego - p. 415
reality principle - p. 415

superego/conscience - p. 415

conflict - p. 415
defense - p. 415
repression - p. 416
unconscious - p. 416

rationalization - p. 416
displacement - p. 416

sublimation - p. 416
projection - p. 416

reaction formation - p. 416

regression - p. 416
moderation - p. 417

erogenous zones - p. 417

fixation - p. 417

months of life, a child is in the _____ stage of development; the most pleasurable activities at this stage center around the _____ . From age 1 1/2 to 3, the child is in the _____ stage; the child's greatest pleasure centers around the _____ function. During the next stage, the _____ stage, pleasure centers on the _____ . It is during this period that the _____ _____ develops. From age 6 until puberty, the child represses all interest in sexual urges and is said to be in the _____ stage. The final stage, which begins at puberty, is concerned with feelings for someone outside the

_____ .
The key objections to Freud's theory are (1) that the pervasive force behind personality is not _____ , (2) the first _____ years of life are not as powerful in shaping personality, (3) the ego and _____ thought play more important roles than Freud believed, and (4) _____ factors are more important than Freud believed. Karen Horney's approach emphasized _____ factors in development. She also believed that the prime motive in human existence was for _____ . She suggested that people usually develop one of the following strategies to cope with anxiety: they either move _____ people, _____ from people, or _____ people. Chodorow's feminist revision of psychoanalytic theory emphasized that women are more likely than men to define themselves in terms of their _____ , while many men use _____ in regard to their relationships. Jung's approach involved the belief that the roots of our personality go back to the beginning of human existence Jung called this common heritage the _____ _____ , and the impressions they have made in the mind were called _____ . Two common archetypes are _____ and animus. Adler's theory, which focused on the uniqueness of every person, is called _____ psychology. He disputed Freud's emphasis on sexual motivation, believing we can _____ monitor our lives. According to Adler, all individuals strive for _____ . In order to overcome real or imagined weaknesses, we use _____ . An exaggerated effort to conceal a weakness is called _____ . A person who exaggerates feelings of inadequacy has an inferiority complex, whereas a person who exaggerates self-importance to mask feelings of inferiority has a _____ complex.

Although many psychologists agree that early experiences are important determinants of personality and that personality should be studied developmentally, the main concepts of psychoanalytic theories have been difficult to _____ . Another criticism of the psychoanalytic perspective is that it portrays people in a _____ light. Behaviorists believe that psychology should examine only what can be directly _____ and measured. Skinner concluded that personality is the individual's _____ , which is determined by the _____ environment; and it does not include _____ or _____ processes. Since personality is learned in the environment, behaviorists believe that changes in the _____ can change an individual's personality. Social cognitive theorists emphasize behavior, environment, and _____ as the key factors in personality. These factors _____ in determining personality. Social cognitive theorists believe that we acquire much of our personality by _____ the behavior of others. They also believe that we can _____ our own behavior. A prominent social cognitive theorist, Walter Mischel, believes that delay of _____ is important in understanding personality. The behavior and social cognitive points of view have been criticized for being too concerned with _____ and for ignoring the _____ determinants of personality.

An approach that stresses the importance of our personal growth, people's positive qualities, and our freedom is the _____ approach. Carl Rogers, a humanistic psychologist, believed that love and praise are often not given unless we conform to _____ or social standards; thus, each of us is a victim of _____ _____ regard. Through an individual's experiences of the world, a _____ emerges. _____-_____ refers to individuals' overall perceptions of their abilities, behaviors, and personalities. Maladjustment results when there are large discrepancies between our _____ self and our _____ self. Rogers believed we should all be valued and feel accepted regardless of our behavior, a situation called _____ _____ regard . Rogers also believed that individuals can develop a positive self-concept if others are _____ and _____ . Rogers stressed the importance of becoming a _____ _____ person. Abraham Maslow, who called the humanistic approach the " _____ _____," believed that people strive for self-actualization. According to Maslow, human needs are arranged in a _____ of motives, ranging from the most basic needs to _____ needs. Self-_____ refers to our evaluative and affective dimension of self-concept. Four ways to improve self-esteem are: identifying the causes of low self-esteem, _____ support and approval, achievement and _____ . A weakness of the humanistic approach is that it is very difficult to test _____ .

_____ theories suggest that personality consists of broad dispositions to respond in particular ways. According to Allport, each of us is unique because of our _____ _____ . Allport argued that traits could be grouped into _____, _____, and _____ . Eysenck found that personality could be explained by three dimensions: introversion-extraversion, stable-unstable, and _____ . Recent studies have revealed the existence of the _____ _____ factors of personality, including emotional _____ , extroversion, _____ , agreeableness and conscientiousness. Research has also focused on the role of the five factors in different cultures and predicting health. One criticism of the trait approach suggests that personality varies extensively from one context to another, a view called _____ . Many psychologists in the field today believe that both person and situation variables are necessary in understanding personality; that is, they are _____ . Cross-cultural psychologists suggest that personality is best understood by considering both the immediate setting and the broader context.

Personality Assessment

"If you make your predictions broad enough, any person can fit the description"; this is the _____ _____ . The personality tests chosen for use by a psychologist frequently depend on the psychologist's _____ orientation. Also, most personality tests measure _____ characteristics. Some tests present individuals with an ambiguous stimulus and then ask for a description or story. These tests are called _____ tests. The purpose of projective tests is to elicit _____ behaviors and conflicts. A well-known projective tests is the _____ _____ Test. Another projective test, which consists of a series of ambiguous pictures about which individuals are asked to tell a story, is the _____ _____ Test. A projective test that uses handwriting analysis to determine an individual's personality traits by asking individuals about their traits is called _____ test. Although many clinical psychologists use the test, researchers have found it to have low _____ and _____ .

Although many early self-report tests were constructed using _____ _____ , these assume that individuals respond honestly. However, even if an individual is honest, he or she may be giving _____ _____ answers. Tests that select items that predict a particular criterion are called _____ _____ tests. A widely used self-report personality test used originally with mentally disturbed patients is the _____ _____ Personality Inventory (MMPI). Much research has found that the MMPI is able to improve the diagnosis of _____ _____ individuals. An assessment technique that observes an individual's behavior directly is called _____ _____ . A test that asks an individual what her thoughts were before getting angry would be an example of _____ assessment.

Comparing Personality Perspectives

Three important issues pertaining to personality theories are (1) whether personality is _____ or learned, (2) whether personality is conscious or _____ , and (3) whether personality is due to _____ or _____ determinants.

Barnum effect - p. 434

theoretical - p. 434
stable (enduring) - p. 435

projective - p. 435
unconscious - p. 435
Rorschach Inkblot - p. 435

Thematic Apperception - p. 435

graphology - p. 436
reliability/validity - p. 436

face validity - p. 436

socially desirable - p. 436
empirically keyed - p. 436

Minnesota Multiphasic - p. 437

mentally disturbed - p. 437-438

behavioral assessment - p. 439

cognitive - p. 439

innate - p. 439
unconscious - p. 440
internal/external - p. 440

Explorations in Psychology

To respond to the questions and exercises presented in this section, please write your thoughts, perspectives, and reactions on a separate piece of paper.

Explorations in Psychology and Life: Freud, da Vinci, and Dali

- How do you react to Freud's assertion that art reflects unconscious wishes?
- What do you think Leonardo da Vinci would say if he found out how Freud evaluated *Mona Lisa*?
- Do you think Freud would also argue that the little pictures or doodles we draw on paper reflect unconscious wishes? Why?
- If Freud were alive today, how would he analyze today's contemporary music?

Explorations in Psychology and Life: Freud's Oedipus Complex: Cultural and Gender Biases

- Given Freud's influence on our culture, what effects has Freud's idea of the Oedipus complex had on how we view males and females and their roles?
- How might Freud react to the study by Malinowski regarding failure to find the Oedipus complex in Trobriand islanders of the Western Pacific?
- The textbook makes the statement, "Many psychologists believed Freud placed far too much emphasis on anatomy's role in personality development." In your view, does anatomy of any kind have any role in personality development?

Explorations in Psychology and Life: Being Skeptical About Graphology

- Why is graphology so readily embraced as a way to assess personality in light of the poor scientific evidence?
- In what way would other pieces of information such as age, gender, autobiographical statements, influence the graphologist's evaluation of a person's handwriting?
- If you were applying for a job and asked to provide a sample of handwriting for analysis, what would be your response? Why?

In Your Own Words

To respond to the questions and exercises presented in this section, please write your thoughts, perspectives, and reactions on a separate piece of paper.

✓ Describe your personality. As you look over what you've written, what perspective have you used to understand your personality?
✓ How would Freud react to you if you said the psychoanalytic perspective was totally wrong and actually represented Freud's own anxieties and conflicts? (Hint: Keep in mind the defense mechanisms!)
✓ Which personality perspective is the "right" one?
✓ Paraphrase the textbook's definition of personality.
✓ Of the names presented in this chapter, which one did you recognize? In what context did you hear that name before?
✓ Look at Figure 12.2 describing defense mechanisms. Select three of them and develop your own examples more relevant to your experiences.
✓ Are there any aspects of the five Freudian stages that you've seen in others?
✓ Describe an experience where your personality was reciprocally determined by behavior, environment, person/cognitive factors.
✓ List some behaviors of others that exemplify conditional positive regard and unconditional positive regard.
✓ Discuss some situations or contexts in which your behavior can change from being shy to being outgoing. How does this relate to situationism?

Correcting the Incorrect

Carefully read each statement. Determine if the statement is correct or incorrect. If the statement is incorrect, make the necessary changes to correct it. Then look directly under the statement for the correct statement and page reference in the textbook.

1.   Personality consists of behavior.
   ❑ *Personality consists of behavior, thoughts, and emotions. (p. 412).*
2.   Much of the information contained in the various personality perspectives is contradictory.
   ❑ *Much of the information contained in the various personality perspectives is complementary. (p. 412)*
3.   The humanistic perspective argues that personality is primarily unconscious.
   ❑ *The psychoanalytic perspective argues that personality is primarily unconscious. (p. 413)*

4. From the psychoanalytic perspective, it is not important to understand the unconscious mind.
   - ❑ *From the psychoanalytic perspective, it is important to understand the unconscious mind. (p. 413)*
5. In developing his theory, Freud conducted scientifically rigorous and well-controlled studies.
   - ❑ *In developing his theory, Freud observed psychiatric patients. (p. 413)*
6. According to Freud, our mind is mostly conscious rather than unconscious.
   - ❑ *According to Freud, our mind is mostly unconscious rather than conscious. (p. 415)*
7. The id refers to the structure of personality that deals with the demands of reality.
   - ❑ *The ego refers to the structure of personality that deals with the demands of reality. (p. 415)*
8. For Freud, personality is very much like an iceberg.
   - ❑ *For Freud, mind is very much like an iceberg. (p. 415)*
9. Regression is the most powerful and pervasive defense mechanism.
   - ❑ *Repression is the most powerful and pervasive defense mechanism. (p. 416)*
10. Fixation occurs when the individual remains locked in a stage because needs are undergratified.
    - ❑ *Fixation occurs when the individual remains locked in a stage because needs are undergratified or overgratified. (p. 417)*
11. The order of the stages in the psychoanalytic perspective is oral, phallic, anal, genital, and latency.
    - ❑ *The order of the stages in the psychoanalytic perspective is oral, anal, phallic, latency, and genital. (p. 417)*
12. During the genital stage, young childen experience the Oedipus complex.
    - ❑ *During the phallic stage, young children experience the Oedipus complex. (p. 418)*
13. Research has found that sexuality is the pervasive underlying force behind personality.
    - ❑ *Research has found that sexuality is not the pervasive underlying force behind personality (p. 419)*
14. Horney emphasized the role of the collective unconscious.
    - ❑ *Jung emphasized the role of the collective unconscious. (p. 420)*
15. An archetype can be an emotionally-laden idea or image in the collective unconscious.
    - ❑ *An archetype can be an emotionally-laden idea or image in the collective unconscious. (p. 420)*
16. Overcompensation, according to Jung, describes what a person does to overcome imagined or real inferiorities by developing one's abilities.
    - ❑ *Compensation, according to Adler, describes what a person does to overcome imagined or real inferiorities by developing one's abilities. (p. 421)*
17. For Skinner, personality is behavior.
    - ❑ *For Skinner, personality is behavior. (p. 423)*
18. The behavioral perspective argues that unconscious motives determine personality.
    - ❑ *The behavioral perspective argues that the environment determine personality. (p. 423)*
19. In social cognitive theory, there are reciprocal influences of behavior, environment, and person/cognitive factors.
    - ❑ *In social cognitive theory, there are reciprocal influences of behavior, environment, and person/cognitive factors. (p. 424)*
20. The humanistic perspective stresses the importance of observable behavior and environmental influences on personality.
    - ❑ *The humanistic perspective stresses personal growth, freedom to choose, and positive qualities. (p. 425)*
21. Conditional positive regard refers to love and praise being withheld unless the person conforms to parental or social standards.
    - ❑ *Conditional positive regard refers to love and praise being withheld unless the person conforms to parental or social standards. (p. 426)*
22. Self-concept and self-esteem refer to the same thing--a person's overall perceptions of their abilities, behavior, and personality.
    - ❑ *Self-concept and self-esteem do not refer to the same thing— self-concept refers to a person's overall perceptions of their abilities, behavior, and personality while self-esteem refers to the evaluative and affective dimension of self-concept. (p. 426-427)*
23. Self-actualization refers to the ability to satisfy all the lower motives in Maslow's hierarchy of motives.
    - ❑ *Self-actualization refers to motivation to develop one's full potential. (p. 427).*

24. Cardinal traits are those limited traits that rarely are shown.
    ❑ *Secondary traits are those limited traits that rarely are shown. (p. 431)*
25. Personality varies across situations.
    ❑ *Personality varies across situations. (p. 432)*
26. Situationism means that the situation has little impact on personality.
    ❑ *Situationism means that the situation has much impact on personality. (p. 432)*
27. Mischel has attacked social cognitive theory, arguing that both person and situation variables are important in understanding personality.
    ❑ *Mischel has attacked trait theory, arguing that both person and situation variables are important in understanding personality. (p. 432)*
28. The Barnum effect refers to broad predictions that are most likely to be true.
    ❑ *The Barnum effect refers to broad predictions that are most likely to be true. (p. 434)*
29. The types of assessment that involve ambiguous stimuli are referred to as objective tests.
    ❑ *The types of assessment that involve ambiguous stimuli are referred to as projective tests. (p. 435)*
30. Most psychologists agree that the Rorschach Inkblot Test meets the criteria of reliability and validity.
    ❑ *Most psychologists agree that the Rorschach Inkblot Test does not meet the criteria of reliability and validity. (p. 435)*
31. The Rorschach Inkblot Test and the Thematic Apperception Test are examples of empirically keyed tests.
    ❑ *The Rorschach Inkblot Test and the Thematic Apperception Test are examples of projective tests. (p. 435)*
32. The test that was developed by giving many statements to both mental patients and normal people was the MMPI.
    ❑ *The test that was developed by giving many statements to both mental patients and normal people was the MMPI. (p. 438)*
33. Behavioral assessment focuses on directly observing an individual's behavior.
    ❑ *Behavioral assessment focuses on directly observing an individual's behavior. (p. 439)*
34. All personality perspectives see personality as being externally determined.
    ❑ *Some personality perspectives see personality as being externally determined. (p. 440, p. 441)*

Practice Test

1. Which of the following is part of the definition of personality?
   a. thoughts
   b. emotions
   c. behaviors
   d. all of the above

a.	no; but you're close
b.	no; however emotions are a part of personality
c.	no; you are only partially correct
d.	GOOD; personality is made up of thoughts, emotions, and behaviors

2. According to psychoanalytic theorists, personality is primarily
   a. unconscious.
   b. shaped by self-actualization
   c. conscious.
   d. acquired through reinforcement and punishment.

a.	THAT'S RIGHT; personality is shaped by unconscious processes
b.	no; this sounds too much like the humanistic perspective
c.	no; remember that personality is mostly out of awareness
d.	no; this option describes the behavioral viewpoint

3. According to Freud, which part of the personality is dominated by the pleasure principle?
   a. the id
   b. the conscience
   c. the ego
   d. the superego

a.	RIGHT; the id is dominated by the pleasure principle
b.	no
c.	no; the ego operates according to the reality principle
d.	no; the superego is often describe as being our conscience

4. According to Freud, the executive branch of the personality is called the
   a. ego.
   b. superego.
   c. id.
   d. conscience.

a.	RIGHT; the ego deals with the demands of reality
b.	no; the superego is the moral branch of the personality
c.	no; the id always seeks pleasure and avoids pain
d.	no; this is not one of the three components of personality according to Freud

5. The moral branch of personality according to the psychoanalytic perspective is
   a. ego
   b. superego
   c. id
   d. regression

a.	the ego deals with the demands of reality
b.	RIGHT; the superego is the moral branch of the personality
c.	the id always seeks pleasure and avoids pain
d.	no; this is not one of the three components of personality according to Freud

6. _____ are the ego's protective methods for reducing anxiety by unconsciously distorting reality.
   a. Sublimations
   b. Archetypes
   c. Defense mechanisms
   d. Cardinal traits

a.	no; sublimation is an example of a defense mechanism
b.	no; archetypes are emotion-laden ideas and images in the collective unconscious
c.	YES; this is the definition of defense mechanism
d.	no; cardinal traits are a type of trait

7. The most powerful and pervasive defense mechanism is
   a. sublimation.
   b. regression.
   c. rationalization.
   d. repression.

a.	no
b.	no
c.	no
d.	YEA; repression is the most powerful and pervasive defense mechanism

8.   In which defense mechanism do we attribute our problems to others?
    a.   sublimation
    b.   projection
    c.   reaction formation
    d.   regression

a.	no; this is when an unacceptable impulse is replaced with a socially acceptable one
b.	GOOD; we project our own problems and shortcomings to others
c.	no; this is when an unacceptable motive is transformed into its opposite
d.	no; regression refers to going back to an earlier developmental period

9.   During the Oedipus complex,
    a.   the child enters the anal stage.
    b.   the child develops an intense desire to replace the parent of the same sex.
    c.   the child represses all interest in sexuality.
    d.   the genital stage begins.

a.	no; the anal stage occurs earlier
b.	THIS IS RIGHT; the child also has the desire to enjoy the affections of the opposite-sex parent
c.	no; this describes the latency stage which appears following the Oedipus complex
d.	no; genital stage is the fifth Freudian stage appearing after the Oedipus complex

10.   During what Freudian stage of development does the child focus on social and intellectual skills?
    a.   the oral stage
    b.   the anal stage
    c.   the latency stage
    d.   the genital stage

a.	no; the mouth is center of pleasure in this stage
b.	no; this is associated with pleasure regarding the eliminative function
c.	YEA; this is related to going to school
d.	no; this coincides with puberty where there is a sexual reawakening

11.   Which of the following is not a criticism of Freud's ideas about personality?
    a.   sexuality is not the pervasive underlying force Freud believed it to be
    b.   experiences after 5 years of age are powerful in shaping adult personality
    c.   unconscious thoughts play little role in our personality
    d.   sociocultural factors are much more important Freud argued

a.	no; this is a criticism
b.	no; this is a criticism
c.	GOOD: in fact, according to Freud, unconscious thoughts play a large role in our personality
d.	no; this is a criticism

12.   If a person tries to conceal her weaknesses in an exaggerated way, she might be showing _____ according to Adler.
    a.   overcompensation
    b.   compensation
    c.   fixation
    d.   situationalism

a.	RIGHT; this is the definition of overcompensation
b.	the key is that she is trying to conceal her weakness, not trying to overcome
c.	no; fixation refers to receiving too much or too little stimulation
d.	no; situationalism is the notion that personality changes according to the situation

13. According to Jung, archetypes
    a.   are conscious events.
    b.   are responsible for hallucinations and delusions.
    c.   are derived from the collective unconscious.
    d.   cause inferiority and superiority complexes.

a.	no	
b.	no	
c.	YEP; archetypes are emotion-laden ideas and images from collective unconscious	
d.	no	

14. People cope with anxiety by moving either toward people, away from people, or against people, according to
    a.   Freud.
    b.   Jung.
    c.   Horney.
    d.   Adler.

a.	no	
b.	no	
c.	THAT'S RIGHT; these are ways that people cope with anxiety	
d.	no	

15. An important difference between the behavioral and social cognitive perspectives relates to
    a.   the unconscious.
    b.   cognition.
    c.   early childhood events.
    d.   the collective unconscious

a.	no; neither places any weight on the unconscious
b.	RIGHT; social cognitive theory suggests that cognitive factors play a role
c.	no; this is not an important difference
d.	no; neither even refers to the collective unconscious

16. "Personality is a collection of observable behavior." Who is most likely to have said that?
    a.   Freud
    b.   Adler
    c.   Skinner
    d.   Chodrow

a.	Freud stressed the role of the unconscious mind on personality
b.	no; Adler's focus is on striving for superiority
c.	CORRECT; for Skinner personality is behavior
d.	her focus is on how people define the self in terms of relationships

17. Which perspective would be most likely to stress the importance of reinforcement and the environment in personality?
    a.   behaviorism
    b.   psychoanalytic
    c.   humanistic
    d.   individual

a.	THAT'S RIGHT; behaviorism focuses on reinforcement and the environment
b.	no; the emphasis is on unconscious processes
c.	no; the humanistic perspective stresses personal growth and freedom to choose
d.	no; Adler stressed our need to strive for superiority

18. Which personality theorists would place the most emphasis on cognitive factors mediating the environment's effects on the personality?
   a. psychoanalysts
   b. behaviorists
   c. social cognitive theorists
   d. humanists

a.	no; unconscious processes play the primary role in personality for psychoanalysts
b.	no; the behaviorists would say that cognitive factors play no role in personality
d.	YES; these theorists would say that behavior, environment, and cognitive factors interact with one another
d.	no; the humanists stress self-actualization, positive regard, and self-concept

19. Which of the following stresses the interaction between behavior, environment, and person/cognitive variables?
   a. humanistic
   b. psychoanalytic
   c. behavioral
   d. social cognitive

a.	no; the humanistic perspective stresses personal growth and freedom to choose
b.	no; unconscious processes play the primary role in personality for psychoanalysts
c.	no; this perspective focuses on the role of the environment in personality
d.	RIGHT

20. According to Bandura, the belief that a person has mastery over a situation and the ability to produce positive outcomes is called
   a. self-efficacy.
   b. self-esteem.
   c. self-concept.
   d. self-actualization.

a.	CORRECT; this defines self-efficacy and it is one of the cognitive/person factors
b.	no; self-esteem is how we evaluate and feel about our self-concept
c.	no; this is an individual's overall perceptions of ability, behavior, and personality
d.	no; this term refers to the motivation to develop one's full potential

21. According to Walter Mischel, a key to understanding personality is the concept of
   a. delay of gratification.
   b. repression.
   c. unconditional positive regard.
   d. central traits.

a.	RIGHT; this refers to the ability to defer immediate gratification for something better in the future
b.	no; repression is an example of defense mechanism from psychoanalytic view
c.	no; this means that acceptance is given to someone without strings attached
d.	no; these are traits that are adequate enough to describe someone's personality

22. According to Rogers, acceptance of another person regardless of the person's behavior is called
    a.   conditional positive regard.
    b.   unconditional positive regard.
    c.   self-actualization.
    d.   hierarchy of motives.

a.	no; in fact, this is acceptance of another when this person conforms to standards
b.	CORRECT
c.	no; this term refers to the motivation to develop one's full potential
d.	no; this is a way to order individual's needs from physiological needs to self-actualization

23. Rogers would describe a person who is open to experience, not very defensive, and sensitive to others as being
    a.   fixed in the anal stage
    b.   receiving conditional positive regard
    c.   a fully functioning person
    d.   striving for superiority

a.	no
b.	no
c.	YES; these characterize a fully functioning person
d.	no

24. The evaluative and affective dimensions of self-concept are referred to as
    a.   self-esteem.
    b.   self-worth.
    c.   self-efficacy.
    d.   all of the above

a.	RIGHT; this is the definition of self-esteem
b.	no
c.	no; this is the belief that one can master a situation and produce desired outcomes
d.	no

25. Unconditional positive regard and conditions of worth are important concepts in
    a.   the behavioral perspective.
    b.   the social cognitive perspective.
    c.   the humanistic perspective.
    d.   trait theory.

a.	no; the behavioral perspective emphasizes reinforcement
b.	no; this perspective underscores learning and cognitive processes
c.	YES; these are important concepts in the humanistic perspective
d.	no; traits stress broad dispositions that lead to characteristics responses

26. Each of the following is considered one of the "Big Five" factors in personality except
    a.   extraversion.
    b.   emotional stability.
    c.   agreeableness.
    d.   intellect.

a.	no; this is one of the "Big Five"
b.	no; this is one of the "Big Five"
c.	no; this is one of the "Big Five"
d.	YES; this not among the "Big Five" factors

27.   The projective tests are designed to elicit
        a.   unconscious feelings and conflicts
        b.   conscious feelings and conflicts
        c.   self-report of traits
        d.   social desirability

a.	CORRECT; the projective tests consist of ambiguous stimuli
b.	no; the psychodynamic perspective emphasizes the unconscious
c.	the projective tests do not allow self-reporting of traits
d.	no; social desirability is a flaw that should be avoided in personality assessment

28.   "This is a test of your imagination. I am going to show you some pictures, and I want you to tell me an interesting story about each one. What is happening, how did it develop, and how will it end?" These instructions are part of the preparation for the
        a.   Thematic Apperception Test.
        b.   Rorschach Inkblot Test.
        c.   MMPI.
        d.   self-report test.

a.	RIGHT; the TAT is made up of pictures that elicit information about personality
b.	no; this test involves asking the individual what they see in inkblots
c.	no; the MMPI is a self-report test
d.	no; these tests directly ask people whether items describe their personality or not

29.   A basic assumption of behavioral assessment is that
        a.   the unconscious always influences behavior.
        b.   personality cannot be evaluated apart from the environment.
        c.   traits are consistent even in varying situations.
        d.   personality is inherited.

a.	no; in fact, this is not assumed in behavioral assessment, but is in psychoanalytic
b.	YES; this is an important assumption of behavioral assessment
c.	no
d.	no

30.   Which type of personality test is designed to elicit the individual's unconscious feeling?
        a.   self-report tests
        b.   the MMPI
        c.   NEO-PI-R
        d.   projective tests

a.	no; these tests directly ask people whether items describe their personality or not
b.	no; the MMPI is an example of self-report test
c.	no; this is an example of self-report test that assesses the Big Five factors
d.	RIGHT; these tests are designed to elicit unconscious feelings

Chapter 13 - Abnormal Psychology

The Big Picture: Chapter Overview

Abnormal behavior refers to behavior that is deviant, maladaptive, or personally distressful. Insanity is a legal term that implies that a person was wholly or partially irrational when the crime took place and that this irrationality affected his/her behavior. The appropriateness of the insanity defense remains controversial. Some states allow a verdict of guilty but mentally ill. The insanity defense is rarely used, and when used is typically not successful.

Biological factors that contribute to abnormal behavior include brain processes and genetic factors. The medical model describes mental disorders as medical disorders with a biological origin; drug therapy is often used to treat abnormal behaviors. Psychological factors such as distorted thoughts, emotional turmoil, and troubled relationships are believed to be causes of abnormal behavior. Socioeconomic status and neighborhood quality influence mental disorders. Gender is also associated with the presence of certain disorders. The interactionist approach suggests that behavior is influenced by biological, psychological, and sociocultural factors.

About one-third of those who participated in a survey said that they had experienced one or more mental disorders in their lifetime; 20% said that they currently had an active disorder.

In 1980 the American Psychiatric Association published the Diagnostic and Statistical Manual, 3rd edition (DSM-III). The DSM is a widely used system for classifying mental disorders. The fourth edition, DSM-IV, was published in 1994. A classification is important for clinicians since it gives professionals a shorthand system for communicating with each other about disorders. In addition, a classification system provides predictive information. The DSM-III did not include the terms neurotic and psychotic, which had been used in earlier editions of the DSM. Moreover, gender- and ethnicity-related diagnoses have been recently added. DSM-IV uses the multiaxial system, which consists of five dimensions, to assess individuals. Critics charge the DSM-IV with depending on a disease model of mental disorders, categorizing everyday problems as mental disorders, and an overemphasis on finding problems or pathology.

Motor tension, hyperactivity, and apprehensive expectations and thoughts characterize anxiety disorders. Generalized anxiety disorder consists of persistent anxiety for at least one month without specific symptoms. Panic disorder involves recurrent and sudden onset of apprehension or terror and may include agoraphobia. Phobic disorders involve an irrational, overwhelming, persistent fear of an object or a situation. Agoraphobia and social phobia are common phobias. Obsessive-compulsive disorder is a mental disorder characterized by obsessions that are anxiety-provoking thoughts that won't go away and compulsions, or ritualistic behaviors, performed in a stereotyped way. The most common compulsions include checking, cleaning, and counting. Post-traumatic stress disorder is an anxiety disorder that develops through exposure to a traumatic event such as sexual abuse and assault.

In somatoform disorders, the psychological symptoms take a physical form, although no evidence of a physical cause can be found. Two types of somatoform disorders are hypochondriasis and conversion disorder. In hypochondriasis, the individual has a pervasive fear of illness and disease. Conversion disorder involves specific physical symptoms (e.g., blindness) even though no physiological problem can be found. Another conversion disorder is glove anesthesia. Dissociative disorders involve a sudden memory loss or change of identity. Dissociative amnesia is memory loss due to extensive psychological stress. Dissociative fugue is amnesia in addition to unexpected travel away from home and the assumption of a new identify. The most dramatic but rarest dissociative disorder is dissociative identity disorder; in this disorder, the individual has two or more distinct personalities or selves, with each having its own memories, behaviors, and relationships. Many individuals with dissociative identity disorder have histories of sexual or physical abuse during early childhood.

Mood disorders include depressive disorders and bipolar disorder. In the depressive disorders, the individual suffers from depression as in major depressive disorder; depressed characteristics (e.g., unhappiness, fatigue, problems in thinking) must be present for at least 2 weeks or longer. The symptoms are so severe that the person's functioning becomes impaired. Dysthmic disorder is a more chronic and less severe form of major depressive disorder. Bipolar depression is characterized by dramatic mood swings that include mania and depression. Biological explanations of mood disorders focus on heredity, brain processes, and neurotransmitters. Psychosocial factors have been suggested as causes of mood disorders. Freud described depression as the turning inward of aggressive instincts. Bowlby suggests that insecure attachment between child and mother plays a role in depression, while Beck suggests negative thoughts as a cause. Learned helplessness, another explanation, occurs when an individual, through prolonged stress, learns that he or she has no control over it, leading to an apathetic state of helplessness.

Distorted thoughts and perceptions, odd communication, inappropriate emotion, abnormal motor behavior, and social withdrawal characterize the schizophrenic disorders. Many schizophrenics have delusions and hallucinations. Disorganized schizophrenia consists of delusions and hallucinations that have little or no recognized meaning. In catatonic schizophrenia, the individual engages in bizarre motor behavior such as being in a completely immobile stupor. Paranoid schizophrenia is characterized by delusions of reference, grandeur, and persecution. In undifferentiated schizophrenia, the symptoms don't meet the criteria for the other types or they meet the criteria for more than one type. Genetics factors have been examined as important in schizophrenia, with the disorder running in families. Imbalances in brain chemistry and distorted cerebral blood flow may also be related to schizophrenia. The diathesis-stress view emphasizes a combination of genetic predisposition and environmental stress as causes of schizophrenia.

Personality disorders are chronic, maladaptive cognitive-behavioral patterns that are thoroughly integrated into the individual's personality. These disorders are grouped into three clusters: odd/eccentric, dramatic and emotionally problematic, and chronic fearfulness/avoidant. Antisocial personality disorder is characterized by guiltless, exploitative, irresponsible, self-indulgent, and interpersonally intrusive behavior. People with this disorder were once called sociopaths or psychopaths, and they commit a disproportionately large percentage of violent and property crimes. Both biological (e.g., genetic predisposition) and psychosocial (e.g., inadequate socialization) explanations for antisocial personality disorder have been suggested. Preferring the older term, psychopath, Robert Hare has shown that such people do not integrate cognition and emotion the way normal people do.

Learning Objectives

When you have studied the material in this chapter, you should be able to:

1. describe the characteristics of abnormal behavior. (p. 448)
2. discuss the legal aspects of mental disorders. (pp. 449-450)
3. describe the views of each of the following perspectives regarding abnormal behavior: biological, psychological, sociocultural, and biopsychosocial perspectives. (pp. 450-452)
4. describe the DSM classification system and each of its five axes. (pp. 452-455)
5. discuss the controversies regarding the DSM classification system. (pp. 453-455)
6. define anxiety disorder and distinguish between the major anxiety disorders listed. (pp.455-459)
   - generalized anxiety disorder
   - panic disorder
   - phobias
   - obsessive-compulsive disorder
   - post-traumatic stress disorder
7. define somatoform disorder and distinguish between hypochondriasis and conversion disorder. (pp. 459-460)
8. define dissociative disorder and distinguish between amnesia, fugue, and multiple personality disorder. (pp. 460-461)
9. define mood disorder and distinguish between major depression, dysthymia, and bipolar disorder. (pp. 463-466)
10. summarize the research attempts to isolate biological causes for mood disorders. (p. 466)
11. explain Beck's concept of negative schema and Seligman's concept of learned helplessness as related to depression. (pp. 466-467)
12. describe the characteristics of the schizophrenia disorders. (pp. 467-469)

13.   compare and contrast disorganized, catatonic, paranoid, and undifferentiated schizophrenia. (p. 469)
14.   discuss biological and psychosocial factors as explanations for schizophrenia. (pp. 469-470)
15.   explain why personality disorders differ from other major mental health disorders. (pp. 472-474)
16.   list and describe the characteristics associated with each cluster of personality disorders. (pp. 472-473)
17.   summarize research into the causes of antisocial personality disorder. Discuss Robert Hare's work on psychopaths. (p. 473)
18.   from *Explorations in Psychology: Some Famous Insanity Plea Cases*, discuss the controversies surrounding the insanity defense. (p. 450)
19.   from *Explorations in Psychology: Suicide*, list the factors that put persons at a higher risk for suicide and discuss appropriate intervention strategies. (p.465)

Guided Review

Understanding Abnormal Behavior

Behavior that is deviant, maladaptive, or personally distressful is called _____ behavior. The legal term that implies that a person is not responsible for his or her actions is called _____. A plea of "not guilty by reason of insanity" is referred to as the _____ _____. In Canada, judges and juries may find defendants "not criminally responsible on account of _____ _____." The appropriateness of the insanity defense remains highly controversial.

The causes of abnormal behavior include _____, psychological, and _____ factors. An approach that views abnormal behavior as the result of a physical malfunction in the body is the _____ approach, which is evident in the _____ model. Emotional turmoil, inappropriate learning, and troubled relationships are examples of _____ factors. Among the sociocultural factors that influence mental illness are _____ _____ and _____ _____ are. Research suggests that individuals who live in _____ _____ neighborhoods have higher rates of mental disorders, although the research does not explain the causes. Women tend to be diagnosed with _____ disorders, in particular _____ disorders and _____. Men are more likely to have _____ _____. Biological, psychological, and social factors interact to produce abnormal behavior according to the _____ approach. Random samples of residents in the United States and Canada found that more than _____ had experienced a mental disturbance during their lifetime. One third of the individuals reporting mental disorders had received treatment in the previous _____ months.

The first edition of the Diagnostic and Statistical Manual (DSM) was published in 1952. Two important categories that were included in DSM-II but not in DSM-III are the terms _____, which refers to relatively mild mental disorders, and _____, which refers to severe mental disturbances and a loss of contact with _____. These terms were dropped because the categories were too broad and ill-defined to be useful. Classification systems for mental disorders allow psychologists to _____ with each other and help psychologists do a better job of _____ psychological disturbances. However, some psychologists believe that labeling individuals encourages them to experience self-fulfilling _____. The most recent edition of the DSM is called _____. DSM-IV uses a _____ _____, which consists of five dimensions, to assess individuals. Some psychologists have been critical of DSM-IV; they have criticized the _____ terminology and the inclusion of everyday problems as mental disorders. Other criticisms focus on whether the manual puts too much emphasis on _____ and problems.

Categories of Mental Disorders

Disorders that are characterized by motor tension, hyperactivity, and apprehensive expectations and thoughts are called _____ disorders. _____ anxiety disorder consists of persistent anxiety for at least 1 month, although the individual is unable to specify the reasons for the anxiety. Recurrent and sudden apprehension or terror characterize _____ disorder and can be diagnosed with _____. Irrational, overwhelming, and persistent fear of an object or a situation is found in _____ disorders. Psychoanalytic theorists believe that phobias develop as _____ _____, whereas learning theorists suggest that classical conditioning and _____ learning explain the development of phobias. Other researchers suggest a possible _____ predisposition for phobias as they find a greater incidence of the disorder among first-generation relatives. An anxiety disorder that consists of anxiety-provoking thoughts that won't go away (called _____) and/or repetitive, ritualistic behaviors performed in a stereotyped way (_____) is referred to a obsessive-compulsive disorder. A mental disturbance that develops through exposure to traumatic events is called _____-_____ _____ disorder. Anxiety symptoms may immediately follow the trauma or be delayed by months or _____. About 15 to 20 percent of _____ veterans experienced post-traumatic stress disorder, as have about 10 percent of Canadian _____.

In some mental disturbances, the psychological symptoms take a physical form, although no evidence of a physical cause can be found. These are called _____ _____. A somatoform disorder characterized by a pervasive fear of illness and disease is _____. In another somatoform disorder, the individual converts anxiety into a specific physical symptom, although no physiological problems can be found. This is called _____ _____. It is quite rare for these disorders to occur without other _____ _____.

Psychological disorders that involve sudden losses of memory or changes in identity are called _____ _____. Memory loss that is due to extensive psychological stress is called _____ _____. A loss of memory in which the individual unexpectedly travels away from home and assumes a new identity is called a _____ _____. A dramatic but less common dissociative disorder is _____ _____ disorder where there are two or more distinct personalities. Many of these individuals have early childhood histories of _____ or _____ _____.

_____ disorders are characterized by wide emotional swings. The _____ disorders involved depression without mania. In _____ _____ disorder, the mood is so severe that the person cannot function. Dysthymic disorder is more _____ and has _____ symptoms than major depressive disorder. Depression is so widespread it is referred to as the _____ _____ of mental disorders. Dramatic mood swings characterize the mood disorder called _____ disorder. The manic episodes typically average _____ weeks. _____ factors are important in bipolar disorder since the risk of developing bipolar disorder is higher when a first degree relative has the disorder. The _____ transmitters have also been implicated in mood disorders. Aaron Beck would suggest that _____ _____ shape the depressed person's experiences. Seligman argues that depressed people have developed _____ helplessness and one contributing factor to it may be that our society emphasizes _____, _____, and individualism. With regard to women's rate of depression, _____ factors may interact with biological and cognitive factors.

monoamine - p. 466

negative thoughts - p. 466
learned - p. 467

self/independence - p. 467
sociocultural - p. 467

The _____ disorders are characterized by distorted thoughts and perceptions, odd communication, inappropriate emotion, abnormal motor behavior, and social withdrawal. About _____ percent of North Americans will develop schizophrenia in their lifetime. Many schizophrenics have false beliefs, called _____ ; they may also hear or see things not actually there, called _____ . They may communicate in incoherent, loose word associations called _____ salad.

schizophrenic - p. 467

1.5 - p. 467

delusions - p. 468
hallucinations - p. 468
word - p. 468

A type of schizophrenia characterized by delusions and hallucinations that have little or no recognizable meaning is _____ schizophrenia. Bizarre motor behavior is the central feature of _____ schizophrenia. In a catatonic state, an individual may show _____ flexibility. The central theme of paranoid schizophrenia is complex, elaborate _____ . The three main types of delusions are _____ , reference, and _____ . A fourth form of schizophrenia, characterized by disorganized behavior, hallucinations, delusions, and incoherence, is _____ schizophrenia. Genetic factors are strongly implicated as a cause of schizophrenia. As _____ similarity to a schizophrenic relative increases, so does the chance of becoming schizophrenic. Among neurological factors, possible causes include brain _____ , a malfunctioning _____ system, and distorted blood flow to the _____ . An environmental factor being given much attention is _____ ; the _____-_____ view suggests that a combination of environmental stress and _____ predisposition is involved. _____ factors are also involved because the type and incidence of schizophrenia varies from culture to culture.

disorganized - p. 469

catatonic - p. 469
waxy - p. 469
delusions – p. 469
grandeur/persecution - p. 469

undifferentiated - p. 469

genetic - p. 469

metabolism/dopamine - p. 469
cerebrum - p. 469-470
stress – p. 470
diathesis-stress - p. 470
biogenetic - p. 470
Psychosocial - p. 470

When personality traits become inflexible and maladaptive, _____ _____ develop. The different personality disorders are clustered around three types of characteristics. One cluster involves odd or _____ behaviors; a second cluster involves fear and _____ , and a third involves dramatic, or erratic behaviors. A pattern of crime, violence, and delinquency with little remorse typifies the _____ personality disorder; people with this disorder were once called sociopaths or _____ . Such people cannot integrate _____ and _____ as normal people do. The disorder typically begins before the age of _____ and is more common in _____ . Since the disorder is more likely to appear in identical twins than in fraternal twins, _____ factors have been suggested. Parental behavior may also play a role in the disorder as parents may be more _____ in their discipline.

personality disorders - p. 472

eccentric - p. 473
avoidance - p. 473

antisocial - p. 473
psychopaths - p. 473
cognition/emotion – p. 473
15 – p. 473
males - p. 473
genetic - p. 473

inconsistent (punitive) - p. 473

Explorations in Psychology

To respond to the questions and exercises presented in this section, please write your thoughts, perspectives, and reactions on a separate piece of paper.

Explorations in Psychology and Life: Some Famous Insanity Plea Cases

- Most people would argue that anyone who murdered his victims and then ate them would be insane. What does this say with regard to how the general public defines insanity and the way the legal system defines insanity?
- Jeffrey Dahmer's lawyer said, "This is not an evil man, this is a mentally sick man." What relationship, if any, do you see between his actions, evilness, and the definition of insanity?
- In the case of Lorena Bobbitt, was her action justified by what she claimed was years of physical and mental abuse from her husband?
- Discuss your views of the verdict of "not criminally responsible on account of mental disorder".

Explorations in Psychology and Life: Suicide

- If a good friend of yours threatened suicide, what would you do?
- Do you think there are any "good" reasons for committing suicide? If so, what are they?
- Is it "abnormal" to think about suicide?

Explorations in Psychology and Life: NIMH--Nora, Iris, Myra, and Hester, the Schizophrenic Genain Quadruplets

- Why is this type of research important in determining the causes of schizophrenia?
- Does the case of the Genain quadruplets support the role of genetics in schizophrenia, while at the same time question the role of the environment?
- What did PET scans of the quadruplets suggest about schizophrenia?

In Your Own Words

To respond to the questions and exercises presented in this section, please write your thoughts, perspectives, and reactions on a separate piece of paper.

- ✓ Give examples of the three criteria of abnormal behavior (i.e., deviance, maladaptiveness, and distress).
- ✓ List some characteristics that you would like to have that are deviant (i.e., atypical). If you had these characteristics, would you be considered abnormal?
- ✓ Besides illness, patients, and mental hospitals, what other words can you think of to illustrate the influence of the medical model in abnormal psychology?
- ✓ Do you have any fears? Are they rational? Would they be considered phobias?
- ✓ When you feel depressed, how does the depression affect you with regard to functioning?
- ✓ Genetic factors appear to play a role in many mental disorders. For instance an identical twin is more likely to develop schizophrenia than a fraternal twin. But what about environmental factors? List some environmental influences that may play a role in mental disorders.
- ✓ Describe something that you do that you consider abnormal. Does it fit the criteria of deviance, maladaptiveness, and distress?
- ✓ Speculate on how nonwesterns might react to hearing about anorexia nervosa. Does this reaction mirror your reaction as you read about amok and windigo in Figure 13.2? What role does this suggest culture plays in defining abnormal behavior?
- ✓ Select one of the mental disorders described in this chapter and create a fictitious case study of an individual with the disorder. Include appropriate background information that is consistent with the disorder.

✓ Why can most people relate to anxiety disorders and mood disorders, but have trouble understanding dissociative disorders and schizophrenic disorders?

Correcting the Incorrect

Carefully read each statement. Determine if the statement is correct or incorrect. If the statement is incorrect, make the necessary changes to correct it. Then look directly under the statement for the correct statement and page reference in the textbook.

1. Abnormal behavior is behavior that is strange or odd.
    - ❑ *Abnormal behavior is behavior that is deviant, maladaptive, or distressful. (p. 448)*
2. Normal and abnormal behaviors are different in kind.
    - ❑ *Normal and abnormal behaviors are not different in kind. (p. 448)*
3. Insanity is a psychiatric term.
    - ❑ *Insanity is a legal term. (p. 449)*
4. The verdict that is used in the insanity defense is "not guilty."
    - ❑ *The verdict that is used in the insanity defense is not criminally responsible on account of mental disorder." (p. 449)*
5. The insanity defense is commonly used and is very successful in helping people avoid punishment.
    - ❑ *The insanity defense is not commonly used and is not very successful in helping people avoid punishment. (p. 449)*
6. The medical model describes mental disorders as medical diseases.
    - ❑ *The medical model describes mental disorders as medical diseases. (p. 450)*
7. Ethnicity plays a stronger role in mental disorders than socioeconomic status.
    - ❑ *Socioeconomic status plays a stronger role in mental disorders than ethnicity. (p. 451)*
8. Men are more likely to experience internalizing disorders.
    - ❑ *Men are more likely to experience externalizing disorders. (p. 452)*
9. About one-half of people surveyed said they had experienced one or more mental disorders in their lifetime.
    - ❑ *About one-third of people surveyed said they had experienced one or more mental disorders in their lifetime. (p. 452)*
10. Most people who currently have a mental disorder received treatment in the past 6 months.
    - ❑ *Few people who currently have a mental disorder received treatment in the past 6 months. (p. 452)*
11. The American Psychological Association publishes the DSM.
    - ❑ *The American Psychiatric Association publishes the DSM. (p. 452)*
12. The DSM dropped the term neurotic, but still continues to use the term psychotic.
    - ❑ *The DSM dropped the term neurotic and the term psychotic. (p. 453)*
13. The DSM-IV has a multiaxial system.
    - ❑ *The DSM-IV has a multiaxial system. (p. 453)*
14. One criticism of the DSM-IV is that it labels mental disorders that are often thought of as everyday problems.
    - ❑ *One criticism of the DSM-IV is that it labels mental disorders that are often thought of as everyday problems. (p. 454)*
15. The main features of the anxiety disorders are motor tension, hyperactivity, and apprehensive expectations and thoughts.
    - ❑ *The main features of the anxiety disorders are motor tension, hyperactivity, and apprehensive expectations and thoughts. (p. 455)*
16. In generalized anxiety disorder, the individual experiences flashbacks that are related to traumatic events.
    - ❑ *In posttraumatic stress disorder, the individual experiences flashbacks that are related to traumatic events. (p. 459)*
17. Panic disorder may also be diagnosed with generalized anxiety disorder.

❑ *Panic disorder may also be diagnosed with agoraphobia. (p. 456-451).*

18. Most people with phobic disorders do not realize that their fear is irrational.
❑ *Most people with phobic disorders do realize that their fear is irrational. (p. 457)*

19. Social phobia is another term for agoraphobia.
❑ *Social phobia is the intense fear of humiliation or embarrassment in social situations. (p. 457).*

20. Obsessions are ritualistic behaviors and compulsions are anxiety-provoking thoughts.
❑ *Compulsions are ritualistic behaviors and obsessions are anxiety-provoking thoughts. (p. 458)*

21. The symptoms of post-traumatic stress disorder typically show up immediately after experiencing the traumatic event or the oppressive situation.
❑ *The symptoms of post-traumatic stress disorder can show up immediately or years after experiencing the traumatic event or the oppressive situation. (p. 459)*

22. People with hypochondriasis accurately react to bodily sensations.
❑ *People with hypochondriasis overreact to bodily sensations. (p. 459)*

23. In hypochondriasis, people are faking so they can get out of fulfilling their roles and responsibilities.
❑ *In hypochondriasis, people are not faking. (p. 459)*

24. Glove anesthesia is an example of conversion disorder.
❑ *Glove anesthesia is an example of conversion disorder. (p. 460)*

25. The dissociative disorders involve distorted thoughts and perception and social withdrawal.
❑ *The dissociative disorders involve loss of memory or change in identity. (p. 460).*

26. Dissociative amnesia consists of memory loss caused by excessive psychological stress.
❑ *Dissociative amnesia consists of memory loss caused by excessive psychological stress. (p. 460)*

27. A person has memory loss, travels, and assumes a new identity in dissociative identity disorder.
❑ *A person has memory loss, travels, and assumes a new identity in dissociative fugue. (p. 460).*

28. Dissociative identity disorder is a fairly common disorder.
❑ *Dissociative identity disorder is a rare disorder. (p. 461)*

29. Dissociative identity disorder is characterized by high rates of sexual or physical abuse during early childhood.
❑ *Dissociative identity disorder is characterized by high rates of sexual or physical abuse during early childhood. (p. 461)*

30. Major depression disorder consists of chronic and less severe depression.
❑ *Dysthymic disorder consists of chronic and less severe depression. (p. 463)*

31. Depression has been called the "common cold" of mental disorders.
❑ *Depression has been called the "common cold" of mental disorders. (p. 464)*

32. Swings of mood from mania to depression typify bipolar disorder.
❑ *Swings of mood from mania to depression typify bipolar disorder. (p. 464)*

33. People in a manic episode have tremendous energy.
❑ *People in a manic episode have tremendous energy. (p. 464)*

34. There is a stronger family link for depressive disorder than for bipolar disorders.
❑ *There is a stronger family link for bipolar disorder than for depressive disorders. (p. 466)*

35. Acetylcholine has been identified as contributing to mood disorders.
❑ *Monoamine has been identified as contributing to mood disorders. (p. 466)*

36. A person has learned to become apathetic and helpless in learned helplessness.
❑ *A person has learned to become apathetic and helpless in learned helplessness. (p. 466-467)*

37. About 3 out of 10 North Americans will develop schizophrenia in their lifetime.
❑ *About 1 out of 10 North Americans will develop schizophrenia in their lifetime. (p. 468)*

38. Delusions include hearing, seeing, feeling, and smelling things that are not there.
❑ *Hallucinations include hearing, seeing, feeling, and smelling things that are not there. (p. 468)*

39. The term "word salad" is used to describe the hallucinations in schizophrenia.
❑ *The term "word salad" is used to describe the speech in schizophrenia. (p. 468)*

40. In catatonic schizophrenia, the person suffers from delusions and hallucinations that have little or no meaning.

❑ *In disorganized schizophrenia, the person suffers from delusions and hallucinations that have little or no meaning (p. 469)*

41. Waxy flexibility is common among people with paranoid schizophrenia.
   ❑ *Waxy flexibility is common among people with catatonic schizophrenia. (p. 469)*
42. The neurotransmitter dopamine may be involved with schizophrenia.
   ❑ *The neurotransmitter dopamine may be involved with schizophrenia. (p. 469-470)*
43. The diathesis-stress view argues that people develop learned helplessness because their instincts have turned inward, which ultimately leads to schizophrenia.
   ❑ *The diathesis-stress view argues that people develop schizophrenia because of stress and biogenetic disposition. (p. 470)*
44. The personality disorders consist of chronic, maladaptive cognitive-behavioral patterns that are thoroughly integrated into the individual's personality.
   ❑ *The personality disorders consist of chronic, maladaptive cognitive-behavioral patterns that are thoroughly integrated into the individual's personality. (p. 472)*
45. There are three clusters of personality disorders: odd/eccentric, dramatic, and emotionally dramatic.
   ❑ *There are three clusters of personality disorders: odd/eccentric, dramatic, and emotionally dramatic. (p. 473)*
46. Someone who has antisocial personality disorder shows behavior that is unstable, anxious, and irritable.
   ❑ *Someone who has antisocial personality disorder shows behavior that is guiltless, exploitive, irresponsible, and self-indulgent. (p. 473).*
47. Research suggests that people with antisocial personality disorder have not learned to delay gratification.
   ❑ *Research suggests that people with antisocial personality disorder have not learned to delay gratification. (p. 473)*

Practice Test

1. According to the text, which of the following is a factor in abnormal behavior?
   a.   biological causes
   b.   psychological causes
   c.   sociocultural causes
   d.   all of the above

a.	no; other factors beside biological causes need to be taken into account
b.	no; certainly psychological causes are important, but so are other types of causes
c.	no; there are other factors as well
d.	YES; abnormal behavior can be explained using all of these types of causes

2. For Irving to be described as exhibiting abnormal behavior, his behavior must be
   a.   excessive.
   b.   atypical.
   c.   maladaptive.
   d.   genetically based.

a.	no; excessive behavior is not necessarily abnormal
b.	no; some atypical behaviors are very desirable
c.	YES; this behavior interferes with the persons ability to function effectively
d.	no; just because some behavior is genetically based does not make it abnormal

3. Which of the following is true of the concept "innocent by reason of insanity"?
   a.   Insanity is a psychiatric term.
   b.   Insanity is a legal term.
   c.   Insanity implies that an individual is not rational to stand trial.
   d.   Insanity is commonly used in court cases.

a.	no; insanity is not a psychiatric term	
b.	YES; insanity is a legal term	
c.	no; insanity refers to the person when the crime is alleged to have occurred.	
d.	no; in fact the insanity defense is not used very often	

4. Which of the following statements about the insanity defense is **true**?
    a. Due to this defense strategy, many innocent people go to prison.
    b. Due to this defense strategy, many guilty people go unpunished.
    c. This defense is not used very often, and it is not very often successful.
    d. Although this defense is not used very often, when it is used, it is usually successful.

a.	no; this is not true
b.	no; the insanity defense is usually not successful
c.	CORRECT; often these defenses are given much attention in the media
d.	no; it is not often used nor is it usually successful

5. Which of the following groups is at risk for mental disorders?
    a. ethnic minority individuals
    b. those living in poverty
    c. people from low income neighborhoods
    d. all of the above

a.	no; but these individuals are at risk
b.	no; but these individuals are at risk
c.	no; but these individuals are at risk
d.	YES; all of these are at-risk of developing mental disorders

6. Each of the following is an axis on the DSM multiaxial system except
    a. personality disorders.
    b. psychological stressors in the individual's recent past.
    c. the individual's highest level of functioning in the past year.
    d. potential treatments for the individual.

a.	no; personality disorders are placed on axis II
b.	no; psychological stressors are indicated on axis IV
c.	no; information on functioning is placed on axis V
d.	CORRECT; treatment options are not among the axes in the DSM

7. If you were to call Janet *neurotic*, you would be implying that she suffers from a relatively
    a. obscure disorder.
    b. mild disorder.
    c. rare disorder.
    d. progressive disorder.

a.	no
b.	THAT'S RIGHT; these individuals are still in touch with reality, yet are distressed
c.	no
d.	no

8. The DSM has dropped which of the following?
    a. Axis VI - Treatment Options
    b. the multiaxial system
    c. the term "psychotic"
    d. "a" and "c" above

a. no; there has never been Axis VI - Treatment Options
b. no; the DSM still has five axes
c. CORRECT; this term is no longer used
d. no; there is a better answer

9. Which of the following is a criticism of the DSM-IV
   a. Five axes are not sufficient for the classification of all mental disorders.
   b. The classification is not comprehensive enough.
   c. The classification is not current enough.
   d. Labels can become self-fulfilling prophecies.

   a. no; this is not a criticism
   b. no; this is not a criticism
   c. no; this is not a criticism
   d. YEP; this is a criticism since the DSM focuses on pathology and problems

10. The DSM-IV has been criticized for each of the following except:
    a. It contains too many characteristics of the medical model.
    b. Many psychologists find the DSM-IV to be confusing.
    c. The focus is on pathology and on finding something wrong.
    d. It contains categories for everyday problems.

    a. no; this is a valid criticism
    b. CORRECT; this is not a criticism of the DSM-IV
    c. no; this is a valid criticism
    d. no; this is a valid criticism

11. Mr. Dodge engages in very rigid and structured behavior. He is preoccupied with cleanliness. He washes his hands more than twenty times per day and brings two changes of underwear to work with him. He would **probably** be diagnosed as suffering from a(n)
    a. conversion disorder.
    b. phobia.
    c. generalized anxiety disorder.
    d. obsessive-compulsive disorder.

    a. no; there are no physical symptoms
    b. no; Mr. Dodge does not complain of an persistent irrational fear
    c. no; he is not experiencing persistent anxiety
    d. YES; obsessive-compulsive disorder included thoughts and rituals

12. Stanley was fearful of developing cancer, which was the cause of the deaths of both of his parents. He avoided any situation where someone might smoke, ate no processed meat or dairy products, and would not even speak with anyone who had been diagnosed as having cancer. Wherever he was, he constantly had thoughts of himself wasting away with cancer. Stanley's thoughts were
    a. obsessions.
    b. compulsions.
    c. a generalized anxiety disorder.
    d. a conversion disorder.

    a. YES; obsessions are thoughts that are anxiety-provoking
    b. no; compulsions are repetitive, ritualistic behaviors
    c. no; he does not experience persistent anxiety
    d. no; there is no evidence of physical symptoms that are unexplainable

13. All somatoform disorders have which characteristic in common?
    a.   antisocial tendencies
    b.   avoidance behavior
    c.   experiencing real physical symptoms
    d.   generalized anxiety

a.	no
b.	no
c.	YOU GOT IT; these disorders involve physical symptoms which are not faked
d.	no

14. A somatoform disorder characterized by a pervasive fear of illness and disease is called
    a.   conversion disorder.
    b.   obsessive-compulsive disorder.
    c.   hypochondriasis.
    d.   dissociative fugue.

a.	no; in this disorder involves physical problems, yet nothing physiologically wrong
b.	no; this disorder involves anxiety-provoking thoughts and ritualistic behaviors
c.	YES; this define hypochondriasis
d.	no; this disorder involves amnesia, unexpected travel, and a new identity

15. What do dissociative identity disorder and fugue have in common?
    a.   They are both conversion disorders.
    b.   They are both dissociative disorders.
    c.   They involve delusions of grandeur and reference.
    d.   They are the most common mood disorders.

a.	no; in this disorder involves physical problems, yet nothing physiologically wrong
b.	YES; in these disorders, there are losses of memory or change in identity
c.	no
d.	no

16. A disorder characterized by unexpected travel away from home and a new identity is called
    a.   dissociative identity disorder.
    b.   dissociative amnesia.
    c.   dissociative fugue.
    d.   hypochondriasis.

a.	no; this disorder refers to two or more distinct personalities in one person
b.	no; this disorder involves amnesia caused by extensive psychological stress
c.	RIGHT; this defines dissociative fugue ("fugue" means flight)
d.	no; hypochondriasis includes a pervasive fear of illness and disease

17. Which of the following is a common characteristic of those individuals diagnosed with dissociative identity disorder?
    a.   sexual abuse
    b.   brain trauma
    c.   fugue.
    d.   growing up in single-parent families

a.	YES; this occurs in about 56% of reported cases
b.	no; this is not a common characteristic
c.	no; fugue is not a common characteristic
d.	no; this is not a common characteristic

18. Which of the following is **not** related to the mood disorders?
    a. bipolar disorder
    b. major depressive disorder
    c. dysthymic disorder
    d. conversion disorder

a.	no; bipolar disorder is a mood disorder	
b.	no; major depressive disorder is a mood disorder	
c.	no; dysthymic disorder is a mood disorder and is more chronic	
d.	CORRECT; conversion disorder is a type of somatoform disorder	

19. Bipolar disorder is characterized by
    a. depressive behavior.
    b. manic behavior.
    c. both of the above.
    d. none of the above.

a.	no; you are partially right	
b.	no; you are partially right	
c.	RIGHT; bipolar involves extreme mood swings of mood (mania and depression)	
d.	no	

20. The "common cold" of mental disorders is
    a. schizophrenic disorder.
    b. depression.
    c. bipolar disorder.
    d. multiple personality.

a.	no	
b.	YES; depression is sometimes referred to the "common cold" since it is widespread	
c.	no	
d.	no	

21. Which of the following individuals is at **highest** risk for developing a mood disorder?
    a. Angela, whose aunt is often moody and withdrawn
    b. Fred, whose father is a diagnosed manic-depressive
    c. Roslyn, who is often in a bad mood
    d. Andrew, whose brother has a personality disorder

a.	no	
b.	THIS IS RIGHT; mood disorders have a strong genetic component	
c.	no	
d.	no	

22. Which of the following refers to a biological cause of mood disorders?
    a. heredity
    b. learned helplessness
    c. personality factors
    d. childhood experiences

a.	CORRECT; heredity refers to genetics and is a biological cause of mood disorders	
b.	no; learned helpless is a psychosocial explanation	
c.	no; personality factors do not refer to biological causes	
d.	no; childhood experiences are not related to biological causes	

23. According to Aaron Beck, a depressed person is **more likely** than a non-depressed person to engage in
   a. productive thinking.
   b. creative thinking.
   c. catastrophic thinking.
   d. reactive thinking.

a.	no; Beck does not make reference to productive thinking
b.	no; Beck does not make reference to creative thinking
c.	AYE; Beck focuses on how negative thoughts shape person's experience
d.	no; Beck does not make reference to reactive thinking

24. Which of the following characterizes a schizophrenic disorder?
   a. hallucinations.
   b. delusions
   c. bizarre motor behavior
   d. all of the above

a.	no; but you are partially right
b.	no; but you are partially right
c.	no; but you are partially right
d.	RIGHT; all of these characterize schizophrenia

25. What is the **main** difference between schizophrenia and dissociative personality disorder?
   a. The schizophrenic has one personality that has disintegrated.
   b. The schizophrenic has one integrated personality.
   c. The schizophrenic never has more than one alternate personality.
   d. The schizophrenic always has more than two alternate personalities.

a.	YES; schizophrenia is not "split personality"
b.	no; in schizophrenia, the personality has disintegrated
c.	no; this is not an accurate description of schizophrenia
d.	no; this is not an accurate description of schizophrenia

26. Paranoid schizophrenia differs from disorganized schizophrenia **primarily** in which way?
   a. the inappropriateness of affect
   b. the complexity and systematic nature of hallucinations and delusions
   c. the disorganization of thought
   d. the extreme bizarreness of motor behavior, ranging from stupor to agitation

a.	no; disorganized schizophrenia includes inappropriateness of affect
b.	THAT'S CORRECT; these two characteristics differentiate these two forms of schizophrenia
c.	no; disorganized schizophrenia includes disorganization of thought
d.	no; this sounds like catatonic schizophrenia

27. Martha has been sitting in a hunched-over position on her hospital bed for several hours. When you speak to her, her position remains unchanged, and she doesn't answer. When you lift her arm, she remains sitting motionless, with her arm in a raised position. Martha is **most likely** suffering from which type of schizophrenia?
   a. paranoid
   b. catatonic
   c. disorganized
   d. undifferentiated

a.	no; there is no indication of delusions
b.	YES; Martha shows bizarre motor behaviors
c.	no; these symptoms do not fit disorganized schizophrenia
d.	no; these symptoms fit a particular type of schizophrenia

28. Which type of schizophrenic disorder is characterized by a "waxy flexibility"?
    a. disorganized schizophrenia
    b. catatonic schizophrenia
    c. paranoid schizophrenia
    d. undifferentiated schizophrenia

a.	no; this disorder has delusions and hallucinations with no meaning
b.	RIGHT; waxy flexibilty is seen sometimes in people with catatonic schizophrenia
c.	no; this type is characterized by delusions of reference, grandeur, and persecution
d.	no; this type does not meet the criteria of any one disorder or more than one

29. Delusions of reference, grandeur, and persecution characterize which type of schizophrenia?
    a. disorganized
    b. catatonic
    c. paranoid
    d. undifferentiated

a.	no; these delusions are not consistent with disorganized schizophrenia
b.	no; catatonic schizophrenia symptoms involve bizarre motor behaviors
c.	CORRECT; these types of symptoms characterize paranoid schizophrenia
d.	no

30. Which theory argues that a biogenetic disposition and stress cause schizophrenia?
    a. diathesis-stress view
    b. disorganized-stress theory
    c. dopamine hypothesis
    d. psychoanalytic theory

a.	THAT'S RIGHT; the diathesis refers to the disposition
b.	no
c.	no; but dopamine is a neurotransmitter that may play a role in schizophrenia
d.	no

31. _____ disorders are chronic, maladaptive cognitive-behavioral patterns that are thoroughly integrated into an individual's personality.
    a. Anxiety
    b. Personality
    c. Schizophrenic
    d. Dissociative

a.	no; these involve motor tension, hyperactivity, and apprehensive expectations
b.	YES; this is the definition of personality disorders
c.	no; these disorders involves disturbances in thought, emotion, and motor behavior
d.	no; dissociative disorders involves changes in memory and identity

32. An individual who engages in stealing and vandalism, who cannot uphold financial obligations, and who shows no remorse after harming someone may be considered to have a(n)
    a. conversion disorder
    b. bipolar disorder.
    c. somatoform disorder.
    d. antisocial personality disorder.

a.	no; in this disorder involves physical problems, yet nothing physiologically wrong
b.	no; this disorder involves extreme moods such as mania and depression
c.	no; these disorders involve physical symptoms
d.	RIGHT; these characterize antisocial personality disorder

33. Which of the following characterizes antisocial personality disorder?
   a. It usually begins in middle adulthood.
   b. It affects males and females equally.
   c. Most adolescents grow out of the disorder.
   d. Those with the disorder show no remorse when harming someone.

a.	no; typically the disorder starts in adolescence
b.	no; this disorders affects more males than females
c.	no; in fact people do not "grow out" of personality disorders
d.	THAT IS RIGHT; people with this disorders show no remorse

34. Andrea has an excessive need to be the center of attention whenever she is with other people. At work, she is highly competitive and gets very angry if anyone criticizes her. She constantly manipulates others, especially younger coworkers. These behaviors are associated with which personality disorder?
   a. paranoid
   b. borderline
   c. schizoid
   d. narcissistic

a.	no; this disorders involves mistrust and suspiciousness
b.	no; it refers to emotional instability and impulsiveness
c.	no; schizoid personality disorder involves problems with social relationships
d.	YES; Andrea shows an exaggerated sense of self-importance

Chapter 14 - Therapies

The Big Picture: Chapter Overview

Psychotherapy is the process used by mental health professionals to help individuals recognize, define, and overcome their psychological and interpersonal difficulties and improve their adjustment. Many early treatments of mental disturbances were inhumane. For instance, in primitive societies trephining was used to let evil spirits escape. After Hippocrates' more human treatment, exorcism was used in the Middle Ages to cast out evil spirits. During the Renaissance, the mentally disturbed were housed in asylums. Pinel believed that mental patients needed to be treated with compassion and initiated a changed in the treatment of mental illness. In the United States, the efforts of Dorothea Dix were instrumental in separating the mentally disturbed from criminals. In Canada, Clarence Hincks founded the Canadian Mental Health Association. The development of new drugs and the deinstitutionalization movement led to a large number of inpatients being transferred to community-based outpatient facilities. Since then in Canada, the Canadian Mental Health Foundation has proposed the Community Resource Base model. In the U.S. managed care has changed mental health care delivery to control health care costs and has been met with much criticism.

There are several mental health professions that vary in degree, education, and nature of training. Society controls individuals who practice psychotherapy through licensing and certification. The theories of personality serve as the foundation for many forms of psychotherapy. For instance insight therapy describes the psychodynamic and humanistic views since the goal is to encourage insight and awareness of one's self.

The psychodynamic therapies stress the importance of the unconscious mind, the role of infancy and childhood experiences, and extensive interpretation by a therapist. Psychoanalysis is a well-known psychodynamic approach. In psychoanalysis, the individual's unconscious thoughts are analyzed. Freud believed that mental disturbances are caused by unresolved unconscious conflicts, often involving sexuality, that originate in early childhood. The therapist may use free association, which is encouraging the patient to say out loud whatever comes to mind no matter how trivial or embarrassing; this would allow for emotional feelings to be released through catharsis. The therapist would also interpret free association, dreams, statements, and behaviors to search for the underlying symbolic meaning. In dream analysis, the therapist analyzes the dream's manifest content to determine its latent content. Transference refers to the person's relating to the therapist in ways that reproduce or relive important relationships. Resistance is a term used to describe unconscious defense strategies that prevent the analyst from understanding the person's problems. An important theme in contemporary psychodynamic theories is the development of the self in social contexts such as early relationships with attachment figures. Few contemporary psychodynamic therapists rigorously follow Freud's guidelines.

In the humanistic therapies, clients are encouraged to understand themselves and to grow personally. The humanistic perspective focuses on conscious thoughts, the present, personal growth, and self-fulfillment. Person-centered therapy was developed by Carl Rogers and creates a warm, supportive atmosphere to improve the client's self-concept and to encourage the client to gain insight about problems. Unconditional positive regard, genuineness, accurate empathy, and active listening are critical in creating this type of atmosphere. Fritz Perls developed Gestalt therapy to help clients become more aware of their feelings and to face their problems. Role playing and confrontation are often used in Gestalt therapy to help clients. Both the humanistic therapies encourage clients to take responsibility for their feelings and actions and to understand themselves.

Behavior therapies are based on the principles of learning to reduce or eliminate maladaptive behavior. Behavior therapists assume that overt maladaptive symptoms are the problem and not unconscious conflicts or inaccurate perceptions. Behavior therapy is based on the learning principles of classical, operant, and social cognitive theories. Systematic desensitization, a technique that makes use of the principles of classical conditioning, has been used to treat phobias; anxiety is treated by getting the person to associate deep relaxation with increasingly intense anxiety-producing situations. Aversive conditioning is used to teach people to avoid such behaviors as smoking, overeating, and drinking. Aversive conditioning consists of repeated pairings of the undesirable behavior with aversive stimuli to decrease the behavior's rewards. Using operant conditioning is based on the idea that maladaptive behavior patterns are learned and therefore, can be unlearned. Behavior modification is a therapy technique that makes use of operant conditioning. It is believe that many problem behaviors are caused by inadequate response consequences. In a token economy, behaviors are reinforced with tokens that can be exchanged for desired rewards. Donald Meichenbaum's cognitive behavior modification integrates behavior therapy with cognitive therapy.

The cognitive therapists emphasize that an individual's cognitions, or thoughts, are the main sources of abnormal behavior. Cognitive therapies focus on changing the individual's thoughts or cognitions to change behaviors. Albert Ellis' rational-emotive therapy is an example of cognitive therapy. In this type of therapy, the therapist disputes the individual's self-defeating beliefs and encourages the client to change his or her belief system. Aaron Beck's cognitive therapy tries to change the illogical thinking of depressed individuals. Beck's approach helps clients to make connections between logical errors and emotional responses.

Group therapies stress that social relationships are important in successful therapy, therefore group interaction may be more beneficial than individual therapy. Other types of therapies include family and couples therapy and self-help support groups. Community psychology focuses on both prevention and treatment of mental disorders.

Much research has been conducted to determine whether or not psychotherapy is effective and if one approach is superior to another. Hans Eysenck concluded that psychotherapy is ineffective and found that neurotic individuals on a waiting list showed marked improvement even though they did not receive psychotherapy. Using meta-analysis, which statistically combines the results of many different studies, researchers found psychotherapy is effective in general. When comparing different approaches, research has found that behavior therapy and insight therapies were superior to no treatment, but did not differ from each other in effectiveness. Some therapies have been found to be more effective in treating some disorders than others. Behavior therapies have been most successful in treating phobias and sexual dysfunctions, while cognitive therapies are effective in treating depression and anxiety. Relaxation training is effective in treating anxiety disorders. The most effective psychotherapies have the common elements of expectations, mastery, and emotional arousal as well as a supportive therapeutic relationship. In the last two decades, psychologists have turned their attention to gender and ethnic concerns in psychotherapy.

Biomedical therapies are designed to alter the way an individual's body functions. The most common type of biomedical therapy is drug therapy. Three major classes of psychotherapeutic drugs are antianxiety (e.g., Xanax, Valium, Librium), antidepressant (e.g., Elavil, MAO inhibitors, Prozac, Paxil, lithium) and antipsychotic (e.g., neuroleptics). Tardive dyskinesia is a major side effect of neurolpetic drugs and involves grotesque, involuntary movements of facial muscles and mouth. Another neuroleptic drug, Clozaril, has toxic effects on white blood cells in some patients. Electroconvulsive therapy (ECT) and psychosurgery are two extreme techniques that are used as last resorts. ECT is mainly used to treat severe depression and involves causing a seizure. Adverse side effects include memory loss or other cognitive impairments. Psychosurgery involves the removal or destruction of brain tissue to improve psychological adjustment.

Most therapists take an eclectic or integrative approach to therapy. In this approach, the therapist is open to using various therapeutic techniques. An example of this is the joint use of psychotherapy and drug therapy. In the future, therapists will pay more attention to ethnic and cultural factors in treating clients.

Learning Objectives

When you have studied the material in this chapter, you should be able to:

1. discuss the early approaches to therapy, including trephining, exorcism, and the use of asylums. (pp. 480-481)
2. explain the deinstitutionalization movement. (pp. 481-482)
3. discuss the challenges of delivering psychotherapeutic services in Canada and the impact of managed care on treatment quality in the U.S. (pp. 482-484)

4.   explain the psychoanalytic approach to psychotherapy and the following techniques: free association, catharsis, interpretation, dream analysis, transference, and resistance. (pp. 484-488)
5.   differentiate between Freudian and contemporary psychoanalysis. (pp. 488-489)
6.   discuss the humanistic approach to therapy. (pp. 489-491)
7.   compare and contrast Rogers' person-centered therapy and Perl's Gestalt therapy. (pp. 489-491)
8.   describe behavioral therapy and differentiate between classical conditioning approaches, operant conditioning approaches, and cognitive behavior modification (pp. 491-494)
9.   describe cognitive behavioral therapy and differentiate Ellis' rational-emotive therapy, Beck's cognitive therapy, and Meichenbaum's cognitive behavior modification (pp. 493-496)
10.   list and describe the features of group therapy. (pp. 497-500)
11.   explain the dynamics of the following group therapy approaches: family and couples therapy and self-help groups. (pp. 498-499)
12.   summarize research evaluating the effectiveness of psychotherapy. pp. 501-502)
13.   discuss the challenges involved in providing psychotherapy for women and ethnic minorities. (pp. 502-504)
14.   list and identify the biochemical mechanisms of drugs used to treat mental illness: antianxiety drugs, antidepressants, and antipsychotics. (pp. 504-506)
15.   indicate when electroconvulsive therapy is appropriate and discuss its benefits and risks. (p. 506)
16.   discuss advances made in psychosurgery and when psychosurgery is indicated. (pp. 507-508)
17.   explain the eclectic approach to psychotherapy and evaluate arguments in favor and disputing the appropriateness of eclecticism. (p. 508-509)
18.   from *Explorations in Psychology: Contemporary Behavior Therapy and the Treatment of Depression - The Lewinsohn Approach*, list the steps involved in treating depression using the Lewinsohn approach. (p. 495)
19.   from *Explorations in Psychology: Guidelines for Seeking Professional Help*, list and discuss important considerations prior to seeking therapy and during the therapeutic process. (p. 503)

Guided Review

The Nature and History of Psychotherapy

_____ is the process mental health professionals use to work with individuals to reduce their problems and improve their adjustment. A wide variety of psychotherapeutic techniques exist today. In primitive societies, a technique called _____ was used for mentally disable people. In the Middle Ages, mentally disabled individuals' "evilness" was treated by _____. During the Renaissance, the mentally disable were housed in _____. Reform in France was led by _____. In the United States the efforts of Dorothea Dix were instrumental in separating the mentally disabled from _____. In Canada, Clarence Hincks founded the _____ _____ _____ _____. The movement that led to the transfer of many inpatients from mental hospitals to community-based facilities where they received outpatient care is called _____. The goals of the community mental health centers were to provide _____-based mental health services and to commit resources to help _____ mental disorders rather than to treat them. A U.S. approach to dealing with increasing mental health costs, involving the use of external reviewers to approve the treatments, is called _____ care.

Mental health professionals differ in their degree and _____. Society controls individuals who practice psychotherapy by _____ and _____. The goal of both the psychodynamic and humanistic therapies is to encourage insight and awareness of self; therefore they are called _____ therapies.

Psychotherapy - p. 480	
trephining - p. 480	
exorcism - p. 480	
asylums - p. 481	
Pinel - p. 481	
criminals – p. 481	
Canadian Mental Health Association – p. 481	
deinstitutionalization - p. 481	
community - p. 481	
prevent - p. 481	
managed - p. 482	
training - p. 483	
licensing/certification - p. 484	
insight - p. 484	

Approaches to Psychotherapies

The types of therapies that stress the importance of the unconscious mind, the role of the infant and childhood experiences, and extensive interpretation by a therapist are called _____ therapies. A well-known psychodynamic approach was developed by Freud; it is called _____. According to this approach, psychological problems can be traced to childhood experiences, often involving conflicts about _____. These conflicts are not _____ to the conscious mind. Special therapeutic techniques help bring these conflicts into _____. One technique in which the patient lies on a couch and is encouraged to talk freely, is called _____ _____. By talking freely, Freud felt that emotional tension could be released, a process called _____. The search for symbolic, hidden meanings in what the client says and does is called _____. Psychoanalysts interpret a client's dreams in the technique called _____ _____. According to Freud, the conscious, remembered aspects of a dream are called the _____ content, whereas the unconscious, symbolic aspects of a dream are called the _____ content. Often, patients relate to the therapist in ways that reproduce important relationships in the patient's life, a process called _____. The client's unconscious defense strategies that prevent an analyst from understanding the client's problems is called _____. Showing up late for sessions or arguing with the

psychodynamic - p 484	
psychoanalysis - p. 484	
sexuality - p. 486	
available - p. 486	
awareness - p. 486	
free association - p. 486	
catharsis - p. 486	
interpretation - p. 487	
dream analysis - p. 487	
manifest - p. 487	
latent - p. 487	
transference - p. 487	
resistance - p. 487	

psychoanalyst are examples of _____ . An important theme in contemporary psychodynamic theories is the development of the self in _____ _____ .

Clients are encouraged to understand themselves and to grow personally in the _____ psychotherapies. One type of humanistic psychotherapy, developed by Carl Rogers, is called _____-_____ therapy. According to Rogers, the positive regard we receive from others has strings attached, a situation he refers to as _____ of _____ . Rogers believes that therapists should create a warm and caring environment, a concept called unconditional _____ _____ . Additionally, Rogers believes that therapists must not hide behind a façade; in other word, therapists must be _____ . Therapists should also try to imagine what it would be like to be the client, an ability Rogers calls _____ _____ . Also, therapists should restate and support what clients say and engage in _____ _____ . In another type of humanistic psychotherapy, therapists question and challenge clients to help them become aware of their _____ . This approach is called _____ therapy and was founded by _____ _____ . In this technique, therapists set examples, and encourage _____ between verbal and nonverbal behavior, and use _____ playing. Gestalt therapy is much more _____ than person-centered therapy.

Behavior therapies use the principles of _____ to reduce or eliminate maladaptive behavior. Two procedures deal with behaviors learned through _____ conditioning. One procedure, which treats anxiety by getting clients to relax as they visualize anxiety-producing situations, is _____ _____ . Research suggests that this technique is an effective way to treat a number of _____ . A second technique that is based on classical conditioning repeatedly pairs undesirable behavior with an negative stimulus; this is called _____ _____ . Other behavior therapy techniques make use of _____ conditioning in order to change the individual's behavior; this process is often called _____ . A behavior therapy technique that allows individuals to earn tokens that can later be exchanged for desired rewards is called a _____ _____ . Cognitive Behavior Modification, which integrates behavior modification with cognitive techniques was developed by _____ _____ .

Cognitive therapists emphasize that the individual's cognitions or _____ are the main source of abnormal behavior. Albert Ellis developed a cognitive therapy called _____-_____ Therapy. In this type of therapy, the therapist _____ the individual's self-defeating beliefs and encourages him or her to change his or her _____ system. The cognitive therapy of Aaron Beck focuses on treating a variety of dysfunctions, especially _____ . Beck's approach helps the individual understand the connection between illogical thinking and _____ _____ .

The following features make group therapy attractive: (1) the individual receives _____ from either the group leader or group members, (2) group members realize that others are suffering also, a feature called _____ , (3) group members can support one another, a feature termed _____ , (4) because a therapy group resembles a family, it provides corrective _____ of the family group, (5) feedback from other group members promotes development of _____ skills, and (6) the group offers a setting for _____ learning. Group therapy with family members is called _____ therapy and stresses that an individual's psychological adjustment is related to a pattern of interaction within the family. Therapy with couples that focuses on their relationship is called couples therapy. Four widely used techniques in family systems therapy are (1) _____ , (2) reframing, (3) _____ change, and (4) detriangulation. Groups that are run on a voluntary basis and without a professional therapist are called _____ - _____ groups. One well-known self-help group is _____ _____ .

Is psychotherapy effective? One well-known study, which used a procedure called _____ to evaluate many other investigations, found psychotherapies to be effective. If a study is using a _____ - _____ control group, it means that there are individuals wanting to see a psychotherapist but who have not yet received psychotherapy. One study found _____ therapies to be most effective in treating specific behavioral problems such as phobias, where as _____ therapies have been successful in treating depression and anxiety. Frank has concluded that effective psychotherapies have the common elements of _____ , mastery, and emotional arousal . In the past 2 decades, psychologists have become sensitive to the concerns of ethnicity and _____ in psychotherapy. An important issue regarding females in therapy focuses on the appropriateness of _____ as a therapy goal. Some have suggested that therapy goals for women should be _____ and connection with others. Ethnic minority individuals generally prefer to discuss problems with friends and _____ rather than with mental health professionals. Research also suggests that _____ _____ individuals are more likely to terminate therapy early when there is an ethnic mismatch between client and therapist.

Biomedical Therapies

Therapies designed to deal with psychological problems by altering the way an individual's body functions are called _____ therapies. A common type of biomedical therapy is _____ therapy. One group of drugs, commonly known as tranquilizers, are the _____ drugs. Drugs used to diminish agitation, hallucinations, and delusions are the _____ drugs. The most widely used antipsychotic drugs are the _____ , which apparently block the _____ system's action in the brain. A major side effect of the neuroleptics is a neurological disorder called _____ _____ . Drugs that regulate mood are called _____ drugs. The three main classes of antidepressant drugs are _____ , _____ and _____ inhibitors. A drug that is widely used to treat bipolar disorder is _____ .

"Shock treatment," more formally known as _____ therapy (ECT) is used to treat severe _____ . One treatment even more extreme than ECT involves removal or destruction of brain tissue to improve an individual's psychological adjustment. It is called

_____ and has become more precise.

Therapy Integration

Most therapists use a variety of approaches to therapy; that is they are _____ . In integrative therapy, the mental health professional will _____ various techniques and methods from diverse therapies. Therapy integrations are conceptually compatible with the _____ model of abnormal behavior.

psychosurgery - p. 507

eclectic (integrative) - p. 509
use - p. 509

biopsychosocial - p. 509

Explorations in Psychology

To respond to the questions and exercises presented in this section, please write your thoughts, perspectives, and reactions on a separate piece of paper.

Explorations in Psychology and Life: Penetrating Mrs. A.H.'s Thoughts

- How would a psychoanalyst interpret Mrs. A.H.'s forgetfulness during the first session in mentioning what turned out to be an important incident?
- After reading this section, would you prefer to have your behaviors, statements, free associations, and dreams evaluated using psychoanalysis?
- Can you relate any aspect of Mrs. A.H.'s behavior or statements in the context of defense mechanisms discussed in Chapter 12?

Explorations in Psychology and Life: Contemporary Behavior Therapy and the Treatment of Depression - the Lewinsohn Approach

- What are the basic principles of the Lewinsohn approach in treating depression?
- When you are feeling down or "blue" do you believe that it is related to too few positive life events?
- Can you reconcile the effectiveness of the Lewinsohn approach that focuses on pleasant events with research showing a biological cause of depression?

Explorations in Psychology and Life: "My Work Is Boring and I Resent It"

- What is the cause of mental disorders according to the cognitive therapies?
- What remarks by the client are especially forceful? Does the client benefit from these remarks?
- If you were the client, would come back to the therapist for the next session?

Explorations in Psychology and Life: Guidelines for Seeking Professional Help

- If you were the person described in this section, what type of mental health professional would you seek out? Why?
- Can you think of any other guideline that might be important in seeking professional help?
- What is the matter with asking a friend for the name of a good therapist?

In Your Own Words

To respond to the questions and exercises presented in this section, please write your thoughts, perspectives, and reactions on a separate piece of paper.
- ✓ Analyze one of your dreams with regard to manifest content and then speculate on its latent content using what you already know about the psychodynamic perspective.
- ✓ How would parents put conditions of worth on their children? List some ways.
- ✓ Look at the hierarchy of situations involving the fear of exams. Assume that you have a similar fear and rearrange the situations to make them more reflective of your fear.

✓ What irrational beliefs or logical thinking errors are you able to notice in yourself?
✓ As you read the section on therapy integration, what aspects of each psychotherapy would you use to treat depression if you were a mental health professional?
✓ How could transferring inpatients from mental hospitals to community-based care help these individuals? In other words, justify deinstitutionalization.
✓ Make up titles of fictitious songs that could have been written by Freud, a behavioral therapist, Rogers, and Ellis. The title of each song should be consistent with the therapeutic approaches of these individuals.
✓ Consider this: A depressed friend of yours is thinking about seeking professional help. He is thinking of going to a psychoanalyst, a psychologist using the Lewinsohn approach, Albert Ellis, Donald Meichenbaum, and a psychiatrist. He knows that you are taking a psychology class and asks you for your views on each. What do you say?

Correcting the Incorrect

Carefully read each statement. Determine if the statement is correct or incorrect. If the statement is incorrect, make the necessary changes to correct it. Then look directly under the statement for the correct statement and page reference in the textbook.

1. In trephining, a small amount of poison is given to a person to kill evil spirits.
   ❑ *In trephining, a small hole was chipped into the skull to allow evil spirits to escape. (p. 480)*
2. Hippocrates advocated the use of trephining.
   ❑ *Hippocrates advocated the use of rest, exercise, and a bland diet. (p. 480)*
3. During the Middle Ages, the mentally ill were care for with kindness and compassion.
   ❑ *During the Middle Ages, the mentally ill were treated by exorcism. (p. 480)*
4. Pinel initiated some changes in the way that the mentally disordered were treated.
   ❑ *Pinel initiated some changes in the way that the mentally disordered were treated. (p. 481)*
5. Deinstitutionalization occurred in the 1860s.
   ❑ *Deinstitutionalization occurred in the 1960s. (p. 481)*
6. Mental health care providers receive the same training.
   ❑ *Mental health care providers do not receive the same training. (p. 483)*
7. The behavioral theories of Skinner were important in developing psychoanalysis.
   ❑ *The psychodynamic theories of Freud were important in developing psychoanalysis. (p. 484)*
8. Freud believed that problems could be traced back to childhood conflicts about sexuality.
   ❑ *Freud believed that problems could be traced back to childhood conflicts about sexuality. (p. 486)*
9. In catharsis, the person is asked to say whatever comes to mind, even if it is trivial or embarrassing.
   ❑ *In free association, the person is asked to say whatever comes to mind, even if it is trivial or embarrassing. (p. 486)*
10. The manifest content of a dream refers to its underlying, symbolic meaning.
    ❑ *The latent content of a dream refers to its underlying, symbolic meaning. (p. 487)*
11. Psychoanalysis tries to encourage resistance.
    ❑ *Psychoanalysis tries to work through resistance. (p. 487)*
12. In person-centered therapy, the therapist creates an atmosphere with many conditions of worth.
    ❑ *In person-centered therapy, the therapist creates an atmosphere with no conditions of worth. (p. 489)*
13. The therapist's role in person-centered therapy is directive.
    ❑ *The therapist's role in person-centered therapy is nondirective. (p. 489)*
14. Perls developed Gestalt therapy to help people focus on their past.
    ❑ *Perls developed Gestalt therapy to help people focus on here and now. (p. 491)*
15. Behavior therapies are based on Freud's theory.
    ❑ *Behavior therapies are based on learning theory. (p. 491)*
16. In systematic desensitization, the person receives tokens for appropriate behavior.
    ❑ *In systematic desensitization, the person learns relaxation with more anxiety-provoking situations. (p. 492)*

17.   Aversive conditioning associates some undesirable behavior with aversive stimuli.
       ❏   *Aversive conditioning associates some undesirable behavior with aversive stimuli.* (p. 492)
18.   An example of procedure based upon operant conditioning is free association.
       ❏   *An example of procedure based upon operant conditioning is token economy.* (p. 493)
19.   A cognitive therapist focuses on how the environment influences her client's behavior.
       ❏   *A cognitive therapist focuses on how thoughts influences her client's behavior.* (p. 494)
20.   Ellis argues that irrational and self-defeating beliefs play a role in psychological problems.
       ❏   *Ellis argues that irrational and self-defeating beliefs play a role in psychological problems.* (p. 494)
21.   Beck abbreviated his approach to therapy as A, B, C, D, and E.
       ❏   *Ellis abbreviated his approach to therapy as A, B, C, D, and E.* (p. 494)
22.   Beck's approach to therapy is much more directive and confrontational than Ellis' approach.
       ❏   *Beck's approach to therapy is much less directive and confrontational than Ellis' approach.* (p. 494-496)
23.   Group therapy takes advantage of relationships that may hold the key to an individual's problems.
       ❏   *Group therapy takes advantage of relationships that may hold the key to an individual's problems.* (p. 498)
24.   The main form of family therapy is the psychodynamic approach.
       ❏   *The main form of family therapy is family systems therapy.* (p. 498)
25.   In self-help groups, a professional therapist tries to uncover communication styles that are maladaptive.
       ❏   *In couples therapy, a professional therapist tries to uncover communication styles that are maladaptive.* (p. 499)
26.   Alcoholics Anonymous is one the best-known cognitive therapies.
       ❏   *Alcoholics Anonymous is one the best-known self-help support groups.* (p. 499)
27.   Hans Eysenck provided evidence that psychotherapy is effective.
       ❏   *Hans Eysenck provided evidence that psychotherapy is ineffective.* (p. 501)
28.   A meta-analysis examines one study in a very detailed way.
       ❏   *A meta-analysis examines one the results of many studies.* (p. 501)
29.   Cognitive therapies seem to be most successful with depression and anxiety.
       ❏   *Cognitive therapies seem to be most successful with depression and anxiety.* (p. 502)
30.   Research shows that therapeutic relationship is less important than the therapist's academic training.
       ❏   *Research shows that therapeutic relationship is more important than the therapist's academic training.* (p. 502)
31.   The goals of therapy should be the same for males and females.
       ❏   *The goals of therapy may not be the same for males and females.* (p. 504)
32.   Drug therapies are often administered to patients by their psychologists.
       ❏   *Drug therapies are often administered to patients by their medical doctors or psychiatrist.* (p. 504)
33.   Antianxiety drugs work by preventing the release of neurotransmitters into the synapse.
       ❏   *Antianxiety drugs work by binding to receptor sites.* (p. 504)
34.   Prozac interferes with the reabsorption of serotonin in the brain.
       ❏   *Prozac interferes with the reabsorption of serotonin in the brain.* (p. 505)
35.   MAO inhibitors are drugs that are most commonly used to treat bipolar disorder.
       ❏   *Lithium is a drug that is most commonly used to treat bipolar disorder.* (p. 505)
36.   A patient with schizophrenia would be given a neuroleptic.
       ❏   *A patient with schizophrenia would be given a neuroleptic.* (p. 505)
37.   There are no significant side effects of ECT.
       ❏   *There are significant side effects of ECT.* (p. 506)
38.   Prefrontal lobotomies are routinely used to control aggressive behavior.
       ❏   *Prefrontal lobotomies are not used to control aggressive behavior.* (p. 508)
39.   In integrative therapy, the therapist uses techniques from several therapies.
       ❏   *In integrative therapy, the therapist uses techniques from several therapies.* (p. 509)
40.   The integrative therapy approach contradicts the biopsychosocial model of abnormal behavior.
       ❏   *The integrative therapy approach is compatible with the biopsychosocial model of abnormal behavior.* (p. 509)

Practice Test

1. In ancient civilizations, what was the **main** intent of trephining?
    a. to restore the chemical balance in the brain
    b. to cure abnormal behavior by letting the evil spirit escape
    c. to restore the balance of body fluids
    d. to torture the individual who displayed abnormal behavior

a.	no
b.	THAT'S RIGHT; go figure.
c.	no
d.	no

2. Which of the following individuals led the movement to reform the treatment of mentally ill peoples?
    a. Pinel
    b. Milgram
    c. Pavlov
    d. Bandura

a.	CORRECT; he believed that the mentally ill should be treated as people not animals
b.	no; Milgram was a social psychologist who studied obedience
c.	no; Pavlov is associated with classical conditioning
d.	no; Bandura is best known for his social cognitive theory

3. What was the original intent of deinstitutionalization?
    a. to increase the hospitalization time for individuals who suffered from severe mental illnesses
    b. to transfer the treatment of mental illness from state and provincial hospitals to community-based clinics
    c. to test the new drugs that had become available in the late 1990s
    d. to use the facilities of state mental hospitals as state prisons

a.	no; deinstitutionalization did just the opposite
b.	RIGHT; this was the original intent of deinstitutionalization
c.	no; the new drugs that revolutionized treatment was in the 1950s
d.	no; this was not the original intent of deinstitutionalization

4. A criticism of the managed health care system for providing psychotherapy is the
    a. emphasis on long-term psychotherapy.
    b. emphasis on short-term psychotherapy.
    c. development of explicit and measurable treatment plans.
    d. lack of certified practitioners.

a.	no; managed care has attempted to eliminate long-term psychotherapy
b.	YES; this is a criticism of managed care
c.	no; this is not a criticism
d.	no; this is not a criticism

5. James dreamed that he went to his neighbor's house at midnight and made himself a sandwich. His psychoanalyst interpreted the dream to mean that James really wanted to go to bed with his neighbor's wife. Making the sandwich was the
    a. symbolic content of the dream.
    b. manifest content of the dream.
    c. latent content of the dream.
    d. resistant content of the dream.

a.	no; the correct for a dream's symbolic content is the latent content
b.	YES: the manifest content refers to the dream's conscious, remembered aspects
c.	no; the latent content refers to the unconscious, unremembered aspects
d.	no

6. The psychoanalytic term to explain a client who suddenly begins missing appointments and becomes hostile in therapy sessions is
   a. resistance.
   b. transference.
   c. free association.
   d. catharsis.

a.	RIGHT; resistance refers to unconscious defense strategies
b.	no; this is the person's relating to the analyst in a way that resembles another relationship
c.	no; in free association the person says aloud whatever comes to mind
d.	no; this is the release of emotional tension when having an emotional experience

7. The experience of a release of emotional tension associated with reliving an emotionally charge experience is called
   a. catharsis.
   b. resistance.
   c. free association.
   d. unconditional positive regard.

a.	YES; this is the release of emotional tension when having an emotional experience
b.	no; resistance refers to unconscious defense strategies
c.	no; in free association the person says aloud whatever comes to mind
d.	no; this is acceptance of another person without any strings attached

8. Which of the following is **not** a focus of humanistic therapy?
   a. conscious thoughts
   b. past experiences
   c. personal growth
   d. self-fulfillment

a.	no; conscious thought is a focus of humanistic therapy
b.	GOOD; humanistic therapy focuses on the present rather than the past
c.	no; humanistic therapy emphasizes personal growth
d.	no; self-fulfillment is a focus of humanistic therapy

9. According to Carl Rogers, person-centered therapy requires all of the following **except** which one?
   a. unconditional positive regard
   b. genuineness
   c. interpretation
   d. active listening

a.	no; this is required in person-centered therapy
b.	no; this is required in person-centered therapy
c.	YES; this is not required since person-centered therapy is nondirective
d.	no; this is required in person-centered therapy

10. Gestalt therapy is similar to psychoanalytic therapy in that they both
    a. assume problems stem from past unresolved conflicts.
    b. assume the client can find solutions in the right atmosphere.
    c. expect resistance and transference to occur.
    d. deny the importance of dreams in understanding a person.

a.	RIGHT; this is an assumption of both Gestalt therapy and psychoanalytic therapy
b.	no; the client cannot finds solutions without the assistance of a therapist
c.	no; Gestalt therapy makes no requirement on resistance and transference
d.	no; psychoanalytic therapy makes use of dream analysis in understanding a person

11. The term "insight therapy" applies to both psychodynamic therapies and
    a. behavior therapies.
    b. humanistic therapies.
    c. biomedical therapies.
    d. aversive conditioning.

a.	no; behavior therapies does not use insight
b.	CORRECT; both therapies assume the client needs to gain insight and awareness
c.	no; insight is not required for the biomedical therapies
d.	no; in this therapy a behavior is paired with some unpleasant stimulus

12. Vigorously challenging and questioning clients about critical issues and forcing them to face their problems are techniques used in
    a. psychodynamic therapy.
    b. humanistic therapy.
    c. Gestalt therapy.
    d. person-centered therapy.

a.	no; this is not a technique in psychoanalysis
b.	no; the humanistic therapies would not be so active in confronting individuals
c.	THAT'S RIGHT; the therapist often confronts individuals
d.	no; person-centered therapy would not be so confrontational

13. Your roommate Rachel has terrifying memories of having been bitten by a pit bull when she was a child. To this day, she gets extremely nervous if a dog is anywhere near her. In order to help Rachel overcome this fear of dogs, you have brought home a puppy and intend to use systematic desensitization. Which of the following **best** describes your procedure?
    a. bringing the puppy closer and closer to Rachel after she has been given time to completely relax
    b. keeping the puppy in a separate room where Rachel does not have to interact with it
    c. forcing Rachel to hold the dog because fear of a puppy is ridiculous
    d. letting young children handle the dog in front of Rachel

a.	RIGHT; the person is gradually exposed to feared object while remaining relaxed
b.	no; this is not systematic desensitization
c.	no; this is not systematic desensitization
d.	no; this is not systematic desensitization

14. The principles of operant and classical conditioning are extensively used by practitioners of
    a. psychoanalysis.
    b. Gestalt therapy.
    c. group therapy.
    d. behavior therapy.

a.   no; psychoanalysis stress the importance of the unconscious mind

b.   no; this therapy includes challenging and confronting the client

c.   no; these principles are not extensively used in group therapy

d.   YES; behavior therapy is based on the idea that maladaptive behaviors are learned

15.   A technique of behavior therapy that pairs an undesirable behavior with an unpleasant stimulus is called

    a.   token economy

    b.   systematic desensitization

    c.   aversive conditioning

    d.   rational-emotion therapy

a.   no; in this technique, behavior is reinforced with tokens that can be later redeemed

b.   no; the technique uses relaxation and anxiety-producing situations

c.   AYE; this is the definition of aversive conditioning

d.   no; this focuses on irrational and self-defeating beliefs as causes of problems

16.   Cognitive therapists are likely to be concerned with

    a.   an individual's thoughts.

    b.   unconditional positive regard

    c.   the manifest content of dreams.

    d.   unconscious motives.

a.   YES; cognitive therapists focus on irrational beliefs and faulty thinking

b.   no; this is a concept from person-centered therapy

c.   no; the manifest content of dreams would be determined in psychoanalysis

d.   no; psychoanalytic therapy would emphasize unconscious motives

17.   Which approach is most likely to be concerned with challenging irrational and self-defeating beliefs?

    a.   Beck's cognitive therapy

    b.   Ellis' rational-emotional therapy

    c.   systematic desensitization

    d.   operant therapy

a.   no; even though Beck does focus on cognitions, the therapy is less directive

b.   YEA; Ellis believed that our self-statements are often irrational and self-defeating

c.   no; the technique uses relaxation and anxiety-producing situations

d.   no; operant therapy primarily focuses on the use of reinforcement in therapy

18.   Research has supported the effectiveness of Aaron Beck's cognitive therapy in treating

    a.   bipolar disorder.

    b.   depression.

    c.   schizophrenia.

    d.   all of the above.

a.   no

b.   no

c.   RIGHT; depression is seen as the result of faulty thinking and errors in logic

d.   no

19.   When a family systems therapist is using validation, a member of the family would hear the therapist

    a.   expressing understanding to a family member.

    b.   telling the family which member is correct about the nature of a problem.

    c.   encouraging the parents to spend more time together.

    d.   trying to encourage the family to have fewer conflicts.

a.	YES; by expressing understanding to a person, their views are validated
b.	no; this is not validation
c.	no; this is not validation
d	no; this is not validation

20. In family systems therapy, teaching family members to view individual problems as family problems is called
   a. validation.
   b. reframing.
   c. structural change.
   d. detriangulation.

a.	no; this refers to expressing understanding to a person to validate their views
b.	CORRECT; this is reframing
c.	no; in structural change, the therapist attempts to change relationships in the family
d.	no, this technique is used to direct attention from a child to the parents

21. Ann and the children feel that they are not getting enough of Jerry's attention. Ann complains that Jerry works too much. Their family therapist told them all that Jerry is not the problem and that they should not complain to or about him for 2 weeks. The therapist is using
   a. restructuring.
   b. detriangulation.
   c. something other than the systems approach.
   d. reframing.

a.	no; this technique refers to the therapist attempting to change relationships
b.	RIGHT; this technique is used to direct attention from one family member, who may be a scapegoat, to other relationships within the family
c.	no
d.	no; teaching family members to view individual problems as family problems

22. Development of social skills is **most immediately** facilitated in which type of therapy approach?
   a. behavior therapy
   b. individual
   c. group
   d. person-centered

a.	no; behavior therapy uses principles of learning to address maladaptive behaviors
b.	no
c.	RIGHT; the development of social skills is facilitated in group therapy
d.	no; this therapy creates an atmosphere where the person can gain insight

23. Based on the most current research, is psychotherapy effective?
   a. yes, overall
   b. no, not very effective
   c. only for those with schizophrenia
   d. only for those with phobias

a.	YES; different therapies are more effective for specific types of problems
b.	no; this is not correct
c.	no; there are psychotherapies that are effective for certain types of disorders
d.	no; other disorders can be effectively treated using psychotherapy

24. An ethnic match between the therapist and the client appears to provide which **main** advantage for psychotherapy?
    a. professional similarity
    b. cultural commonality
    c. educational similarity
    d. socioeconomic commonality

a.	no; an ethnic match would probably not result in professional similarity
b.	CORRECT; cultural commonality may make the therapy more effective since the client is likely to be more comfortable with the therapist and be less likely to drop out early
c..	no; this not likely to occur
d.	no; probably ethnic match would not result in socioeconomic commonality

25. What is the **primary** reason for using drug therapy as a treatment for psychological disorders?
    a. to sedate mental patients
    b. to correct neurochemical imbalances
    c. to be able to release patients from mental hospitals
    d. to enable patients to sleep through the night

a.	no; this is not a primary reason for using drug therapy
b.	THAT'S RIGHT; drugs affect behavior and mood by altering the neurochemicals
c.	no; most patients are not treated in mental hospitals
d.	no; sleeping is not a primary reason for drug therapy

26. Neuroleptics are widely used to reduce symptoms of
    a. depression.
    b. schizophrenia.
    c. bipolar disorder.
    d. multiple personality.

a.	no; neuroleptics are antipsychotic drugs and depression is a mood disorder
b.	RIGHT; neuroleptics are antipsychotic drugs
c.	no; neuroleptics are antipsychotic drugs and bipolar disorder is a mood disorder
d.	no; neuroleptics are antipsychotic drugs and this disorder is a dissociative disorder

27. In a study by Seligman, it was shown that electroconvulsive therapy is
    a. the most effective treatment for major depressive disorder.
    b. comparable in effectiveness to cognitive therapy and drug therapy.
    c. is more effective than cognitive therapy, but not as effective as drug therapy.
    d. less effective than both cognitive therapy and drug therapy.

a.	no; this is not a conclusion of the study
b.	CORRECT; ECT is comparable to cognitive therapy and drug therapy
c.	no; this ECT is not more effective than cognitive therapy or less effective as drugs
d.	no; this is not conclusion of the study

28. Electroconvulsive therapy is used in treating severe
    a. schizophrenic disorder.
    b. bipolar disorder.
    c. multiple personality.
    d. depression.

a.	no; antipsychotic drugs are used to treat schizophrenic disorders
b.	no; lithium is generally used to treat bipolar disorder
c.	no; ECT is not used to treat multiple personality
d.	RIGHT; ECT is used to treat depression

29. Research on the effectiveness of different therapies has found that phobias and sexual dysfunctions were most successfully treated by
   a.   behavior therapy.
   b.   cognitive therapy.
   c.   psychoanalysis.
   d.   Gestalt therapy.

a.	YES; using the principles of learning, these disorders are effectively treated using behavior therapy
b.	no; cognitive therapy is effective in treating depression and anxiety
c.	no; psychoanalysis are not as effective as behavior therapy
d.	no; Gestalt therapy is less effective than behavior therapy

30. What is the **main** advantage of an integrative approach to psychotherapy?
   a.   It is usually more cost effective.
   b.   It is usually less time consuming.
   c.   It requires less formal training on part of the psychotherapist.
   d.   It utilizes the strengths of a variety of approaches to meet the specific needs of the client.

a.	no; while this could be an advantage, it is not the main one
b.	no; this is not an advantage
c.	no; in fact the psychotherapist must be competent in several diverse therapies
d.	GOOD; this the main advantage of integrative psychotherapy

31. If you were to consider seeking professional psychological help, you would do all of the following **except** which one?
   a.   research the services offered by potential therapists
   b.   identify the professional credentials of potential therapists
   c.   pick a therapist from the *Yellow Pages* and make an appointment
   d.   set specific therapy goals and frequently assess whether these goals are being met

a.	no; this would sensible advice
b.	no; this is an appropriate thing to do
c.	THAT'S GOOD; this is not a very good way to pick a psychologist
d.	no; seeking professional psychological help would involve setting specific goals

Chapter 15 - Health Psychology

The Big Picture: Chapter Overview

Historically, physical illness was viewed in just biological terms, not in terms of mental factors. Health psychology is a field of psychology that specializes in promoting and maintaining health and preventing and treating illness. As an interdisciplinary field, behavioral medicine focuses on developing and integrating behavioral and biomedical knowledge to promote health and reduce illness. Chronic illnesses are the main contributors to disability and death today compared to a century ago, when acute diseases were more important. Psychological and social factors play important roles in chronic illnesses.

One of the main areas of interest is the relationship between stress and illness. Stress is the response to circumstances and events that threatens us or taxes our coping abilities. According to Selye, the body's reaction to stress is called the general adaptation syndrome and consists of the alarm stage, the resistance stage, and the exhaustion stage. Selye also described eustress as the positive features of stress. The neuroendocrine-immune pathway describes the relationship between the endocrine system and immune system; cortisol can have a negative effect on the immune system. The sympathetic nervous system pathway describes how the release of hormones during the fight-or-flight response can be harmful over time. The field that explores the relationship between psychological factors, the nervous system, and the immune system is called psychoneuroimmunology. Research supports the connection between the immune system and stress. Psychological factors also play a role in stress. Type A behavior is a cluster of characteristics such as competitiveness, hostility, and impatience and Type B behavior refers to characteristics such as calmness and being easygoing. Type A behavior cluster was thought by many psychologists to be related to the incidence of heart disease. Now the component of hostility is believed to be most consistently associated with coronary disease. Hardiness refers to a personality style characterized by a sense of commitment, control, and a perception of problems as being challenges. According to Lazarus, stress depends on how individuals cognitively appraise and interpret events in their lives. As we interpret a situation, we go through primary appraisal and secondary appraisal. Environmental factors can produce stress. Overload occurs when the stimuli become so intense that we can no longer cope with them; this can lead to burnout. Conflict occurs when we must decide between options and can be of these types: approach/approach conflict, avoidance/avoidance conflict, and approach/avoidance conflict. We experience frustration when we cannot reach a goal. Life events and daily hassles are major sources of stress.

Stress is also produced by acculturation stress, the negative contact between two distinct cultural groups. John Berry proposed that people can adapt to acculturation in four ways: assimilation, integration, segregation, and marginalization. Marginalization and separation are the least adaptive responses to acculturation. Poverty can also cause considerable stress and is related to threatening and uncontrollable life events. Ethnic minority families are disproportionately among the poor.

Coping refers to managing taxing circumstance, expending effort to solve life's problems, and seeking to master or reduce stress. In problem-focused coping, individuals squarely face their troubles and try to solve them. When we use emotion-focused coping, we respond to stress in an emotional manner, especially using defensive appraisal. Depending on the context, either approach may be adaptive. Cognitive restructuring refers to modifying the thoughts, ideas, and beliefs that maintain a person's problems. Self-talk is mental speech we use when we think, plan, or solve problems. Illusions are related to one's sense of self-esteem. The ideal overall orientation may be an illusion that is mildly inflated. Sometimes defensive pessimism may actually work best in handling stress, however, optimism is the best strategy. Rod Martin argues that humor is an important component of a positive outlook. Self-efficacy is the belief that one can master situation and produce positive outcomes; self-efficacy can improve an individual's ability to cope and mental health. Social support provides information and feedback from others that one is loved and cared for, esteemed and valued, and included in a network of communication and mutual obligations. The benefits of social support include tangible assistance, information, and emotional support. Assertive behavior illustrates how we can deal with conflict in social relationships. Stress management programs teach people how to appraise stressful events, how to develop skills for coping with stress, and how to put these skills into use in everyday life. Other ways to cope with stress include meditation, relaxation, and biofeedback. Multiple strategies in coping with stress work better than a single strategy.

Aerobic exercise, even to a moderate degree, can reduce the risk of heart attacks and provide positive benefits for self-concept, anxiety, and depression. Proper nutrition is vital in maintaining good health. Many of us are unhealthy eaters. There is a link between fat intake and cancer. A sound diet includes fat, carbohydrates, protein, vitamins, minerals, and water. Smoking has significant effects on health. Although the adverse consequences of smoking have been widely publicized, smoking is still widespread because it is addictive and reinforcing. Four methods have been developed to help smokers quit, nicotine substitutes, stimulus control, aversive conditioning, and going "cold turkey." Making healthy decisions with regard to sexuality is important. Making the correct decisions is dependent on having accurate knowledge about sex, contraception, STDs, and AIDS.

Learning Objectives

When you have studied the material in this chapter, you should be able to:

1. explain the goals of behavioral medicine and health psychology. (pp. 516-517)
2. define stress. (pp. 517-518)
3. outline Hans Selye's general adaptation syndrome and the physiological processes occurring in each stage. (pp. 518-519)
4. differentiate between the neuroendocrine-immune pathway and the sympathetic nervous system pathway in response to stress. (pp. 519-520)
5. explain the goals of neuroimmunology. (pp. 519-521)
6. distinguish between type A and Type B personality factors and their relationship to coronary disease. (p. 521)
7. explain the concept of hardiness and its relationship to health. (p. 522)
8. discuss the cognitive appraisal of stress. (pp. 522-523)
9. define burnout and factors associated with burnout. (p. 523)
10. differentiate between the three types of conflict: approach-approach, avoidance-avoidance, and approach-avoidance. (pp. 523-524)
11. list the responses to acculturative stress identified by John Berry and the outcome of each response. (pp. 525-526)
12. differentiate between problem-focused and emotion-focused coping. (pp. 527-529)
13. discuss the benefits of cognitive restructuring, positive self-talk, positive self-illusion, and humor. (pp. 529-531)
14. define self-efficacy and discuss its relationship to health. (p. 532)
15. summarize the results of studies finding a correlation between social support and health. (pp. 532-533)
16. explain why assertive behavior benefits mental health. (pp. 533-534)
17. discuss how meditation and biofeedback decrease arousal and increase relaxation. (pp. 535-536)
18. summarize the benefits of regular exercise and proper nutrition. (pp. 537-540)
19. describe the challenges in helping people to stop smoking. (pp. 540-542)
20. evaluate the importance of sexual knowledge and education regarding contraception and sexually transmitted diseases as part of health psychology. (pp. 542-544)
21. from *Explorations in Psychology: Jen and Nick: Faces of Welfare Poverty in Canada*, relate the stories of Jen and Nick to information on stress and resilience. (p. 527)

Guided Review

The Scope of Health Psychology

_____ psychology is a field of psychology that specializes in promoting and maintaining health and preventing and treating illness. _____ _____ develops and integrates behavioral and _____ knowledge to promote health and reduce illness. A century ago, _____ diseases like small pox and influenza caused death. Now _____ illness are the main contributors to disability and death.

Health - p. 516

Behavioral medicine - p. 516
biomedical - p. 516
acute - p. 517
chronic - p. 517

Stress

Stress refers to the response of individuals to the circumstances and events, called _____ , that threaten them and tax their coping abilities. According to Selye, the body's reaction to stress is called the _____ _____ Syndrome. The GAS consists of three stages: (1) the body enters a temporary state of shock in the _____ stage, (2) an all-out effort is made to combat stress in the _____ stage, and (3) wear and tear on the body increase in the _____ stage. According to Selye, not all stress is bad. The positive features of stress are called _____ . _____ is a steroid that, over time, can suppress the immune system; it is part of the neuroendocrine-immune system. When the sympathetic nervous system is activated, the hormones _____ and _____ are released; these can put us at-risk for illness and disease. The field that explores the relationships between psychological factors, the nervous system, and the immune system is called _____ . Among the biological systems that are activated by stress are the _____ , endocrine, and the _____ _____ systems. Stress affects the immune system in the following ways: acute stressors produce _____ changes, chronic stressors impair the functioning of the _____ system, and research with cancer patients has linked _____ of life with immunity.

stressors - p. 518

General Adaptation - p. 518

alarm - p. 518
resistance - p. 518
exhaustion - p. 518
eustress - p. 518
Cortisol - p. 519

epinephrine - p. 519
norepinephrine - p. 519

psychoneuroimmunology - p.519
immune/central nervous - p. 519

immunological - p. 520
immune - p. 520
quality - p. 520

A cluster of characteristics, such as excessively competitive, hard-driven, impatient, and hostile, that are thought to be related to the incidence of heart disease is called _____ _____ behavior. The component of type A that is especially related to heart disease is _____ . A personality style characterized by a sense of commitment, control, and a perception of problems as being challenges is called _____ .

Type A - p. 521

hostility - p. 521

hardiness - p. 522

A term suggested by Lazarus that describes individuals' interpretations of their lives and their determination of whether they have the resources to cope is called _____ _____ . According to Lazarus, in _____ appraisal, people interpret whether an event involves harm, threat, or challenge. In _____ appraisal, they evaluate their resources and determine how to cope with the event. A hopeless, helpless feeling brought on by relentless work-related stress is called _____ . Burnout usually occurs as a result of a _____ of stress rather than from one or two incidents. Burnout is also a problem with _____ _____ . Conflicts in

cognitive appraisal - p. 522
primary - p. 522
secondary - p. 522

burnout - p. 523
gradual accumulation - p. 523
university students - p. 523

which an individual must choose between two attractive stimuli or circumstances are called _____ conflicts. Conflicts in which individuals must choose between two unattractive stimuli or circumstances are called _____ conflicts. A conflict in which a single stimulus or circumstance has both positive and negative characteristics is called _____ conflict. Another stress-producing circumstance, in which a person cannot reach a desired goal, is called _____. Significant _____ _____ have been proposed as a major source of stress. A widely used scale to measure life events and their possible impact on illness is the _____ _____ _____ _____. People who experience clusters of life events are more likely to become _____. Psychologists are increasingly considering the nature of _____ _____ and their effects on stress.

_____ _____ refers to the negative consequences of continuous, first-hand contact between two distinct cultural groups. _____ occurs when individuals relinquish their cultural identity and move into the larger society. In contrast, _____ implies the maintenance of cultural integrity and the movement to become part of the larger culture. A self-imposed withdrawal from the larger culture is called _____, but when it is imposed by the larger dominant society, it is referred to as _____. The term that refers to the process in which groups are out of contact with both their traditional society and the dominant society is _____. Two adaptive outcomes of acculturative stress are _____ and _____. Poverty creates considerable stress for individuals and families; _____ _____ families are disproportionately among the poor. Poverty is also related to threatening and uncontrollable _____ _____, such as crime and violence.

Coping
The process of managing taxing circumstances and seeking to master, minimize, reduce, or tolerate stress and conflict is called _____. According to Lazarus, individuals who cope with stress by facing their problems and trying to solve them engage in _____-_____ coping, whereas those who cope with stress in an emotional, defensive manner engage in _____-_____ coping. Over the long term, it is best to use _____-focused coping more.
The process of modifying the thoughts, ideas, and beliefs that maintain an individual's problems is called _____ _____. The soundless, mental speech we use, called _____-_____, is often helpful in cognitive restructuring. Although mental health professionals have long recommended an accurate view of reality, recent research has demonstrated the value of _____ _____-_____. In other situations a strategy of imagining negative outcomes, called _____ _____, is best for handling stress. Seligman recommends that individuals who wish to develop an optimistic outlook should consider _____ _____. Cognitive therapists suggest avoiding self-pity and disputing _____ thoughts. The belief that one can master a situation and produce

positive outcomes is called _____-_____ . Self-efficacy beliefs can be increased if you (1) select something you expect to be able to do; (2) distinguish between your _____ performance and _____ project; (3) keep good _____ ; (4) pay close attention to your _____ ; (5) list the kinds of situations likely to be most difficult and least difficult and begin with the _____ tasks.

self-efficacy - p. 532

past - p. 532
present/records - p. 532
successes - p. 532
easier - p. 532

Information from others that one is loved, esteemed and valued, and included in a network of others is called _____ _____ . The benefits of social support stem from tangible assistance, information, and _____ support. Individuals learn how to appraise stressful events and develop skills for coping with stress in _____ _____ programs. A system of thought designed to attain bodily or mental control, as well as enlightenment, is called _____ . The most popular form of meditation in the North America is called _____ meditation. Researchers disagree as to whether the benefits of meditation are superior to those derived from _____ . A process of monitoring an individual's muscular or visceral activities and providing the information to individuals so they can learn to control the physiological activities is called _____ . When facing stress, _____ coping strategies are often better than using a single strategy.

social support - p. 532

emotional - p. 532

stress management - p. 535

meditation - p. 535
transcendental - p. 535

relaxation - p. 535

biofeedback/multiple - p. 536/537

Promoting Health

Sustained exercise, such as jogging, swimming, or cycling, that stimulates heart and lung activity is called _____ exercise. Researchers generally agree that even moderate exercise can reduce the risk of _____ _____ . Exercise also provides positive benefits for depression , anxiety, and _____-_____ . A well-balanced diet provides more energy, can lower _____ _____ , cancer risk, and tooth decay. Although the adverse consequences of smoking have been highly publicized, smoking is still widespread because it is _____ and _____ . Four methods can be effective in helping smokers to quit: nicotine substitutes, _____ , aversive conditioning, and going _____ _____ . With regard to sexual knowledge, there is much that we _____ _____ . _____ influences the choice of contraceptive method. AIDS is caused by _____ which destroys the body's immune system. About _____ percent of Canadian and U.S. AIDS cases occur among _____ males and intravenous drug users.

aerobic - p. 537

heart attack - p. 537
self-concept - p. 539
blood pressure - p. 540

pleasurable/reinforcing - p. 541
stimulus control - p. 541
cold turkey - p. 541
don't know - p. 542
Age - p. 543
HIV - p. 543
90 - p. 543
homosexual - p. 543

Explorations in Psychology

To respond to the questions and exercises presented in this section, please write your thoughts, perspectives, and reactions on a separate piece of paper.

Explorations in Psychology and Life: Jen and Nick: Faces of Welfare Poverty in Canada

- What is most likely to happen to Jen and Nick?
- Suggest some ways people like Jen and her children and Nick can be saved from their environment.
- What do the characteristics of resiliency give children?
- Do you know people who grew up in poverty and violence and were able to survive because of resiliency? How do they explain their fortune?

Explorations in Psychology and Life: Using Optimistic Thinking To Go From Sausage-Stuffer to Supersalesman

- What role does optimistic thinking play in your life? Would you benefit from optimism like Bob Dell did?
- Is it possible that optimism leads us to think in unrealistic ways?
- Are optimistic people unnecessarily setting themselves up for pessimism when they ultimately do fail?

In Your Own Words

To respond to the questions and exercises presented in this section, please write your thoughts, perspectives, and reactions on a separate piece of paper.

- ✓ Before reading this chapter, how would you define stress? Was your definition similar to the one presented in the chapter?
- ✓ Have you noticed a relationship between health and stress in yourself or your friends? For instance, do you get colds during final exam week?
- ✓ Paraphrase the chapter's definitions of primary appraisal and secondary appraisal in more personally relevant terms.
- ✓ When have you experienced overload and frustration?
- ✓ Develop some examples for each of the types of conflict presented in the chapter that you have experienced.
- ✓ Do you use problem-focused coping and/or emotion-focused coping as you are assigned papers and projects and face exams? In these contexts, what are the advantages and disadvantages of each?
- ✓ How do appraise exams? Center your answer on primary and secondary appraisal and on problem-focused and emotion-focused coping.
- ✓ Can you add to the strategies presented in the chapter that are effective in protecting against AIDS and other STDs?
- ✓ Of those ways described in the chapter on methods of coping with stress (e.g., optimism, self-efficacy, social support, assertive behavior), which one is your greatest strength? Which one do you need to develop further?

Correcting the Incorrect

Carefully read each statement. Determine if the statement is correct or incorrect. If the statement is incorrect, make the necessary changes to correct it. Then look directly under the statement for the correct statement and page reference in the textbook.

1. Most cases of death and disability today are due to acute diseases.
    ❑ *Most cases of death and disability today are due to chronic diseases. (p. 517)*
2. Stress is defined as the response of individuals to circumstances and events that threaten them and tax their coping abilities.
    ❑ *Stress is defined as the response of individuals to circumstances and events that threaten them and tax their coping abilities. (p. 518)*
3. Bandura developed the General Adaptation Syndrome.
    ❑ *Selye developed the General Adaptation Syndrome. (p. 518)*
4. The General Adaptation Syndrome consists of three stages: alarm, resistance, and marginalization.
    ❑ *The General Adaptation Syndrome consists of three stages: alarm, resistance, and exhaustion. (p. 518)*
5. Eustress refers to the positive features of stress.
    ❑ *Eustress refers to the positive features of stress. (p. 518)*
6. The neuroendocrine-immune pathway focuses on the effects of the activation of the sympathetic nervous system on the immune system.
    ❑ *The sympathetic nervous system pathway focuses on the effects of the activation of the sympathetic nervous system on the immune system. (p. 519)*
7. Cortisol is a steroid that can suppress the immune system.
    ❑ *Cortisol is a steroid that can suppress the immune system. (p. 519)*
8. Acute stressors can produce immunological changes, but only in ill individuals.
    ❑ *Acute stressors can produce immunological changes in healthy individuals. (p. 520)*
9. Type B personality is associated with heart disease.
    ❑ *Type A personality is associated with heart disease. (p. 521)*
10. The components of hardiness are commitment, control, and challenge.
    ❑ *The components of hardiness are commitment, control, and challenge. (p. 522)*
11. Cognitive appraisal refers to the individual's interpretation of events.
    ❑ *Cognitive appraisal refers to the individual's interpretation of events. (p. 522)*
12. In secondary appraisal, individuals evaluate their resources and determine how effectively they can be used to cope with the stressor.
    ❑ *In secondary appraisal, individuals evaluate their resources and determine how effectively they can be used to cope with the stressor. (p. 522)*
13. An approach/approach conflict occurs when the individual must choose between two unattractive stimuli or circumstances.
    ❑ *An approach/approach conflict occurs when the individual must choose between two attractive stimuli or circumstances. (p. 523)*
14. Frustration refers to any situation in which a person cannot reach a desired goal.
    ❑ *Frustration refers to any situation in which a person cannot reach a desired goal. (p. 524)*
15. Life events checklists provide important information about a person's psychological makeup.
    ❑ *Life events checklists do not provide important information about a person's psychological makeup. (p. 525)*
16. Life's major events are the primary sources of stress.
    ❑ *Life's major events may not be primary sources of stress. (p. 525)*
17. Separation and marginalization are the most adaptive responses to acculturation.
    ❑ *Separation and marginalization are the least adaptive responses to acculturation. (p. 526)*
18. Acculturative stress refers to the negative consequences of the third stage of the General Adaptation Syndrome.
    ❑ *Acculturative stress refers to the contact between two distinctive cultural groups. (p. 525)*

19. Poor women are more likely to experience crime and violence than are middle-class women.
   ❑ *Poor women are more likely to experience crime and violence than are middle-class women.* (p. 526)

20. Denial is an example of problem-focused coping.
   ❑ *Denial is an example of emotion-focused coping.* (p. 529)

21. Most people use either problem-focused coping or emotion-focused coping.
   ❑ *Most people use both problem-focused coping or emotion-focused coping.* (p. 529)

22. Self-talk is a sign of serious psychological disturbance.
   ❑ *Self-talk is helpful in cognitive restructuring.* (p. 529)

23. Most mental health professionals believe that seeing reality as accurately as possible is the best path to mental health.
   ❑ *Most mental health professionals believe that some positive illusions may helpful for mental health.* (p. 530)

24. A strategy of defensive pessimism is never a good way to deal with stress.
   ❑ *A strategy of defensive pessimism may be a good way to deal with stress.* (p. 530)

25. Pessimism can be overcome through cognitive therapy.
   ❑ *Pessimism can be overcome through cognitive therapy.* (p. 531)

26. Self-efficacy is the belief that one can master a situation and produce positive outcomes.
   ❑ *Self-efficacy is the belief that one can master a situation and produce positive outcomes.* (p. 532)

27. Smokers who have unsuccessfully tried to quit will have high self-esteem to try to quit again.
   ❑ *Smokers who have unsuccessfully tried to quit will have low self-esteem to try to quit again.* (p. 532)

28. Social support gives us benefits in three ways: tangible assistance, information, and emotional support.
   ❑ *Social support gives us benefits in three ways: tangible assistance, information, and emotional support.* (p. 532)

29. The more diverse the social support is, the less effective it is in helping us cope with stress.
   ❑ *The more diverse the social support is, the more effective it is in helping us cope with stress.* (p. 533)

30. One way to become more assertive is to state problems in terms of their consequences for you.
   ❑ *One way to become more assertive is to state problems in terms of their consequences for you.* (p. 534)

31. Stress management programs teach us how to avoid stress.
   ❑ *Stress management programs teach us how to cope with stress.* (p. 535)

32. Biofeedback is effective at reducing an individual's muscle tension.
   ❑ *Biofeedback is effective at reducing an individual's muscle tension.* (p. 536)

33. Multiple coping strategies are preferred over a single coping strategy.
   ❑ *Multiple coping strategies are preferred over a single coping strategy alone.* (p. 537)

34. Only intense aerobic exercise has any real effect on reducing risk for heart disease.
   ❑ *Moderate aerobic exercise has any real effect on reducing risk for heart disease.* (p. 539)

35. Mice fed a high-fat diet are more likely to develop breast cancer than mice fed on a low-fat diet.
   ❑ *Mice fed a high-fat diet are more likely to develop breast cancer than mice fed on a low-fat diet.* (p. 540)

36. There is no difference in cancer rates between Japan and North America.
   ❑ *There is a difference in cancer rates between Japan and North America.* (p. 540)

37. Nicotine is a stimulant that increases the smoker's energy and alertness.
   ❑ *Nicotine is a stimulant that increases the smoker's energy and alertness.* (p. 541)

38. Most people know that erection problems begin with physical problems.
   ❑ *Two-thirds of people do not know that erection problems begin with physical problems.* (p. 542)

39. A majority of adolescents do not use contraception during their first sexual intercourse experience.
   ❑ *A majority of adolescents do not use contraception during their first sexual intercourse experience.* (p. 543)

40. HIV destroys the immune system.
   ❑ *HIV destroys the immune system* (p. 543)

Practice Test

1. Health psychologists are concerned with
   a. promoting health.
   b. maintaining health.
   c. preventing and treating illness.
   d. all of the above

a.	no; but there is a better option
b.	no; while are concerned with maintaining health, there's more
c.	no; you are partially correct
d.	THAT'S RIGHT; health psychologists have an interest in health and illness

2. A model that is used in the field of health psychology emphasizes a combination of influences on health. This model is called the _____ model.
   a. psychodynamic
   b. general adaptation syndrome
   c. hardiness
   d. biopsychosocial

a.	no; this option emphasizes unconscious causes
b.	no; this model describes the effects of stress
c.	no; hardiness is a personality trait that influences how we cope with stress
d.	RIGHT; you can see in the term a reference to several types of causes

3. Dr. Livingston is interested in studying the relationship between the degree to which people follow doctor's orders and health care outcomes. Of the following, Dr. Livingston **most likely** works in which field?
   a. clinical psychology
   b. behavior modification
   c. psychoanalysis
   d. behavioral medicine

a.	no; she may be a working in clinical psychology, but there's a better option given her interest
b.	no; she may be using behavior modification, but this is not a field
c.	no; she is the least likely to be working in psychoanalysis since there's no reference to unconscious or therapy
d.	CORRECT; she is integrating behavioral and biomedical knowledge

4. _____ is the response of individuals to the circumstances and events that threaten them and tax their coping abilities.
   a. Frustration
   b. General adaptation syndrome
   c. Stress
   d. Appraisal

a.	no; frustration is the response
b.	no; this syndrome describes the biological factors involved in stress
c.	YES; this is the definition of stress
d.	no; this refers to interpretation of events

5.	Which of the following is the **best** example of a stressor?
	a.	taking a vacation
	b.	talking to a friend
	c.	getting an A on an exam
	d.	being fired from a job

a.	no; for some, a vacation can threaten or tax coping abilities; but there is better example of a stressor
b.	no; this probably does not threaten nor tax coping abilities
c.	no; this probably does not threaten nor tax coping abilities
d.	RIGHT; being fired from a job is threatening and taxes our coping abilities

6.	If you were a psychoneuroimmunologist, you would be most likely to read which fictitious journal?
	a.	*Journal of Humanistic Psychology*
	b.	*Journal of Motor Skills*
	c.	*Journal of Dream Analysis*
	d.	*Journal of Behavior and Health*

a.	no; humanistic psychology is probably of not much interest to you
b.	no; more than likely you don't have much interest in motor skills
c.	no; more than likely you don't have much interest in analyzing dreams
d.	YEA; since you are interested in the relationships among psychological factors, the nervous system, and the immune system

7.	Which of the following cancer patients would you predict to have the **weakest** immune system?
	a.	Meagan: she is a university graduate, has a good job, and a loving family.
	b.	Charles: he is homeless, sleeps and eats at shelters whenever he can, and is generally alone.
	c.	Anita: she has raised three children and enjoys spending time with her grandchildren.
	d.	James: he owns a business, has many friends, but lives by himself.

a.	no; Meagan seems to have adequate resources such as close relationships
b.	YES; these characteristics put Charles' immune system at risk
c.	no; she has a social support and close relationships
d.	no; he has a social support

8.	Seyle's three-stage pattern of reaction to stress is known as the
	a.	cognitive appraisal scale.
	b.	social readjustment scale.
	c.	personality adjustment system.
	d.	general adaptation syndrome.

a.	no
b.	no; this is a scale that measures how much stress has been experienced
c.	no
d.	CORRECT; the GAS consists of three stages

9. According to Selye, the immune system effectively fights off infection in the _____ stage of the general adaptation syndrome?
   a. alarm stage
   b. resistance stage
   c. exhaustion stage
   d. none of the above

   a. no; there is often a temporary state of shock when resistance drops
   b. THAT'S RIGHT; hormones are released that reduce inflammation
   c. no; there may be exhaustion and vulnerability to disease increases
   d. no

10. Dennis always feels like he is running out of time. He rarely takes a vacation and finds it hard to relax at home. He demands perfection of himself and is competitive in all arenas of his life. Dennis can be described **best** as a(n)
    a. avoidant personality.
    b. Type A personality.
    c. Type B personality.
    d. bulimic personality.

    a. no
    b. YES; Type A personality consists of competitiveness, impatient, and hostile
    c. no; Type B personality refers to people who are relaxed and easygoing
    d. no

11. Each of the following is characteristic of the Type A behavior pattern except
    a. hostility.
    b. competitiveness.
    c. impatience.
    d. a general sense of satisfaction with life.

    a. no; this is a characteristic
    b. no; Type A behavior pattern does include competitiveness
    c. no; impatience is a characteristic of the Type A behavior pattern
    d. no; a general sense of satisfaction with life does not characterize Type A

12. If you have a sense of commitment, control, and perceive problems as challenges, then you have the personality factor of _____.
    a. appraisal
    b. Type B
    c. hardiness
    d. self-talk

    a. no; appraisal refers to interpretation of events
    b. no; Type B personality refers to people who are relaxed and easygoing
    c. RIGHT; these three components characterize hardiness
    d. no; this is the soundless mental speech we use as we think or plan

13. According to Lazarus, in primary appraisal, people assess whether an event involves each of the following except
    a. fear.
    b. harm.
    c. threat.
    d. challenge.

a. CORRECT; we do not appraisal an event as fear
b. no; we may appraise an event as harmful
c. no; we may appraise an event as a threat
d. no; we may appraise an event as a challenge

14. Lazarus suggests that in secondary appraisal individuals
    a. evaluate their resources for dealing with stress.
    b. unconscious recall other similar stressful events
    c. engage in the use of defense mechanisms.
    d. experience resistance and then exhaustion

a. YES; we also determine how to use our resources to cope with stress
b. no; this is not what happens in secondary appraisal
c. no; secondary appraisal does not include the use of defense mechanisms
d. no; these are two stages of the general adaptation syndrome

15. What do primary appraisal and secondary appraisal have in common?
    a. They both take about the same amount of time.
    b. They both are cognitive activities.
    c. They both occur at the same time.
    d. They both are basically passive activities.

a. no; obviously primary appraisal occurs before secondary appraisal
b. THAT'S RIGHT; interpretation is a cognitive activity
c. no; obviously primary appraisal occurs before secondary appraisal
d. no; interpretation is a very active process

16. Burnout appears to be a widespread phenomenon among university students. In order to avoid this situation, a university student should do all of the following **except** which one?
    a. take well-balanced class loads
    b. avoid class overloads
    c. use available campus support resources
    d. plan to graduate in three years

a. no; doing this would reduce the risk of burnout
b. no; doing this would reduce the risk of burnout
c. no; doing this allow the student get the needed support, reducing burnout
d. RIGHT; graduating in three years is difficult and not likely and this could lead to burnout

17. Psychologists refer to the inability to reach a desired goal as
    a. burnout.
    b. conflict.
    c. frustration.
    d. overload.

a. no; burnout is related to relentless work-related stress
b. no; conflict occurs when we must decide on two goals
c. RIGHT; this is how frustration is defined
d. no; overload occurs when stimuli becomes so intense that we cannot cope

18. Jane is experiencing stress. Both of her boyfriends have asked her out for the same night. Assuming she is equally attracted to both, which source of stress is Jane experiencing?
   a. approach/avoidance conflict
   b. approach/approach conflict
   c. avoidance/avoidance conflict
   d. none of the above

a.	no; this refers to a single circumstance and Jane has two boyfriends
b.	CORRECT; Jane must chose between two equally attractive options
c.	no; this is a conflict that involves two unattractive circumstances
d.	no

19. Kenneth can't decide whether or not to ask Debra to marry him. He really loves her, but he knows his parents will object if he marries her before he finishes university. Kenneth's situation exemplifies which type of conflict?
   a. active/coping
   b. approach/avoidance
   c. avoidance/avoidance
   d. approach/approach

a.	no; this is not a type of conflict
b.	RIGHT; Kenneth's conflict involves both approaching Debra and avoiding displeasing his parents
c.	no; this is a conflict that involves two unattractive circumstances
d.	no; this conflict involves two attractive circumstance

20. You take a break from studying and find yourself staring into the refrigerator. The only thing you see is an old piece of leftover pizza and some old jello. You would rather not eat either, but you are very hungry. The stress you are experiencing is called
   a. approach/approach conflict.
   b. avoidance/avoidance conflict.
   c. approach/avoidance conflict.
   d. burnout.

a.	no; this conflict involves two attractive circumstance
b.	YES; this is a conflict that involves two unattractive circumstances
c.	no; this conflict involves a single circumstance with positive and negative characteristics
d.	no; this is not a type of conflict .

21. Sangrita feels that she does not fit within any cultural group and that she has lost her identity. Sangrita is experiencing
   a. assimilation.
   b. separation.
   c. marginalization.
   d. integration.

a.	no; assimilation occurs when individuals give up their cultural identity and move into the larger society
b.	no; separation is self-imposed withdrawal from the larger culture
c.	RIGHT; marginalization occurs when groups are put out of contact with both their traditional and the dominant society
d.	no; integration is when the group becomes an integrate part of the larger culture but still maintains their cultural integrity

22. According to the text, the healthiest, least stressful adaptation to acculturation is
   a. integration.
   b. marginalization.
   c. separation.
   d. assimilation.

a.	CORRECT; integration is the healthiest, least stressful response
b.	no; marginalization and separation are the least adaptive responses
c.	no; marginalization and separation are the least adaptive responses
d.	no; but assimilation can be a healthy response, but there is some cultural loss

22. Emotion-focused coping involves
   a. using defense mechanisms.
   b. facing your troubles and trying to solve them.
   c. a rational approach to solving problems.
   d. none of the above

a.	RIGHT; defense mechanisms are used in emotion-focused coping
b.	no; this sounds more like problem-focused coping
c.	no; this sounds more like problem-focused coping
d.	no

23. Imagining potential problems as a strategy for dealing with or preventing negative outcomes is used in which of the following?
   a. problem-focused coping.
   b. biofeedback.
   c. defensive pessimism.
   d. self-efficacy.

a.	RIGHT; in problem-focusing coping, we are squarely facing one's troubles and trying to solve them
b.	no; biofeedback allows people to learn control over physiological activities
c.	no
d.	no; self-efficacy is the belief that one can master a situation and produce positive outcomes

24. The process of changing the thoughts and beliefs that maintain one's problems is referred to as
   a. self-efficacy.
   b. self-talk.
   c. cognitive restructuring.
   d. positive self-illusion.

a.	no; self-efficacy is the belief that one can master a situation and produce positive outcomes
b.	no; this is the soundless mental speech we use as we think or plan
c.	RIGHT; this attempts to modifying thoughts, ideas, and beliefs that maintain a person's problems
d.	no; this refers to one's options about self, work, and events

26. Rick is one of those people who always sees "the glass as half empty." His thoughts are dominated by negative themes and pessimism. What method could be used to improve Rick's negative thoughts about himself and the world around him?
    a.   biofeedback
    b.   cognitive restructuring
    c.   behavior modification
    d.   psychoanalysis

a.	no; biofeedback allows people to learn control over physiological activities
b.	YES; this attempts to modifying thoughts, ideas, and beliefs that maintain a person's problems
c.	no; this focus on using principles of learning to modify behavior
d.	no; psychoanalysis focuses on unconscious conflicts and motives

27. Individuals who have high self-efficacy are **least likely** to do which of the following?
    a.   persist in the face of obstacles
    b.   expend effort in coping with stress
    c.   experience less stress in challenging situations
    d.   perceive that they have no control over the situation

a.	no; high self-efficacy allows people to persist in the face of obstacle
b.	no; those with high self-efficacy are likely to expend effort
c.	no; people with high self-efficacy experience less stress in these situations
d.	CORRECT; in fact, high self-efficacy will lead to a sense of control

28. Tangible assistance, emotional support, and information are potential benefits derived from
    a.   assimilation.
    b.   self-efficacy.
    c.   social support.
    d.   biofeedback.

a.	no; this is a type of adaptation to acculturative stress
b.	no; self-efficacy is the belief that one can produce a desired outcomes
c.	RIGHT; social support provides effective ways to cope with stress
d.	no; biofeedback refers to a technique to learn control over physiological activities by using instruments

29. Assertive coping has beneficial effects on mental health because it
    a.   is a method of active and effective coping that reduces stress.
    b.   relies on defense mechanisms.
    c.   requires the internalization of anger.
    d.   makes others feel guilty for not meeting their responsibility.

a.	RIGHT; assertive coping is a way to dealing with conflict in relationships
b.	no
c.	no
d.	no; this is not a benefit

30. What is the **best** way to cope with stress?
    a.   positive self-talk
    b.   problem-focused coping
    c.   biofeedback
    d.   multiple coping strategies

a.	no; while this can be effective, it is not the most effective
b.	no; while this can be effective, it is not the most effective
c.	no; while this can be effective, it is not the most effective
d.	CORRECT; multiple coping strategies give individuals more choice

31. A process involving the use of instruments to learn to control physiological activities is called
    a. behavior modification.
    b. meditation.
    c. biofeedback.
    d. the relaxation response.

a.	no; this is the use of the principles of learning to modify behavior
b.	no; even though meditation can help into controlling physiological activities, it does not use instruments
c.	AYE; biofeedback involves learning to control processes such as heart rate by receiving feedback from instruments
d.	no; this does not use instruments

32. Most experts recommend that adults engage in _____ minutes or more of moderate-intensity physical activity on most days of the week.
    a. 5
    b. 15
    c. 30
    d. 60

a.	no
b.	no
c.	YES
d.	no

33. The **best** nutritional plan consists of a
    a. diet high in fibers.
    b. low fat and low cholesterol diet.
    c. well balanced diet that includes all nutrients we need.
    d. high vitamin and high mineral diet.

a.	no; while a diet high in fibers is good, it may ignore other nutrients
b.	no; while a low fat diet is good, a well balanced diet is even better
c.	YES; this is the best nutritional plan
d.	no; this diet may not include other important nutrients

34. The best predictor of getting an sexually transmitted disease is
    a. being homosexual
    b. having sex with multiple partners
    c. living in a large urban city
    d. being between the ages of 16 and 22

a.	no; while this is a risk factor, it is not the best predictor of getting an STD
b.	YES; having sex with multiple partners is the best predictor
c.	no
d.	no

Chapter 16 - Social Psychology

The Big Picture: Chapter Overview

Social psychology studies social thinking, social influence, and social relationships. Attribution theory suggests that we are motivated to discover the underlying causes of behavior. We use both external attributions (e.g., social pressure, luck) and internal attributions (e.g., personality, intelligence, moods). Attributions can also be stable or unstable. Another dimension is whether a cause is controllable or uncontrollable. We are susceptible to several attribution errors and biases since attribution is not a logical, rational process. The fundamental attribution error is the tendency to overestimate the importance of traits and to underestimate the importance of the situation in explaining another's behavior. The self-serving bias is described as attributing our success to internal factors and attributing our failures to external factors. Social perception refers to our judgments about others; these impressions are both unified and integrated. We have an implicit personality theory, which is our conception of how personality traits go together in an individual. We use prototypes to evaluate others, and the primacy effect suggests that first impressions are enduring. Social comparison is a process in which individuals evaluate their thoughts, feelings, behaviors, and abilities in relation to other people. Impression management refers to the process of individuals striving to present themselves as a certain sort of person. Some people are more concerned about the impressions they give to others; these individuals have strong self-monitoring.

Attitudes are beliefs and opinions about a people, objects, and ideas. Foot-in-the-door and door-in-the-face are two strategies devised to change attitudes. Psychologists believe that a stronger association of attitudes and behavior exists when attitudes are strong, when we are aware of our attitudes, and when attitudes are relevant to the behavior. Much evidence exists that changes in behavior precede changes in attitude. One explanation, our need for consistency, is a major component of Festinger's theory of cognitive dissonance. Bem's theory, called self-perception theory, suggests that individuals make inferences about their attitudes by perceiving their own behavior.

Conformity is a change in an individual's behavior to coincide more with a group standard. Conformity to rules and regulations is necessary for society to run smoothly. Solomon Asch found that the pressure to conform is strong when even the group response is incorrect. Normative social influence and information social influence are factors that contribute to conformity. Conformity rates vary across cultures depending upon whether the culture is individualistic or collectivistic. Obedience is behavior that complies with the explicit demands of the individual in authority. Milgram's experiments demonstrated the power of obedience, although they raised important questions about the ethics of psychological research. As we go through our lives, we are both conformists and nonconformists.

All groups have norms or rules that apply to all its members; groups also have roles, which are rules and expectations that govern certain positions in the group. Social psychologists have also studied relationships within groups and between groups. Among the factors that influence individuals in group settings are social facilitation, social loafing, deindividuation, the risky shift, the group polarization effect, and groupthink. Psychologists have studied leadership traits. Two theories that attempt to explain leadership are the great-person theory and the contingency model of leadership. In groups, the minority can still have influence through informational pressure. Certain individuals in the minority may play specific roles. Conflicts among ethnic groups are common around the world. A variety of important phenomena affect relations between groups; these include prejudice, stereotypes, and ethnocentrism. Mark Zanna identified prejudice as arising from four inter-related factors: stereotypes, symbolic beliefs, emotions, and past experience. According to social identity theory, we tend to think of the group we're a part of as the in-group. We can improve our self-image by enhancing personal or social identity. Sherif found that superordinate goals are effective in bringing groups of people together to cooperate in reaching some goal. A strategy devised by psychologists to encourage cooperation instead of conflict between groups is called the jigsaw classroom. Intimate contact with a shared language can improve interethnic relations. An example of intimate contact is living in integrated housing, which can diminish in-group/out-group distinctions.

Aggression has been explained by focusing on biological influences (e.g., ethology, death instinct, genetic, hormones). Culture also plays a role in aggression; some cultures are more violence-prone than others. The frustration-aggression hypothesis states that frustration always leads to aggression; the hypothesis was later revised to show that other responses to frustration do occur. Aversive circumstances can lead to aggression, and may include environmental variables (e.g., noise, weather). The psychological variables of equity, intentions, and responsibility influence whether we respond aggressively. Aggression can also be learned through observational learning and reinforcement; there is question as to whether TV and videogame violence causes aggression. Catharsis has been suggested as a way to reducing aggression, however, social learning theorists argue against catharsis as an effective way to reduce aggression. Males tend to be more aggressive than females. Biological and cultural factors influence male-female differences in aggression.

Altruism refers to an unselfish interest in helping someone else. The evolutionary psychologists view some forms of altruism as being important in perpetuating our genes. Some psychologists have suggested that altruism has never been demonstrated among humans. Others suggest an important distinction between altruism and egoism. The bystander effect, in which individuals who observe an emergency are less likely to help when others are present, has been studied by social psychologists. University students in the past several decades have shown a decreased concern for the well-being of others. Females and males are likely to show altruism in different contexts.

Psychologists have studied the factors that are involved in our attractions to each other. Such factors as proximity, similarity, and physical attraction have been implicated in interpersonal attractions. Love can take the form of romantic love and affectionate love. Sternberg's triangular theory of love proposes the following three elements: passion, intimacy, and commitment. Females tend to have stronger interest in relationships than males. Males tend to prefer report talk, while females prefer rapport talk. Loneliness is found in life's transitions. University students are especially prone to loneliness. Males and females tend to attribute their loneliness to different sources.

Learning Objectives

When you have studied the material in this chapter, you should be able to:

1. define attribution theory and identify attributional errors and biases. (pp. 550-552)
2. discuss the following dimensions of developing impressions of others: unification and integration, implicit personality theory and prototypes, and social comparison and self-perceptions. (pp. 552-554)
3. explain how impression management and self-monitoring affect the impressions we give others. (pp. 555-556)
4. describe the relationship between attitudes and behavior in terms of cognitive dissonance and self-perception theory. (pp. 557-558)
5. list factors likely to lead to conformity. (p. 559)
6. describe the Milgram experiments and their relationship to obedience. (pp. 562-565)
7. explain group motivation in terms of the following concepts: norms and roles, social facilitation and social loafing, and deindividuation. (pp. 565-566)
8. explain how groups arrive at decisions based on the risky shift hypothesis, group polarization effect, and groupthink. (pp. 566-567)
9. describe how leadership emerges in groups in terms of the great-person theory, the situation view, the contingency model, and majority and minority influences. (pp. 567-569)
10. discuss why conflicts emerge as a result of prejudice, stereotyping, ethnocentrism, and social identity theory. Discuss Mark Zanna's theory of prejudice. (pp. 569-572)
11. propose several ways to improve interethnic relations. (pp. 572-574)
12. summarize the research regarding biological, environmental and cultural influences in the development of aggression. (pp. 576-579)
13. explain how social learning theorists believe aggression can be reduced. (p. 580)
14. identify differences in aggression between males and females. (p. 580)

15.   summarize research regarding biological, environmental, and psychological influences on the development of altruism. (pp. 580-584)
16.   explain why we tend to initiate relationships with people that are familiar and similar. (p. 584)
17.   differentiate between the importance of physical attraction for men versus women. (pp. 584-585)
18.   distinguish between the characteristics of romantic love and affectionate love. (pp. 585-586)
19.   describe the differences cited by Gilligan and Tannen in how men and women approach and communicate in relationships. (pp. 586-588)
20.   explain the factors involved in loneliness. (p. 588)
21.   list five strategies for combating loneliness. (p.589)
22.   from *Explorations in Psychology: Impression and Management and Job Hunting*, describe tactics that can be applied in job interviews to the probability of getting the job. (p. 555)

Guided Review

Social Thinking

We are motivated to discover the causes of behavior as part of our interest in making sense out of the behavior, according to _____ _____. One important distinction relating to attribution is whether we attribute the causes of our behavior to the environment, called a(n) _____ _____, or to our personality, referred to as a(n) _____ _____. Our explanations can also focus on whether a cause is permanent or temporary, which is _____-_____. The third dimension of causality is controllable-uncontrollable causes. Our tendency to overestimate the importance of traits and underestimate the importance of situations in seeking explanations of an actor's behavior has been called the _____ _____ error. In the _____-_____ bias, we attribute our success to internal factors, while _____ are attributed to external factors. The judgments we form about the qualities of others is called _____ _____. When we form impressions of others, those impressions are both _____ and _____. We also have a notion of how personality traits go together in an individual; this is referred to as _____ _____ theory. The strong inclination to evaluate individuals as "good" or "bad" is termed the _____ _____. Abstract characterizations of the traits that describe a personality type are called _____. Although we tend to simplify our impressions of others by categorizing them, as we interact with others, we may change our initial impression; thus, we change to a more _____ orientation. First impressions are often enduring; psychologists refer to this as the _____ effect. A process in which individuals evaluate their thoughts, feelings, behaviors, and abilities in relation to other people is called _____ _____. The process in which individuals strive to present themselves as a certain sort of person is called _____ _____. Individuals' awareness of the impression they make on others and degree to which they fine-tune their performance accordingly is called _____-_____.

Beliefs and opinions that predispose individuals to behave in certain ways are _____. Two different strategies exist for presenting the strongest points of communication. The _____-in-the-_____ strategy suggests presenting the strongest point later in the presentation; the _____-in-the-_____ strategy, however, suggests presenting the strongest point first. Psychologists have been interested in the relationship between attitudes and _____. Psychologists have found that a stronger association of attitudes and behavior occurs when attitudes are based on _____ experiences and when we think about our _____. Ample evidence shows that changes in behavior sometimes precede changes in _____. One explanation is that we have a need for cognitive _____. This view is central to Festinger's concept of _____ _____. This concept suggests that we develop _____ for our actions. We also have a need to justify the effort we put forth in life, termed _____.

_____ . Our most intense effort justification occurs when our _____-_____ is involved. Some psychologists believe that the dissonance view relies too heavily on _____ factors. Bem's theory, called self-perception theory, suggests that individuals make inferences about their attitudes by perceiving their own _____ .

Social Influence

When individuals change their behavior to coincide more with a group standard, they experience _____ . The power of conformity was demonstrated by Asch's study on judgment of line lengths. _____ _____ influence refers to the influence that other people have on us because we seek their approval or avoid their disapproval. In _____ _____ influence other people influence us because we want to be right. People are more likely to conform when group opinion is _____ . Conformity also increases for those with low _____ and if group members are experts, attractive, or _____ to the individual. Conformity rates have been found to be lower in _____ cultures.

Behavior that complies with the explicit demands of an individual in authority is _____ . In Milgram's classic experiment, subjects obeyed even though they believed they were _____ someone. Milgram's research raises important questions regarding _____ in psychology experiments.

All groups have rules that apply to all members; these are called _____ . Some rules govern only certain positions in the group; these are _____ . Our performance on well-learned tasks usually improves in the presence of others; this is labeled _____ _____ . In some groups we can reduce our effort and not be detected. The lessened effort exerted in a group because of reduced monitoring is called _____ _____ . In some groups, we lose our individual identity and take on the identity of the group; this is known as _____ . When decisions are made in groups, there is often a tendency to make a riskier decision than when we are alone; this has been called the _____ _____ . Although group decisions are not always riskier, group discussion usually strengthens the position we initially held; this is termed the _____ _____ effect. Sometimes group members seek to maintain harmony and unanimity among the group members; this may lead to _____ , in which individual differences of opinion are stifled. Although in most group decision-making the majority wins, when the minority presents its views consistently and confidently, its views are more likely to be heard; this has been labeled _____ _____ . Some individuals have certain traits that are best suited for leadership positions, according to the _____ _____ theory. A contrasting view that takes into account both personality characteristics and situational influences is called _____ _____ of leadership. According to this model, if a group is working under very favorable or very unfavorable conditions, a _____-oriented leader is best. However, if the conditions are more moderated, a _____-oriented leader is better.

An unjustified negative attitude toward an individual because of the individual's membership in the group is called _____ . An

oversimplified generalization about a groups' characteristics is a
_____ . The tendency to favor one's group over other groups is
referred to as _____ . Mark Zanna's theory identified prejudice as
arising from four inter-related factors: _____, _____,
_____, and _____ . Another theory that explains prejudice
and conflict between groups is called _____ _____ theory.
This theory suggests that when individuals are assigned to a group,
they invariably think of the group as an _____ . Sherif found that
promoting in-groupness at a summer camp for boys created
_____ between two groups. Positive relations between the two
groups were created when the groups were required to carry out
cooperative, _____ tasks. This cooperative strategy was applied
in a classroom setting called the _____ _____ . Research has
also suggested that interethnic relations can be improved by
_____ contact.

Social Interaction and Relationships

According to ethologists, certain stimuli act as _____
_____ of an organism's response. In evolution theory, the most
_____ individuals were probably the survivors. Freud believed
that aggression was related to the _____ instinct. The part of the
brain that may be involved in aggression is the _____ , which is
part of the _____ system. Humans are less susceptible to
_____ influences than animals.
The _____-_____ hypothesis, states that when we are
frustrated we will become aggressive. The psychological factors of
_____, _____, expectations, and responsibility are used to
determine if we respond aggressively in an aversive situation.
Bandura would argue that _____ learning plays an important role
in aggression. Most psychologists would say that TV violence
_____ aggressions or antisocial behavior. _____ is the release
of anger or aggressive energy by directly engaging in anger or
aggression. With regard to gender, _____ tend to be more
aggressive.
An unselfish interest in helping someone else is called
_____ . According to evolutionary psychologists, some types of
altruism are important in perpetuating our genes. These psychologists
emphasize the importance of altruistic acts that encourage the survival
of _____ . Two important psychological aspects of altruism are
_____ and _____ . Some psychologists argue that altruism has
never been demonstrated. Others suggest an important distinction
between altruism and _____ . The degree of altruistic motivation
is influenced by characteristics of the _____ . Individuals who
observe an emergency are less likely to help when someone else is
present; this is called the _____ _____ . Bystanders are less
likely to intervene when the situation might lead to _____
_____ , when helping takes time, when a situation is _____ ,
when struggling individuals are _____, when a victim is drunk,
and when bystanders have no history of being victimized themselves.
Males are more likely to help when a perceived _____ is present
and they feel _____ to help. Females have a stronger orientation
than males toward _____ .

We like to associate with people who are _____ to us. Forming close relationships with others similar to ourselves is rewarding because it provides consensual _____ of our own attitudes and behaviors. Physical _____ is an important factor in determining that we like someone. Research suggests, however, that we choose as a mate someone who is close to our level of attractiveness, a process referred to as the _____ _____. As relationships endure over time, physical attractiveness probably becomes _____ important.

_____ love is also referred to as passionate love or Eros. It often predominates in the _____ part of a romantic relationship. Affectionate love is also called _____ love. It is characterized by a desire to have the other person near and by a deep, caring affection for the other person. Sternberg's triangular theory of love suggests the following three elements: _____ , _____ , and _____ .

_____ talk refers to language of establishing connections and is preferred among _____. Report talk is talked designed to give _____, for which _____ have a strong preference.

Loneliness is associated with life's _____. Men tend to blame loneliness on _____ factors, while women attribute loneliness to _____ factors. Men are socialized to _____ relationships, while women are socialized to _____. To become better connected to others, one might want to draw a diagram of the _____ _____.

similar - p. 584

validation - p. 584
attraction - p. 584

matching hypothesis - p. 585

less - p. 585
Romantic - p. 585
early - p. 585
companionate - p. 586

passion, intimacy - p. 586
commitment - p. 586
Rapport - p. 588
women - p. 588
information/men - p. 588
transitions - p. 588
internal - p. 589
external/initiate – p. 589
wait - p. 589

social networks - p. 589

Explorations in Psychology

To respond to the questions and exercises presented in this section, please write your thoughts, perspectives, and reactions on a separate piece of paper

Explorations in Psychology and Life: Impression Management and Job Interviewing

- As you think about impression management, what is the single most important thing you can do?
- Have you ever encountered someone who was overdoing his or her impression management? What was your reaction to that person?
- Ask someone who knows you well whether you practice good impression management.

In Your Own Words

To respond to the questions and exercises presented in this section, please write your thoughts, perspectives, and reactions on a separate piece of paper.
- ✓ In the past 24 hours what attributions have you made about the people around you? Have you committed the fundamental attribution error? How you experienced the self-serving bias?
- ✓ Name some people who you believe are skilled at impression management. What do they do to be evaluated positive by you?
- ✓ What are some historical events or figures that illustrate obedience or disobedience?
- ✓ What stereotypes exist for individuals who share your appearance, gender, ethnicity, religion, and major?
- ✓ Have you ever done group work in which there was social loafing? Was anything done to reduce it?
- ✓ In what ways can university students show a concern for the well-being of others?
- ✓ As you think about your friends, are they physically near you and similar to you (e.g., characteristics, values, lifestyle, physical appearance)?

✓ Do your experiences match the gender preferences with rapport talk and report talk?
✓ Do you experience cognitive dissonance? Have you ever done something that you knew was wrong? How did you justify your actions or beliefs?
✓ What would our society be like if there were perfect conformity and perfect obedience?
✓ If television is found to actually cause aggression in children, what steps should be taken?

Correcting the Incorrect

Carefully read each statement. Determine if the statement is correct or incorrect. If the statement is incorrect, make the necessary changes to correct it. Then look directly under the statement for the correct statement and page reference in the textbook.

1. Attributions focus on the causes of behavior.
   ❑ *Attributions focus on the causes of behavior. (p. 550)*
2. There are three dimensions of causality: internal-external, stable-unstable, optimistic-pessimistic.
   ❑ *There are three dimensions of causality: internal-external, stable-unstable, controllable-uncontrollable. (p. 551)*
3. An external attribution would be a person's intelligence or attitudes.
   ❑ *An internal attribution would be a person's intelligence or attitudes. (p. 551)*
4. The fundamental attribution error describes how we attribute success to internal causes and failures to external causes.
   ❑ *The self-serving bias describes how we attribute success to internal causes and failures to external causes. (p. 552)*
5. Impressions tend not to be unified or integrated.
   ❑ *Impressions tend to be unified or integrated. (p. 553)*
6. In social comparison, we tend to compare ourselves with others even when there are objective standards.
   ❑ *In social comparison, we tend to compare ourselves with others. (p. 554)*
7. The recency effect describes the enduring quality of initial impressions.
   ❑ *The primacy effect describes the enduring quality of initial impressions. (p. 554)*
8. A person who self-monitors is skilled at reading the facial expressions of others.
   ❑ *A person who self-monitors is skilled at reading the facial expressions of others (p. 556).*
9. In the foot-in-the-door strategy, the strongest point or request is made first followed by a weaker point or request.
   ❑ *In the foot-in-the-door strategy, the weakest point or request is made first followed by a weaker point or request. (p. 556)*
10. Cognitive dissonance is experienced when we have two consistent thoughts.
    ❑ *Cognitive dissonance is experienced when we have two inconsistent thoughts. (p. 557)*
11. Intense justification takes place when our self-esteem is involved.
    ❑ *Intense justification takes place when our self-esteem is involved. (p. 558)*
12. Self-perception suggests that we are motivated toward consistency between attitude and behavior and away from inconsistency.
    ❑ *Cognitive dissonance theory suggests that we are motivated toward consistency between attitude and behavior and away from inconsistency. (p. 557)*
13. Conformity occurs when a person changes behavior in response to an explicit demand of a person in authority.
    ❑ *Obedience occurs when a person changes behavior in response to an explicit demand of a person in authority. (p. 562)*
14. Milgram studied conformity by using a real subject and several accomplices.
    ❑ *Asch studied conformity by using a real subject and several accomplices. (p. 561)*
15. When we seek the approval of others, or when we avoid their disapproval, we are experiencing normative social influence.
    ❑ *When we seek the approval of others, or when we avoid their disapproval, we are experiencing normative social influence. (p. 561-562)*

16. Informational social influence occurs when we are influenced because we want to be right.
   - ❑ *Informational social influence occurs when we are influenced because we want to be liked. (p. 562)*
17. In the Milgram study, two of every three subjects stopped at 100 volts.
   - ❑ *In the Milgram study, two of every three subjects stopped at 450 volts. (p. 563)*
18. The Milgram experiments were criticized because of ethical issues.
   - ❑ *The Milgram experiments were criticized because of ethical issues. (p. 564)*
19. Norms are rules that apply to all members of the group.
   - ❑ *Norms are rules that apply to all members of the group. (p. 565)*
20. Social facilitation occurs on poorly learned tasks.
   - ❑ *Social facilitation occurs on well-learned tasks. (p. 566)*
21. Social loafing can sometimes increase the group's performance.
   - ❑ *Social loafing decreases the group's performance. (p. 566)*
22. Individual members of a group that is rioting probably experience risky shift that makes them more likely to engage in irresponsible behavior.
   - ❑ *Individual members of a group that is rioting probably experience deindividuation that makes them more likely to engage in irresponsible behavior. (p. 566)*
23. Groupthink refers to impaired decision making and avoidance of realistic appraisal to maintain group harmony.
   - ❑ *Groupthink refers to impaired decision making and avoidance of realistic appraisal to maintain group harmony. (p. 567)*
24. A person believes she has the necessary traits best suited for a leadership position; this is most consistent with the contingency model of leadership.
   - ❑ *A person believes she has the necessary traits best suited for a leadership position; this is most consistent with the great-person model of leadership. (p. 568)*
25. If a group is working under very favorable conditions, the best leadership style is task-orientation.
   - ❑ *If a group is working under very favorable conditions, the best leadership style is task-orientation. (p. 568)*
26. Leaders must distinguish themselves in various ways from the rest of the group.
   - ❑ *Leaders must distinguish themselves in various ways from the rest of the group. (p. 568)*
27. Prejudice is an unjustified generalization about a group's characteristics that does not consider any variation from one individual to the next.
   - ❑ *A stereotype is an unjustified generalization about a group's characteristics that does not consider any variation from one individual to the next. (p. 570)*
28. Ethnocentrism is an unjustified negative attitude toward an individual based on that person's membership in a group.
   - ❑ *Prejudice is an unjustified negative attitude toward an individual based on that person's membership in a group. (p. 570)*
29. The in-group is us.
   - ❑ *The in-group is us. (p. 571)*
30. Noncompetitive contact between groups is effective in reducing prejudice.
   - ❑ *Intimate contact between groups is effective in reducing prejudice. (p. 574)*
31. The jigsaw method is a way to teach about social influence.
   - ❑ *The jigsaw method is a way to reduce interethnic conflict. (p. 573)*
32. Aggression is learned according to ethologists.
   - ❑ *Aggression is biologically-based according to ethologists. (p. 577)*
33. After much research, frustration has been found to always lead to aggression.
   - ❑ *After much research, it has been found that frustration may lead to aggression. (p. 578)*
34. Whether you respond aggressively will depend on equity, intention, and responsibility.
   - ❑ *Whether you respond aggressively will depend on equity, intention, and responsibility. (p. 579)*
35. There is no difference between males and females on levels of aggression.
   - ❑ *There is a difference between males and females on levels of aggression. (p. 580)*
36. Altruism is an unselfish interest in helping someone else.
   - ❑ *Altruism is an unselfish interest in helping someone else. (p. 580)*

37. All altruism is motivated by reciprocity.
    - *All altruism is not motivated by reciprocity. (p. 582)*
38. The case of Kitty Genovese illustrates the importance of knowing first aid.
    - *The case of Kitty Genovese illustrates the importance of the bystander effect. (p. 582)*
39. The more people who witness an emergency, the more likely someone will help.
    - *The more people who witness an emergency, the less likely someone will help. (p. 582)*
40. Females have a stronger orientation than males toward caregiving.
    - *Females have a stronger orientation than males toward caregiving. (p. 584)*
41. Opposites attract.
    - *Opposites tend not to attract. (p. 584)*
42. Consensual validation involves validating our attitudes because other people hold them as well.
    - *Consensual validation involves validating our attitudes because other people hold them as well. (p. 584)*
43. We end up choosing someone who is close to our own level of attractiveness; this is called affectionate love.
    - *We end up choosing someone who is close to our own level of attractiveness; this is called the matching hypothesis. (p. 585)*
44. Compassionate love involves the desire to have the other person near and to have a deep caring affection for the person.
    - *Affectionate love involves the desire to have the other person near and to have a deep caring affection for the person. (p. 586)*
45. The triangular theory of love includes the dimensions of passion, affection, and trust.
    - *The triangular theory of love includes the dimensions of passion, intimacy, and commitment. (p. 587)*
46. Men prefer rapport talk.
    - *Women prefer rapport talk. (p. 588)*
47. Rapport talk establishes connections and negotiating relationships.
    - *Rapport talk establishes connections and negotiating relationships. (p. 588)*
48. Loneliness is related to a lack of compassionate love and altruism.
    - *Loneliness is related to life's transitions. (p. 588)*

Practice Test

1. What are the three dimensions that are used in the attributions people make?
   a. internal or external, stable or unstable, and controllable or uncontrollable
   b. internal or external, primary or secondary, and chronic or acute
   c. stable or unstable, controllable or uncontrollable, and primary or secondary
   d. stable or unstable, primary or secondary, and interpersonal or intrapersonal

a.	YEA; these are the dimensions used in making attributions
b.	no
c.	no
d.	no

2. People are interested in discovering the causes of behavior, according to
   a. cognitive dissonance.
   b. self-perception theory.
   c. attribution theory.
   d. catharsis.

a.	no; this is the motivation to reduce the discomfort caused by inconsistent thoughts
b.	no; this theory says that we make inferences about our own attitudes by perceiving our behavior
c.	YES; attributions are explanations for behavior
d.	no; this is the release of anger by directly engaging in anger or aggression

3. Which of the following **most** clearly illustrates an internal attribution?
    a. John believes his sister plays the piano to make a good impression on others.
    b. Larry believes that his father is hostile because of the difficulties at work.
    c. Maria believes Rob gossips about others because of a mean and spiteful streak.
    d. Diane believes her son lies to her to avoid possible punishment.

a.	no; John is attributing his sister's playing to some external factor
b.	no; Larry is attributing his father's hostile behavior to some external cause
c.	CORRECT; Maria is attributing Rob's behavior to a personality or disposition
d.	no; Diane is attributing her son's lying to an external factor

4. "Whenever I do well on an exam, it is because I studied hard. Whenever I do poorly on an exam, it is because the test was unfair." This demonstrates
    a. the fundamental attribution error
    b. implicit personality
    c. prototypes
    d. self-serving bias

a.	no; this is the tendency to overestimate the importance of traits and underestimate the importance of the situations when explaining someone's behavior
b.	no; implicit personality is how a layperson understand how traits go together
c.	no; these are abstract categorizations of traits that describe a particular personality type
d.	GOOD; we attribute successes to internal factors and failures to external factors

5. Which of the following is a component of social perception?
    a. developing impressions of others
    b. gaining self-knowledge from our perceptions of others
    c. presenting ourselves to others to influence them
    d. all of the above

a.	no; that is part of social perception
b.	no; however, you are partially right
c.	no, this is more to social perception
d.	THAT'S CORRECT

6. Another name for impression management is
    a. attribution formation.
    b. self-perception.
    c. self-presentation.
    d. risky shift

a.	no; attribution refers to the causes that we give to explain behavior
b.	no; this theory describes how we infer attitudes from behavior
c.	YEP; in self-presentation we try managing the impression others have of us
d.	no; this describes the tendency of groups to make more risky decisions

7. Suppose you are interviewing for a job. Based on what you know about the primacy effect, you should
    a. present yourself honestly so that the interviewer does not expect too much from you.
    b. make sure that the interviewer first notices your positive traits.
    c. present your positive and negative qualities at the same time.
    d. use the foot-in-the-door technique.

a.	no
b.	RIGHT; the primary effect refers to the tendency to remember initial information
c.	no
d.	no; this is a technique used to change people's attitudes

8. "First impressions are lasting impressions" according to
    a. the primacy effect.
    b. the latency effect.
    c. attribution theory.
    d. the social comparison theory.

a.	RIGHT; the primary effect refers to the tendency to remember initial information
b.	no; the latency effect refers to the tendency to remember information that is presented later
c.	no; attribution theory describes how we explain behavior
d.	no; this theory describes how we compare our thoughts, behaviors to other people

9. You have a friend who is very much aware of the impressions she is making on others. You would say that this person has a high level of
    a. self-promotion.
    b. self-monitoring
    c. cognitive dissonance
    d. self-serving bias

a.	no
b.	YES; she pays much attention to the impression she makes on other
c.	no; this is the motivation to reduce the discomfort caused by inconsistent thoughts
d.	no; this is the tendency to attribute successes to internal factors and failures to external factors

10. _____ are beliefs or opinions about people, objects, and ideas.
    a. Attributions
    b. Altruisms
    c. Stereotypes
    d. Attitudes

a.	no; attributions are the suspected underlying causes of behavior
b.	no; altruism is an unselfish interest in helping someone else
c.	no; stereotypes are generalizations about a group's characteristics that ignores individual variation
d.	CORRECT; this is the definition of attitudes

11. Which of the following is **true** of individuals experiencing cognitive dissonance?
    a. They show an inability to make up their mind.
    b. They have lost their sense of self and the ability to make decisions.
    c. They are preoccupied with how they are perceived by others.
    d. They are experiencing a conflict between their attitudes and behavior.

a.	no	
b.	no	
c.	no; this sounds like a very high level of self-monitoring	
d.	YES; we are motivated to reduce the dissonance when there is inconsistency	

12. Self-perception theory
   a.   suggests that individuals do not commit the fundamental attribution error.
   b.   helps explain interpersonal attraction.
   c.   suggests that individuals make inferences about their attitudes by perceiving their behavior.
   d.   both "a" and "c"

a.	no
b.	no
c.	RIGHT; we look to our own behavior to determine our attitudes
d.	no

13. "Start small and build" best describes the
   a.   door-in-the-face strategy
   b.   face-in the-door strategy
   c.   foot-in-the-door strategy
   d.   foot-in-the-face strategy

a.	no; this is when the strongest demand at first, followed by a weaker one
b.	no
c.	THAT'S CORRECT; start with a small request followed by a stronger one
d.	no

14. If a person's changes their behavior to better fit with a group standard, then _____ is said to have occurred.
   a.   obedience
   b.   conformity
   c.   groupthink
   d.   ethnocentrism

a.	no; obedience is behavior that complies with explicit demands of an authority
b.	GOOD: this is the definition of conformity and it can take many different forms
c.	no; groupthink is the tendency of groups to make impaired decisions
d.	no; this refers to the tendency to favor one's own group over other groups

15. Conformity is greatest
   a.   when group opinion is unanimous.
   b.   among individuals with low self-esteem.
   c.   if group members are experts.
   d.   all of the above

a.	no; actually this is a variable that makes conformity more likely
b.	no; there are other variables as well that increase the chance of conformity
c.	no; you are partially correct
d.	CORRECT; all of these increase the odds of conforming

16. Cansas changed her plans and decided to go on a trip to Banff because she thought that her sister was going to pressure her to go. Cansas was influenced by
   a. deindividuation.
   b. foot-in-the-door.
   c. conformity.
   d. door-in-the-face.

a.	no; this refers to losing sense of one's identity	
b.	no; this is a technique to change attitudes	
c.	RIGHT; Cansas changed her behavior to fit her sister's standard	
d.	no; this is a technique to change attitudes	

17. The type of social influence that involves seeking approval or avoid disapproval is called _____.
   a. obedience
   b. social facilitation
   c. informational social influence
   d. normative social influence

a.	no; obedience is behavior that complies with an authority figure's explicit orders
b.	no; this describes an individual's performance improves in the presence of others
c.	no; this is social influence that involves the desire to be right
d.	YEP; we conform in order to be liked and accepted by others

18. In Milgram's classic study, the "teacher" was
   a. a confederate.
   b. shocked by the "learner."
   c. the subject.
   d. afraid of the "learner."

a.	no; the "learner" was the confederate
b.	no; the "teacher" allegedly shocked the "learner"
c.	RIGHT; the "learner" was a confederate
d.	no

19. In Milgram's research, it was discovered that obedience decreased
   a. as people were paid more to participate.
   b. when the authority figure was perceived to be legitimate.
   c. when the authority figure was close by.
   d. when the victim was made to seem more human.

a.	no
b.	no; this tends to increase obedience
c.	no; this tends to increase obedience
d.	RIGHT; this tended to encourage disobedience

20. Which of the following is true regarding Milgram's research on obedience?
   a. Milgram found lower levels of obedience than he had predicted prior to conducting the research.
   b. Milgram's research failed to debrief participants.
   c. Milgram found surprisingly high levels of obedience.
   d. Milgram found vastly different results when he conducted his research in a more natural environment.

a.	no; Milgram found just the opposite
b.	no; Milgram conducted extensive debriefing of the subjects
c.	CORRECT; over 60% of the "teachers" (i.e., subjects) stopped after 450 volts
d.	no; in different settings, there was still high levels of obedience

245

21. Paula is a good racquetball player whose performance seems to improve as the crowd watching her gets larger. The **best** explanation for this pattern is
    a.   the bystander effect.
    b.   deindividuation.
    c.   social facilitation.
    d.   egoism.

a.	no; the bystander effect describes helping behavior
b.	no; deindividuation refers to a lost of identity when in the presence of a group
e.	RIGHT; social facilitation occurs when individual performance increased in the presence of others
d.	no; egoism describes helping behavior that provides benefits to the person helping

22. Omar is frustrated because there are people in his committee who are just not pulling their weight and doing their assigned tasks. This lack of effort is called
    a.   social loafing
    b.   social facilitation
    c.   deindividuation
    d.   groupthink

a.	RIGHT; social loafing occurs when individuals do not expend much effort when in a group because of reduced monitoring
b.	no; this describes an individual's performance improves in the presence of others
c.	no; deindividuation refers to a lost of identity when in the presence of a group
d.	no; this describes how groups make poor decisions

23. When individuals make decisions on their own, their decisions tend to be more conservative than the decision they will agree to in a group. The tendency for a group's decision to be more daring is called
    a.   deindividuation.
    b.   emergent boldness.
    c.   disinhibition.
    d.   the risky shift.

a.	no; deindividuation refers to a lost of identity when in the presence of a group
b.	no
c.	no
d.	THAT'S GOOD; this is the definition of the risky shift

24. The failure of Canada's national leadership to respond effectively to the Quebec nationalist forces in the last Quebec referendum, nearly resulting in a "No" vote illustrates the consequences of _____.
    a.   rapport talk
    b.   groupthink
    c.   altruism
    d.   foot-in-the-door

a.	no; this is a style of talking that establishes connections and negotiates relationships
b.	YES; in groupthink there is impaired decision making and avoidance of realistic appraisal to maintain group harmony
c.	no; altruism in an unselfish interest in helping someone else
d.	no; this is a method to change people's attitudes

25. According to the great person theory of leadership,
    a.   a good leader in one circumstance will not necessarily be a good leader in another circumstance.
    b.   leaders have certain traits that are best suited for leadership positions.
    c.   a combination of personality characteristics and the situation helps determine who will become a leader.
    d.   leaders using information social influence

a.	no; the great person theory says that the situation is not relevant
b.	RIGHT; there is some person with certain traits that are best suited for leadership
c.	no; this sounds like the contingency model of leadership
d.	no; while this might be true, the great person theory does not say this

26. The fifth-grade teacher was surprised when her Japanese-Canadian student, Hiroko, performed poorly in math. The teacher's reaction was due to
    a.   polarization.
    b.   stereotyping.
    c.   groupthink.
    d.   deindividuation.

a.	no; this describes the solidification of a group's position
c.	GOOD; a stereotype is a generalization about a group's characteristics that ignores individual variation
d.	no; in groupthink there is impaired decision making and avoidance of realistic appraisal to maintain group harmony
d.	no; deindividuation refers to a lost of identity when in the presence of a group

27. The statement "I don't trust that guy. He is a used car salesmen and used car salespeople are not trustworthy" reflects (a)
    a.   prejudice.
    b.   stereotype.
    c.   deindividuation.
    d.   both "a" and "b"

a.	no; but you are close
b.	no; you are partially correct
c.	no; deindividuation refers to a lost of identity when in the presence of a group
d.	THAT'S GOOD; there is generalization (i.e., stereotype) and an unjustified negative attitude (i.e., prejudice)

28. Tajfel's social identity theory provides an explanation for
    a.   prejudice.
    b.   the risky shift.
    c.   group leadership.
    d.   social loafing.

a.	YES; we tend to think of our group as an in-group and other groups as out-groups
b.	no
c.	no
d.	no

29. Why does intimate contact tend to facilitate interethnic relations?
    a.   It allows people to discover their similarities.
    b.   It allows people to confirm their stereotypes.
    c.   It encourages people to re-categorize others.
    d.   It reinforces ethnic and cultural differences.

a.	CORRECT; we discover that there is more similarity with the out-group than difference
b.	no; this would tend to deteriorate interethnic relations
c.	no; this would reinforce our perceptions of an in-group and out-group
d.	no; this could reinforce stereotypes and encourage prejudice

30. Research on improved interethnic relations in shared facilities underscore the importance of
   a. superordinate goals.
   b. the jigsaw classroom.
   c. intimate contact.
   d. all of the above

a.	no; however, when two groups work together on some common goal, interethnic relations can improve
b.	no; however, the jigsaw classroom requires that all individuals make contributions
c.	no; however, intimate contact allows others to see people as individuals
d.	YES; all of these have been found to improve interethnic relations

31. Ethologists say that aggression is _____ based.
   a. cognitively
   b. culturally
   c. biologically
   d. psychologically

a.	no
b.	no
c.	YES; ethologists believe that certain stimuli act as innate releasers of aggressiveness
d.	no

32. According to Dollard, what triggers aggression?
   a. pain
   b. culture
   c. socioeconomic status
   d. frustration

a.	no
b.	no
c.	no
d.	CORRECT; Dollard developed the frustration-aggression hypothesis

33. What do social learning theorists argue about the cause of aggression?
   a. Aggression is biologically based
   b. Aggression is the result of unconscious needs that go unmet
   c. Aggression is learned through observational learning and reinforcement
   d. Aggression is the result of frustration

a.	no; this sounds like the view that ethologists take
b.	no; a psychoanalyst would adopt this argument
c.	AYE; social learning focuses on the role of observational learning and reinforcement
d.	no; this is most consistent with the frustration-aggression hypothesis

34. Which of the following statements about Maccoby and Jacklin's research on gender differences in aggression is **incorrect?**
   a. Males are more aggressive than females in all cultures.
   b. More aggression by males than females is found in animals as well as humans.
   c. Males are found to be more aggressive than females as early as two years of age.
   d. In verbal aggression, no differences are found between adult males and females.

	a.	no; this is a correct statement
	b.	no; this is a correct statement
	c.	no; this is a correct statement
	d.	RIGHT; the type of aggression is important to consider when examining gender differences in aggression (females tend to display more verbal aggression)

35. What is the unselfish interest in helping someone else called?
   a. agoism
   b. egoism
   c. altruism
   d. catharsis

	a.	no
	b.	no; this is just the opposite
	c.	YES
	d.	no; catharsis is the release of anger or aggressive energy

36. Dan spends all day volunteering with others to pick up roadside garbage. That evening, he confides to a roommate that his motivation to volunteer was to impress his girlfriend. Dan's behavior is an example of
   a. reciprocity
   b. social exchange
   c. altruism
   d. egoism

	a.	no
	b.	no
	c.	no; altrusim is the unselfish interest in helping someone else
	d.	YES; Dan helped for selfish reasons

37. Don was in need of help on a very busy highway. No one stopped to help. No one accepted responsibility since everyone assumed that someone else would stop. This is best explained by
   a. the bystander effect
   b. risky shift
   c. groupthink
   d. the matching hypothesis

	a.	YES; the presence of others reduces the chance that any one person will help
	b.	no; groups tend to make more risky choices
	c.	no; groupthink refers to impaired decision making in a group
	e.	no; this refers to the tendency we have to choose someone who is close to our own level of attractiveness

38. Which of the following cliches has been supported by the research in interpersonal attraction?
   a. opposite attract
   b. birds of a feather flock together
   c. killing two birds with one stone
   d. time flies

	a.	no; just the opposite
	b.	YES; similarity says that we tend to associate with people who are similar to us
	c.	no
	d.	no

39. Our own attitudes and behavior are supported when another's attitudes and behavior are similar to ours, according to
    a.   the matching hypothesis.
    b.   consensual validation.
    c.   altruistic theory.
    d.   all of the above

a.	no; this refers to the tendency to select others who have similar level of attractiveness as we do
b.	RIGHT; others' attitudes and behaviors validate our attitudes and behaviors
c.	no; altruism is unselfish interest in helping others
d.	no

40. Similarity and familiarity have been used by social psychologists to explain
    a.   loneliness.
    b.   cognitive dissonance.
    c.   interpersonal attraction.
    d.   social prejudice.

a.	no
b.	no
c.	THIS IS CORRECT; we are attracted to others who are similar to us
d.	no

41. The matching hypothesis of attraction states that
    a.   individuals prefer a person more attractive than themselves.
    b.   individuals are uncomfortable around attractive people.
    c.   individuals chose someone close to their level of attractiveness.
    d.   in enduring relationships, physical attractiveness becomes more important

a.	no; this may be true in the abstract, but is not the matching hypothesis
b.	no; this may be true, but does not summarize the matching hypothesis
c.	CORRECT; we choose others who are close to our own level of attractiveness
d.	no; in fact, attractiveness becomes less important

42. Ken and Barbie have a love relationship characterized by passion, intimacy, and commitment. According to Sternberg, this is called
    a.   a temporary situation.
    b.   infatuation.
    c.   consummate love.
    d.   affectionate love.

a.	no
b.	no; infatuation includes passion
c.	RIGHT; consummate love includes passion, intimacy, and commitment
d.	no; affectionate love includes intimacy and commitment

43. When it comes to relationships, women tend to emphasize
    a.   independence.
    b.   autonomy.
    c.   connectedness.
    d.   focus on self.

a.	no
b.	no
c.	RIGHT; women prefer to engage in rapport talk which stresses connectedness
d.	no

44.   In explaining loneliness, women tend to blame _____ factors.
       a.   external
       b.   internal
       c.   psychological
       d.   unconscious

a.	YES; external factors include other people
b.	no
c.	no
d.	no

45.   Which of the following individuals is **most** at risk for loneliness?
       a.   Vera: she and her family are moving into a new house.
       b.   Rod: he was promoted to manager within his company.
       c.   Jennifer: she just broke up with her boyfriend.
       d.   Allen: he is moving to a new city where he knows no one.

a.	no; Vera has others to rely upon
b.	no; Rod still fall back on relationships that are already established
c.	no; Jennifer can still interact with her other friends for support
d.	CORRECT; Allen is in a new city where there is no social support network for him